Davidson
2014

THE DRAMA OF REFORM

THE DRAMA OF REFORM

Theology and Theatricality, 1461–1553

by

Tamara Atkin

BREPOLS

British Library Cataloguing in Publication Data

Atkin, Tamara, 1981- author.
The drama of reform : theology and theatricality, 1461-1553.
-- (Late medieval and early modern studies)
1. Religion and drama--History--To 1500.
2. Religion and drama--History--16th century.
3. Christian drama, English (Middle)--History and criticism.
4. Mysteries and miracle-plays, English--History and criticism.
5. Religious drama, English--History and criticism.
6. Religion in literature.
7. Theology, Doctrinal, in literature.
8. Theater in propaganda--England--History--To 1500.
9. Theater in propaganda--England--History--16th century.
I. Title
II. Series
822.2'09382-dc23

ISBN-13: 9782503546513

© 2013, Brepols Publishers n.v., Turnhout, Belgium

D/2013/0095/170
ISBN: 978-2-503-54651-3
Printed in the E.U. on acid-free paper

Contents

ACKNOWLEDGEMENTS

This book began as a doctoral thesis in the English Faculty of the University of Oxford under the supervision of Vincent Gillespie and Emma Smith. I am indebted to them both in innumerable ways, but especially for their unshakeable support, guidance, and encouragement. My interest in late medieval and early Tudor drama goes back to my time as an undergraduate at Trinity College, Dublin where Gerald Morgan, Amanda Piesse, and John Scattergood prompted me to ask the questions that lie at the heart of this study. More recently, Julia Boffey has helped to steer this project from manuscript to print and I am thankful for her many kindnesses as a friend and colleague. Any infelicities or errors of phrase or fact are all my own, but this book is much the better for her thoughtful comments.

A number of people have read all or parts of this book, and I owe particular thanks to my DPhil examiners, Mishtooni Bose and Greg Walker, and the anonymous reader at Brepols for their keen questions and helpful suggestions. My thinking has been enlivened by conversations with friends and colleagues in Dublin, Oxford, and London. I am expecially grateful to Ruth Ahnert, Shahidha Bari, Venetia Bridges, Ed Clarke, Aidan Crawshaw, Matilda Culme-Seymour, Tony Edwards, Mary Flannery, Alfred Hiatt, Annie Janowitz, Francis Leneghan, Phoebe Ling, Jacqueline Rose, Richard Rowley, and Eric Stanley, from whom I have learned and continue to learn so much.

Much of this book was written in the Bodleian and British Libraries and I thank the helpful staff of the Upper Reading Room, Duke Humfrey's Library, Rare Books and Music Room, and Manuscripts Room, where I have spent many happy hours. I gratefully acknowledge the support of the AHRC, without which this project might never have got off the ground. The staff and students of University College, Oxford and the Department of English at Queen Mary, University of London have provided help of many varieties, but perhaps most importantly, have offered a sense of belonging. For seeing this project through to completion, I am indebted to Guy Carney and Simon Forde at Brepols.

Above all others I thank my family, my brother for his friendship, and my parents for their unerring care. This book is for my grandparents from whom all things follow.

ABBREVIATIONS

EEBO   Early English Text Society

ELH   *English Literary History*

JMEMS   *Journal of Medieval and Early Modern Studies*

PL   *Patrologia cursus completus: series latina*, ed. by Jacques-Paul Migne, 221 vols in 222 (Paris: Migne, 1844[–64])

SEL   *Studies in English Literature*

STC   *A Short-Title Catalogue of Books Printed in England, Scotland & Ireland and of English Books Printed Abroad, 1475–1640*, ed. by A. W. Pollard and others, 2nd edn, 3 vols (London: Bibliographical Society, 1976–91)

Foxe, TAMO   Foxe, John, *The Unabridged Acts and Monuments Online or TAMO* (Sheffield: HRI Online Publications, 2011) <http//www.johnfoxe.org> [accessed 18 April 2013]

NOTES TO THE READER

Quotations and Proper Names

All English quotations in the text and notes appear as in their original sources, except in the case of prose where I have not recorded line ends. Quotations from other languages have been translated and the original text given in the notes. Unless otherwise noted, transcriptions and translations are my own. The modern and, where appropriate, English versions of place names are given.

Early Printed Books

Where appropriate and unless otherwise noted, all references to early printed books are to the first complete extant editions. Where it has not been possible to discern the chronology of extant editions the STC numbers of all the earliest editions are given, with the STC number of the edition cited indicated in the notes. In such cases, and unless otherwise noted, the edition with the lowest STC number has been consulted. Attributions and publication details, unless otherwise noted, follow the STC. To distinguish between those printers who share a common surname, both first and second names are given in the Bibliography under the subheading Early Printed Materials.

INTRODUCTION

In his great anti-theatrical work, *Histrio-mastix The players scourge, or, actors tragedie* (1633; STC 20464), William Prynne, Puritan pamphleteer and lawyer, translates part of the entry *De tragoediis* from *Gemma animae* (1100), in which the twelfth-century theologian Honorius Augustodunensis links medieval liturgy with classical theatre:

> Wee must know that those who rehearsed Tragedies on Theaters, did represent unto the people by their gestures, the acts of fighters. So our Tragedian *(thus hath he stiled the Masse-Priest, how aptly the ensuing words enforme us)* represents unto the Christian people by his gestures, the combate of Christ in the Theater of the Church, and inculcates into them the victory of his Redemption. Therefore when the Presbyter saith, (Pray ye,) he acteth or expresseth Christ, who was cast into an agony for us, when he admonished his Apostles to pray. By his secret silence, he signifieth Christ led to the slaughter as a Lambe without a voyce. By the stretching out of his hands, he denotes the extension of Christ upon the Crosse. By the Song of the Preface, be expresseth the cry of Christ, hanging vpon the Crosse, &c.[1]

---

[1] Prynne, *Histrio-mastix* (1633; STC 20464), pp. 113–14. It has been suggested that *Histrio-mastix* was in fact published late in 1632. See Dillon, 'Theatre and Controversy, 1603–1642', p. 379; and Greg, *A Companion to Arber*, p. 85. The Latin original reads: 'Sciendum quod hi qui tragoedias in theatris recitabant, actus pugnantium gestibus populo repraesentabant. Sic tragicus noster pugnam Christi populo Christiano in theatro Ecclesiae gestibus suis repraesentat, eique victoriam redemptionis suae inculcat. Itaque cum presbyter *Orate* dicit, Christum pro nobis in agonia positum exprimit, cum apostolos orare monuit. Per secretum silentium, significat Christum velut agnum sine voce ad victimam ductum. Per manuum expansionem, designat Christi in cruce extensionem. Per cantum praefationis, exprimit clamorem Christi in cruce pendentis.' See *PL*, CLXXII (1854), cols 570a–b.

Honorius explains that classical tragedy involves the representation of actions by gestures to an audience in a theatre (*actus pugnantium gestibus populo repraesentabant*), and it is on the basis of this definition that the Mass-priest is compared to a tragic actor who represents the actions of Christ's passion, crucifixion, and resurrection to his audience, the congregation, in the theatre of the church. Ever since O. B. Hardison's influential *Christian Rite and Christian Drama* (1965), theatre historians and literary critics have suggested that *De tragoediis* indicates the importance of liturgical allegory to the history of drama. According to Hardison, the drama described by Honorius 'has a coherent plot based on conflict (*duellam*) between a champion and an antagonist. The plot has a rising action, culminating in the Passion and entombment. At its climax there is a dramatic reversal, the Resurrection, correlated with the emotional transition from the Canon of the Mass to the Communion. Something like dramatic catharsis is expressed in the *gaudiam* of the Postcommunion.'[2] Given that the *Poetics* was completely unknown in the West until the mid-thirteenth century, Hardison's argument that *De tragoediis* approaches a definition of the Mass as Aristotelian tragedy, complete with peripeteia, anagnorisis, and catharsis, has, on the whole, been rejected or revised by subsequent critics.[3] Nonetheless, as Donnalee Dox has noted, Hardison's analysis does raise important questions about the role of impersonation in dramatic performance. 'To what extent [...] did the celebrant and congregation role play in the ceremonial reenactment of Christ's crucifixion and resurrection?'[4] Clearly Honorius's definition of tragedy as the representation of actions approximates the Aristotelian

---

[2] Hardison, *Christian Rite and Christian Drama*, p. 40.

[3] On 17 March 1256, Hermannus Alemannus finished a Latin translation of the twelfth-century Arabic philosopher Averroes' *Middle Commentary* on Aristotle's *Poetics*, that was, for more than two hundred years, the major source of Aristotelian poetic doctrine in the West. Twelfth-century Arabic culture had no theatrical tradition, so when Averroes confronted the terms 'tragedy' and 'comedy' in the *Poetics* he translated them as 'eulogy' and 'satire'; terms familiar to his Muslim audience. When Hermannus translated the commentary he retained Averroes' mistranslation. For Averroes' paraphrase and commentary see Averroes, *Middle Commentary on Aristotle's Poetics*, ed. by Butterworth. For Hermannus Alemannus's Latin translation see Averroes, *De arte poetica*, trans. by Alemannus.

[4] Dox, '*De tragoediis* and the Redemption of Classical Theatre', p. 44. See also Hardison, *Christian Rite and Christian Drama*, p. 78. Dox has written substantially on liturgical allegory, arguing that the idea of theatre and its use as an analogy for the representational practices of the liturgy reflects the changing status of the mechanical arts tradition in the ninth to twelfth centuries. See Dox, *The Idea of the Theater in Latin Christian Thought*; Dox, 'Roman Theatre and Roman Rite'; and Dox, 'The Eyes of the Body and the Veil of Faith'.

categorization of drama as the imitation (μίμησις) of an action and his use of the verbs 'to represent' (*representare*), 'to convey' (*exprimere*), 'to signify' (*significare*), and 'to denote' (*designare*) suggest that the celebrating priest in *De trageodiis* symbolizes, represents, or impersonates Christ.[5]

Hardison argued that Honorius's allegorical interpretation of the Mass was strongly influenced by the work of his ninth-century predecessor, Amalarius of Metz.[6] In the *Prooemium* to his *Liber officialis*, Amalarius describes the Eucharist in dramatic terms:

Sacraments should have a likeness to the things of which they are a representation. Therefore the priest should be like Christ, just as the bread and liquid are like the body of Christ. So the sacrifice of the celebrant at the altar is like the sacrifice of Christ on the cross.[7]

Though he does not specifically compare the celebrant to an actor, the church building to a theatre, or the Mass to a tragedy, Amalarius's allegory clearly proposes a mimetic relationship between the Mass-priest and Christ. Whether the function of his allegory was pedagogical or exegetical, the suggestion of mimetic embodiment provoked the criticisms of Deacon Florus of Lyons and Archbishop Agobard of Lyons, who accused him of making the Mass theatrical.[8] Although their criticisms were at least partly motivated by a mutual desire to curtail his influence in the diocese of Lyons, Florus's and Agobard's attacks on Amalarius's imaginative embodiment of biblical events reflect an ontological antipathy toward his allegorical method, as well as an ethical concern about the effects of allegorical interpretation on Christian belief. Like Augustine, Amalarius's detractors sought to distance Christian ritual from pagan practice and therefore took issue with the proximity of his imaginative allegory to the idolatrous practice of theatre.[9] Since the theatre was historically associated with

[5] 'Ἔστιν οὖν τραγῳδία μίμησις πράξεως σπονδαίας' ('Tragedy is, then, an imitation of an action'). Aristotle, *Ars poetica*, ed. by Kassel, 1449b. 24.

[6] Hardison, *Christian Rite and Christian Drama*, p. 41.

[7] 'Sacramenta debent habere similitudinem aliquam earum rerum quarum sacramenta sunt. Quapropter, similis sit sacerdos Christo, sicut panis et liquor similia sunt corpori Christi. Sic est immolatio sacerdotis in altari quodammodo ut Christi immolatio in cruce.' *PL*, cv (1864), col. 989a.

[8] See Florus, *Opuscula adversus Amalarium*, in *PL*, cxix (1852); and Agobard, *De Correctione Antiphonarii*, in *PL*, civ (1864). On the authorship and purpose of Agobard's text see Acker, 'Introduction', pp. xx–xxxvii.

[9] See Cabansis, *Amalarius of Metz*, p. 90. For Augustine's critique of theatre see Augustine, *Confessions*, ed. by O'Donnell, i: *Introduction and Text*, pp. 23–25, iii.2.2-iii.3.5; and Augus-

polytheism, licentious behaviour, and worldly materiality, Amalarius's critics had an ethical responsibility to undercut the similarities that he had noted between the representational practices of the ancient theatre and the Christian Mass. But they were equally troubled by the fact that the terms of his allegory prioritized sensual signs over the Bible in the communication of spiritual truth.[10] As the author of liturgical allegories, Amalarius was regarded as a poet of likenesses — a producer of simulations — and his critics, on Augustine's authority, condemned his interpretations as corrupted and corrupting, concerned with worldly appearance rather than spiritual reality.[11] No matter how similar the sacraments are to the things they represent, man-made signs can only represent man-made things, and Amalarius's critics accused him of advancing a form of representation that would encourage worshippers to mistake the signs of things for the things themselves.[12] To paraphrase the Augustinian philosopher James K. A. Smith, this ontological critique of the allegorical method is, in a sense, iconoclastic.[13]

While several important ninth-century ecclesiastical critics cited theatricality as evidence of Amalarius's heretical theology, in the twelfth century Honorius was able to make a far more explicit comparison between the Mass and tragic drama without suffering the same consequences. Nonetheless, for most Latin writers, from Augustine and Isidore, through Gerhoch von Reichersberg and Herrad von Landsberg, to Aelred of Rievaulx, the idea of theatre (*theatrum*) carried negative associations. Following the ethical argument against theatre as a site of irreverent behaviour, Latin clerical usage throughout the Middle Ages employed drama as a rhetoric of abuse to label certain beliefs or practices

---

tine, *De civitate Dei contra paganos libri XXII*, ed. by Welldon, I, 64–66, 265–69, II.9, VI.9. For English translations see Augustine, *Confessions*, ed. and trans. by Chadwick, pp. 35–38; and Augustine, *The City of God*, ed. and trans. by Bettenson, pp. 56–58, 243–48. For a consideration of Augustine's anti-theatrical bias see Asher, 'The Dangerous Fruit of Augustine's *Confessions*'; Fendt, 'The (Moral) Problem of Reading *Confessions*'; and Smith, 'Staging the Incarnation'.

[10] As Dox has noted, Agobard's *De Correctione Antiphonarii* emphasizes the centrality and authority of the Bible, warning that songs and scenarios reminiscent of ancient theatre worked to the detriment of scripture. Dox, 'The Eyes of the Body and the Veil of Faith', p. 35. See also *De Correctione Antiphonarii*, in *PL*, CIV (1864), col. 334c.

[11] In his *Opuscula adversus Amalarium*, Florus attacks Amalarius's project of presenting invisible things in visible forms, ultimately accusing him of 'fabricating fantastic errors and perverse doctrine'. Dox, 'The Eyes of the Body and the Veil of Faith', p. 38. See also *Opuscula*, in *PL*, CXIX (1852), cols 74b, 80c.

[12] See Cabansis, *Amalarius of Metz*, p. 86.

[13] Smith, 'Staging the Incarnation', p. 128.

immoral.[14] Ancient theatre was perceived to be the site of lewd action, bawdy
song, and indecorous behaviour, and its derogatory connotations in authoritative texts like Augustine's *Confessions* and Isidore's *Etymologies* might explain
why the word 'theatre' seldom appears in Middle and Early Modern English.
However, the 1576 opening of London's first successful commercial theatre,
The Theatre, gave the word new currency, and for a vocal coterie of anti-theatrical writers theatre ceased to be a metaphor for idle or worldly behaviour and
was blamed as the reason for it.[15] To its critics the early modern theatre was a
kind of alternative church or anti-church: '[l]ike the real church, it had its own
buildings, and like the real church it held regularly scheduled performances on
Sundays, a practice that was loudly condemned by preachers and magistrates
alike as a profanation of the Sabbath.'[16] And to those reformers who opposed
the stage, the theatre, like the unreformed Catholic Church, was 'sathans
synagogue'.[17] What is more, since both drama and Catholicism were perceived
as encouraging moral degeneracy, idolatry, and sacrilege, to go to a play was
akin to attending Mass. Consequently, simply by quoting Honorius's twelfth-
century allegory in his 1633 anti-theatrical tract, Prynne is able to condemn
both the Catholic Church and the theatre as objects worthy of abuse.

In *De tragoediis*, writes Prynne, 'a Roman *Masse-priest* becomes a *Player*, and
in stead of preaching, of reading, acts christs Passion in the Masse; which this
Author stiles, a *Tragedy*.'[18] The charge that the Mass-priest performs rather than
recites Christ's passion clearly echoes Florus's and Agobard's accusations that
Amalarius's allegories undermined the authority of the Bible by focusing on the
symbolic meaning of the Mass. But unlike Agobard and Florus, who were pow-

---

[14] For further discussion about theatre as a rhetoric of abuse in medieval Europe, see Barish,
The Antitheatrical Prejudice, pp. 38–79; Barnes, 'Christians and the Theater'; Briscoe, 'Some
Clerical Notions of Dramatic Decorum'; Clopper, *Drama, Play, and Game*, pp. 25–62; Henshaw,
'The Attitude of the Church toward the Stage'; Jones, 'Isidore and Theatre'; Marshall, '*Theatre* in
the Middle Ages'; and Schnusenberg, *The Relationship between the Church and the Theatre*.

[15] Records survive for an earlier, failed attempt to establish a permenant structure for the
performance of plays at Whitechapel. The Red Lion, which opened in 1567 and may only have
survived for a couple of months, was backed and built by Burbage's younger brother-in-law,
John Brayne, who went on to supply most of the necessary funds for The Theatre. The first anti-
theatrical tract, Gosson, *The shoole [sic] of abuse*, appeared in 1579 (STC 12097), just three years
after the opening of Richard Burbage's Theatre.

[16] White, *Theatre and Reformation*, p. 172.

[17] Stubbes, *The anatomie of abuses* (1583; STC 23376), sig. L7ᵛ.

[18] Prynne, *Histrio-mastix*, p. 114.

erful members of Amalarius's own diocese, Prynne was a puritan Protestant, and his citation of Honorius serves the dual purpose of highlighting both the idolatry of the Carolingian theatre and theatricality of Roman Catholic liturgy. In fact, the charge of theatricality had first been levelled at the Roman Church by William Tyndale, one of England's earliest reformers, some one hundred years earlier. In *The practyse of prelates* (1530; STC 24465), Tyndale, like Honorius, compares the Mass-priest to a player.[19] But, echoing the kinds of criticism levelled by Agobard and Florus at Amalarius, the allegory is presented in wholly negative terms:

> [I]f a man axe you [i.e. the Catholic priesthood], what youre meruelous fassioned playengcotes and youre other popatrye meane, and what youre disfigured heedes and all youre apesplaye meane, ye knowe not: and yet are they but signes of thinges which ye haue professed.[20]

Like Amalarius's critics, who accused him of shifting attention from the spiritual to the worldly, Tyndale blames the Roman Church for presenting carnal and sensual objects as spiritual truths.[21] Like the costumes, props, and performances in a piece of drama, the vestments ('playengcotes'), symbols ('popatrye'), and rituals of the Catholic Church ('apes playe'), are signs rather than referents. However, unlike a play, the referents of Christian worship — the body and blood of Christ, for instance — are invisible, mystical, but real spiritual truths. With its use of elaborate, visual symbols, Tyndale argues that the Roman Church seduces people into mistaking signs for referents — bread for body, wine for blood — encouraging them to confuse man-made things for divine truths.

Given the reformed equation of Catholicism with theatricality, the argument first made by E. K. Chambers and generally upheld by subsequent scholarship, that early English reformers were encouraged and at times commissioned to produce propagandistic religious drama, may read like something of a

[19] Tyndale makes the same comparison in two further texts: Tyndale, *That fayth the mother of all good works iustifieth vs* ([1528]; STC 24454), often referred to, and printed in later editions as Tyndale, *The parable of the wicked mammon*, and *The obedie[n]ce of a Christen man* (1528; STC 24446).

[20] Tyndale, *The practyse of prelates* ([1530]; STC 24465), sigs A3ᵛ–A4ʳ. This passage is discussed at greater length in Chapter 2, pp. 83–84.

[21] Dox has argued '[b]ecause Amalarius extended the transformative power of the host to other aspects of the Mass, he (from the point of view of his Lyons critics) encouraged people to mistake signs for *res*, the very mistake Augustine had feared.' Dox, 'The Eyes of the Body and the Veil of Faith', p. 39.

paradox.[22] However, while reformers were evidently alive to drama's ontological dangers — its potential to confuse, corrupt, and deceive — a number of surviving plays suggest that for a time drama was used to propagate an anti-Catholic agenda. In fact, it seems that some reformed dramatists went so far as to exploit the phenomenal pressures of the stage, using the visual resources of drama to highlight the dangerous sensuality of Catholicism. Plays like John Bale's *Three Laws* ([*c.* 1547]; STC 1287) and Lewis Wager's *The Life and Repentaunce of Mary Magdalene* (1566; STC 24932) present the sumptuous iconography and elaborate rituals of the Roman Church in order to discredit them as idolatrous and theatrical. By taking the signs of Catholic worship out of the Catholic Church's sacred places and into secular playing spaces, reformed playwrights were able to subvert their conventional meanings. What is more, by assigning them new referents, reformed dramatists exposed the instability of visual signs as vehicles for truth, satirizing Catholicism's dependence on spectacular display.

When Amalarius of Metz suggested that the Mass-priest should be like Christ, he recognized that the Church presents Christian truth in a similar fashion to the way the theatre presents dramatic truth. An actor resembles but is not the same as the character he portrays, and a stage prop is like but not the same as the object it represents. Three hundred and fifty years later, Honorius Augustodunensis rendered this analogy between the Church and the stage yet more explicit when he compared the Mass-priest not to Christ but to an actor playing Christ. In the sixteenth century, reformed playwrights like Bale also recognized the phenomenal similarities between the (Roman Catholic) Church and drama. Literalizing the equation between clerics and actors, they enlisted players to perform the elaborate rituals of the old faith in order to demonstrate the extent to which the representational practices of Catholicism mimicked the representational practices of theatre. But in doing so they risked aligning their drama with the excessive practices of the Roman Church. This may explain, at

---

[22] The argument is first proposed in Chambers, *The Mediæval Stage*, II (esp. ch. 25). It is extended in Chambers, *The Elizabethan Stage*, I (esp. ch. 8). A similar case is made in Collinson, *The Birthpangs of Protestant England*, ch. 4. The argument that the first English Protestants did not reject drama outright has been explored and developed in book-length studies by Paul Whitfield White and Greg Walker. See White, *Theatre and Reformation*; Walker, *Plays of Persuasion*; and Walker, *The Politics of Performance*. The notion that the Reformation was not inimical to drama is the foundational premise of work by Peter Happé, Glynne Wickham, Bernard Spivack, and David Bevington on the topical, rhetorical, and dramaturgical features of Protestant moral interludes. See, for instance, Happé, 'The Protestant Adaptation of the Saint Play'; Wickham, 'The Staging of Saint Plays in Europe'; Spivack, *Shakespeare and the Allegory of Evil*; and Bevington, *Tudor Drama and Politics*.

least in part, why the pro-theatrical consensus eventually broke down in the 1570s and 1580s.[23] But for a period in the second quarter of the sixteenth century drama was used propagandistically to promote religious reform. So rather than reject all drama as idolatrous, reformed dramatists attempted to devise new modes of playing distinct from the histrionic displays of the Catholic Church.

This book is about the relationship between drama and religious reform before and during the English Reformation. I am interested in the way that religious change affected the subjects chosen for dramatic presentation. But, perhaps more crucially, I am concerned with the impact of religious reform on drama as a representational practice. I suggest that the attempts of reformed dramatists to distinguish their drama from the rituals of the Catholic Church resulted in the emergence of new modes of playing. The idea that English reformers developed their own dramatic forms to replace the idolatrous spectacles of the Roman Church is not new. Following Richie Kendall's thesis that the new faith relied heavily on dramatic genres and theatrical modes of presentation, Huston Diehl has suggested that '[b]y inspiring new kinds of rituals, spectacles, and dramas, the reformed religion [...] contributes to the formation of a uniquely Protestant theater in early modern England.'[24] But Diehl's study is about the impact of this 'didactic, polemical, Calvinist, and vehemently anti-Catholic dramatic tradition' on the development of the drama written for the commercial Elizabethan and Jacobean playhouses.[25] Her decision to focus on the impact of religious change on drama produced for the commercial theatres is typical of much recent criticism, and an overwhelming majority of scholars have ignored the wide range of plays patronized and promoted by influential reformers in the first half of the sixteenth century. The obvious exceptions are

---

[23] Chambers argued that the enforcement of the Proclamation of 16 May 1559, which prohibited the dramatic treatment of religious and political subjects, brought an end to the use of drama by theologians and politicians as a propagandistic tool. In turn he suggested that state-imposed censorship was the result of shifts within the Established Church that saw 'the substitution of a Calvinist for a Lutheran bias in the conduct of the Reformation'. See Chambers, *The Elizabethan Stage*, I, 242. White has refined Chambers's original argument by pointing out that it is 'impossible to sustain the view of a Lutheran-oriented English Protestantism generally supportive of the stage up to the 1560s and a Calvinist-oriented Protestantism generally antagonistic towards it afterwards'. See White, *Theatre and Reformation*, pp. 3–4. The decline of religious drama may in fact have as much to do with differing reactions to the emergence of the commercial theatres in the 1570s as with the perceived anti-theatricalism of the Puritan factions within the Elizabethan government.

[24] Kendall, *The Drama of Dissent*; Diehl, *Staging Reform, Reforming the Stage*, p. 5.

[25] Diehl, *Staging Reform, Reforming the Stage*, p. 7.

Paul Whitfield White and Greg Walker. In *Theatre and Reformation*, White shows that from Thomas Cromwell and John Bale in the 1530s to William Cecil and William Wager in the 1560s, reformed leaders and teachers extended the medieval practice of using drama to influence and shape public opinion. He argues that writers and patrons 'were drawn to the theatre by its proven capacity (under Catholic authority) to internalise religious belief and practice, but newly devised it for iconoclastic purposes'.[26] Reformation drama, he argues, revealed the image centredness of Catholicism by presenting 'sumptuously dressed priests and their elaborate rituals on the stage, where (according to Protestants) such pageantry belonged in the first place'.[27] Within this broad thesis, White seeks to outline the material conditions in which Reformation drama operated; to establish exactly what connections and associations existed between playwrights, play texts, acting troupes, and patrons. Greg Walker's two books, *Plays of Persuasion* and *The Politics of Performance*, concern the role of pre-playhouse drama in the shaping of political and religious policy. Like White, Walker addresses the relationship between playwrights and patrons. But where White implicitly endorses a 'top-down' model of patronage, in which reformed writers produced plays designed to instruct audiences in the new faith at the behest of their reformed patrons, Walker explores the possibility that Reformation drama might have equally represented a negotiation between playwrights and patrons, players and audience members, over a variety of contested religious and political issues.[28]

Like these studies by White and Walker, this book is about the polemical use of drama in the century before the opening of the theatres. And like them, I work from the premise that reformed playwrights, like other reformed propagandists, produced texts that were active in the dissemination of reformed practices and beliefs.[29] Reading Reformation plays as agents of reform, I propose that reformed dramatists sought to undermine the rituals, symbols, plays, and processions of the Roman Church and promote reformed alternatives. Consequently, I also argue that the reception of reformed theology and

---

[26] White, *Theatre and Reformation*, p. v.

[27] White, *Theatre and Reformation*, p. v.

[28] Walker, *Plays of Persuasion*; and Walker, *The Politics of Performance*.

[29] A number of critics and historians have examined the relationship between patrons and writers in the spread of reformed doctrine and anti-papal polemic. See, for instance, King, *English Reformation Literature*. Also relevant, although dealing largely with the period post-dating this book are, Bennett, *English Books and Readers*; van Dorsten, 'Literary Patronage in Elizabethan England'; and Rosenberg, *Leicester: Patron of Letters*.

its eventual incorporation into state policy had a direct impact upon dramaturgy as playwrights rejected the spectacular, histrionic modes of playing of the
Catholic Church for new, reformed dramas based on the Word of God. But
attempts to reform drama were only partially successful; in exposing the theatricality of the old faith and dramatizing reform, playwrights like John Bale and
Lewis Wager were forced to confront the proximity of their art to the practices
they sought to condemn.

This book begins with a study of the Croxton *Play of the Sacrament*, a late
fifteenth-century dramatic text that survives in a mid-sixteenth-century manuscript. In it I explore the possibility that spectacular drama was used to refute
late medieval heresy and affirm orthodox doctrine. Showing how the Croxton
Play is different from its continental analogues, I argue that the play's writer or
writers were influenced by Nicolas Love's *De sacramento*, a eucharistic treatise
appended to copies of his translation of the Pseudo-Bonaventuran *Meditationes
vitae Christi, The Mirror of the Blessed Life of Jesus Christ* (c. 1410). Drawing
on accounts of late medieval heresy trials, I suggest that the play, like Love's
Mirror, responds directly to heretical assaults on traditional religion in general and the doctrine of transubstantiation in particular, offering direct, visual
proof of Christ's real presence in the Eucharist. Given its treatment of orthodox eucharistic theology it is perhaps surprising that the play survives in a mid-
sixteenth-century manuscript, and I conclude this chapter by offering some
speculative contexts for its late transcription. Might the play's histrionic sense
of display have appealed to reformers eager to demonstrate the theatricality of
the old faith?

Two middle chapters examine plays written during the reigns of Henry VIII
and Edward VI, and argue that drama continued to be used to manipulate religious belief. During the 1530s Thomas Cromwell encouraged Bale to write
plays which popularized the royal supremacy and undermined papal authority,
and in the second chapter I explore Bale's use of drama to reveal and discredit
the theatricality of Catholic practice as described in Tyndale's anti-papal tracts.
Although Bale is active in the dissemination of reformed ideas, the thrust of
his dramatic propaganda is directed against the Roman Church. Lewis Wager
is less interested in anti-papal polemic, and in the third chapter I argue that his
play, *The Life and Repentaunce of Mary Magdalene*, offers Calvinist teachings
on the primacy of the Bible, the relationship between Mosaic and Christian
law, repentance, and justification by grace through faith. I conclude these chapters by suggesting that the iconic status of drama as an art of the body compli-
cates the attempts made by both playwrights to distinguish their own reformed
drama from the theatricality of Catholicism.

In Amalarius's ninth-century dramatic metaphor, the eucharistic bread is like the body of Christ in the same way that a stage prop is like the object that it represents. Both are signs that stand for, or carry across the meaning of, the referent they represent. But after the Fourth Lateran Council (1215), during which the dogma of transubstantiation was adopted as orthodox doctrine, Christ's presence in the Eucharist ceased to be metaphorical; now when the priest intoned the words of institution the bread became the body of Christ. These two modes of presence — the one figurative, the other substantive — offer competing ritual experiences, and during the Reformation the nature of Christ's presence in the Eucharist was the theologoumenon over which Catholics and reformers most clearly disagreed. This book concludes with a consideration of the Edwardian play *Jacke Jugeler*, in which I argue that the play's subject of mistaken identity mediates in the contemporary conflict between the Archbishop of Canterbury, Thomas Cranmer, and the conservative Bishop of Winchester, Stephen Gardiner, about the nature of Christ's presence in the sacrament of the Eucharist.[30] But unlike Bale and Wager who attempt to separate their drama from the drama they condemn as Catholic, the author of *Jacke Jugeler* recognizes that all drama is energized by an epistemology of deceit, and I conclude by suggesting that the play is at once concerned with and mistrustful of theatricality.

Because the nature of so much of the evidence of Reformation dramatic activity is fragmentary, this book does not purport to offer a master narrative about the impact of religious change on drama. Instead it treats five plays as 'bore holes' through which the cultural interactions between theology and theatricality might be observed. So Chapter 1 focuses on the Croxton *Play* because its histrionic mode of presentation clearly relates to its chosen subject: the miracle of transubstantiation. Chapters 2 and 3 focus on Bale and Wager because their attempts to dramatize reformed theology necessarily result in their related attempts to reform drama. And Chapter 4 examines *Jacke Jugeler* because its treatment of mistaken identity dramatizes competing versions of stage and eucharistic presence. At the same time, in tracing the dramatic treatment of arguments concerning the interpretation of the sacraments, the relationship between priests and players, and the use and abuse of imagery and drama in religious worship, *The Drama of Reform* draws on a rich variety of contextual mate-

---

[30] The debate between Cranmer and Gardiner extended over three printed volumes: Cranmer, *A defence of the true and catholike doctrine of the sacrament* (1550; STC 6000); Gardiner, *An explicatio[n] and assertion of the true catholique fayth* ([1551]; STC 11592); and Cranmer, *An answer of Thomas archebyshop of Canterburye* (1551; STC 5991).

rials, including liturgical texts; heresy trial accounts; dramatic treatises; polemical tracts; and religious laws. So Chapter 1 examines Love's eight eucharist miracle narratives alongside the Croxton *Play*'s dramatic miracle, arguing that the
play seeks to embody what these narratives can only describe. Chapter 2 argues
that Bale's plays literalize William Tyndale's equation of theatricality with
Catholicism by presenting priests as players in real plays. Chapter 3 proposes
that Wager's *Mary Magdalene* performs the conversion of the Magdalene as the
promotion of Martin Bucer's definition of honest playing as outlined in his *De
regno Christi* (c. 1550). And Chapter 4 suggests that by dramatizing the eucharistic debate between Cranmer and Gardiner, *Jacke Jugeler* refocuses discussions
about the relationship between eucharistic and theatrical modes of presence,
between Catholic and reformed rituals and stagecrafts. Performing what other
texts merely narrate, the plays examined in this book enact, sometimes uncomfortably, the proximity between the representational practices of the Catholic
Church and the stage. The result is a direct, if uneasy, confrontation between
the phenomenal and functional features of drama as representational practice.

A Note about Terminology

When Honorius compared the church building to a theatre, he recognized
that theatre was the focal point of ancient pagan society in the same way that
the church was the focal point of contemporary Christian society. But the
reformed polemicists of the sixteenth century do not equate Catholicism with
ancient theatre but with contemporary dramatic practice. Mass-priests are not
likened to tragic actors but to players and jugglers; the Mass is not compared
to a tragedy performed in a theatre, but to a play performed in a contemporary
playing space. Ancient theatres were structures that contained a platform, the
stage, on which the actions were performed; an auditorium from which the
audience could stand and watch the drama unfold; and a scene behind which
the actors could change costume. In England, such formal conditions did not
exist until the successful establishment of commercial playhouses in London
in the 1570s. In the fifteenth and and early sixteenth centuries, drama was performed in a variety of different spaces: royal and aristocratic households; academic institutions; churches and chapels; and inn-yards and market places.[31]

---

[31] Many of these spaces continued to be used for performance long after the opening of the
commercial playhouses. The material aspects of some aspects of pre-playhouse performance are
discussed in: Boas, *University Drama in the Tudor Age*; Motter, *The School Drama in England*;
Southern, *The Staging of Plays before Shakespeare*; Tydeman, *The Theatre in the Middle Ages*;

In other words, plays were enacted in places that were not specifically designed for the performance of drama. Given this absence of any physical structures resembling ancient or modern theatres, I have avoided the use of the words 'theatre' and 'stage' throughout this book, preferring instead 'playing space' as a generic term to refer to the site of performance, and 'player' to describe the men and boys who took part in drama. Nonetheless, it is clear that when reformed propagandists liken Catholic priests to players they draw on the negative connotations of the word 'theatre' as it was used by Latin clerics throughout the Middle Ages. Latin clerical usage recognized theatre as a sign system founded on hypocrisy, deception, and falsehood, in which one thing masqueraded in the likeness of another thing. Because reformed polemicists so clearly invoke these charges when they accuse Catholic priests of mimicry, I retain the words 'theatrical' and 'theatricality' when discussing the criticisms levelled by reformed playwrights at the Roman Church. However, I also use these terms more generally in describing the nature of drama as a representational practice.

In his *A defence of the true and catholike doctrine of the sacrament of the body and bloud of our sauior Christ* (1550; STC 6000), Cranmer uses the word 'catholic' in both the non-ecclesiastical sense to mean 'universally prevalent' and as an epithet to describe his reformed interpretation of the Eucharist 'as the proper continuation in England' of the doctrine of the Ancient Church.[32] To put it another way, the term 'catholic' or universal, was retained by reformers who claimed historical continuity with the Ancient Church as the whole communion of the saved and the saintly. However, in this book I use the word 'Catholic' for Roman Catholic, to designate the unreformed Latin Church, the ecclesiastical body that remained under the Roman obedience after Henry VIII was proclaimed head of the Church of England. Prior to the Reformation the term 'Catholic' was rarely applied to the Church of Rome. Consequently, in my first chapter, which focuses on a play that was composed and most likely performed before the spread of reformed theology, I use the word 'orthodox' to refer to the beliefs and practices 'of, belonging to, or in accordance with the accepted theological or ecclesiastical doctrines' of the Catholic Church.[33] Opinions and doctrines not in accordance with those recognized as orthodox I

Tydeman, *English Medieval Theatre, 1400–1500*; Westfall, *Patrons and Performance*; and White, *Theatre and Reformation*, pp. 130–62.

[32] 'catholic, *adj.*, I., 2, 6. a', in *The Oxford English Dictionary*, 2nd edn, <http://dictionary.oed.com/cgi/entry/50034670> [accessed 5 June 2013].

[33] 'orthodox, *adj.*, 1. a', in *The Oxford English Dictionary*, 2nd edn, <http://dictionary.oed.com/cgi/entry/00334152> [accessed 5 June 2013].

have labelled as 'heterodox' or 'heretical', referring to the men and women who held such beliefs as 'heretics', 'Wycliffites', or 'Lollards'.

At this juncture it may be useful to make a couple of observations about the terms 'Lollard' and 'Lollardy' and 'Wycliffite' and 'Wycliffism' and my use of them in this book. In the introduction to *The Premature Reformation: Wycliffite Texts and Lollard History*, Anne Hudson writes:

> A curriculum vitae of the Lollard movement can be readily, if roughly, outlined: born c.1380 in Oxford, father John Wyclif, educated in Oxford until about 1410 though with frequent excursions further afield especially in the southern half of England; left Oxford because of the persistent hostility of archbishop Arundel; suborned, or even perhaps hijacked, into support of Sir John Oldcastle's revolt of 1414. Because of that indiscretion, compelled by secular as well as ecclesiastical persecution to become a fugitive, even in some circumstances an exile. Increasingly enfeebled, Lollardy according to some versions of the legend, effectively died in the 1430s. But to account for the irrefutable reports of sightings in the 1490s and the early sixteenth century, more reliable versions specify that the decline was followed by a brief, attenuated revival. The patient then gladly relinquished life to his lustier successors, Tyndale, Barnes, Frith, and others. Whether his will was ever read by these is held doubtful, despite the testimony of Bale and Foxe affirming it.[34]

As this playful account implies, Hudson makes no distinction between the terms 'Wycliffite' and 'Lollard'. Rejecting the conventional division between the academic disciples of Wyclif and the later, provincial Lollards, she proposes that 'Wyclif must be regarded as the progenitor of views that, even a century after his death, are argued by the Lollards'.[35] Following Hudson I do not differentiate between the two terms in this book, using the words 'Wycliffism' and 'Lollardy' interchangeably to describe the views about the sacraments, images, the cult of the saints, and the ecclesiastical hierarchy expressed in recorded accounts of heterodox beliefs from the last two decades of the fifteenth century and the first two of the sixteenth. This strategy accords with the terminology used to refer to heresy trial defendants in the episcopal records for the period before the spread of Lutheran theology and ecclesiology in the late 1520s and 1530s.[36]

[34] Hudson, *The Premature Reformation*, p. 1.

[35] Hudson, *The Premature Reformation*, p. 2. However, she does argue that between 1385 and 1450 it is possible to trace a distinction between the way the two words were used. During this period it seems that 'Lollard' was a clearer mark of opprobrium, 'Wycliffite' potentially a more neutral label. See Hudson, *The Premature Reformation*, p. 3.

[36] Hudson discusses the difficulties involved in differentiating between late Lollards and early Protestants. See Hudson, *The Premature Reformation*, pp. 494–507.

The English Reformation is traditionally dated to the 1534 Act of Supremacy, which made King Henry VIII Supreme Head of the Church of England. However, following the publication of Christopher Haigh's *English Reformations* in 1993 it has become increasingly common to think of the various attempts to reform the English Church throughout the sixteenth century as Reformations. As Haigh has argued, '[t]hese English Reformations took some ideas from *the* Reformation; they could happen as they did because they coincided with it. But they were not *the* Reformation, exported across the Channel and installed in England by Luther, Calvin, and Co. Ltd.'[37] In Chapters 2, 3, and 4 I have, for the most part, avoided the use of terms like 'Lutheran', 'Calvinist', and 'Zwinglian' to refer to the beliefs and practices of English men and women who rejected the teachings of the Roman Church. Although it is indisputable that the doctrines of Luther, Calvin, Zwingli, and their followers impacted upon the development of English Protestantism, England's earliest reformers express views that are often idiosyncratic and that may be as indebted to an indigenous tradition of nonconformity as they are to the reform movements on the continent. Consequently I employ the word 'reformed' to describe the beliefs and practices of those 'reformers' who repudiated papal authority. Lower case is used to distinguish these men and women and their faith from the 'Reformers' who followed the 'Reformed' faith of the Swiss and Rhineland theologians Ulrich Zwingli, Martin Bucer, and Heinrich Bullinger.[38] While generic labels can dangerously smooth over or eradicate difference, I have at all times tried to identify those people, books, and ideas that were most instrumental in shaping the beliefs and practices of the men and women who sponsored, wrote, performed, or watched the plays that are the subject of this book. Sometimes this influence came directly from the continent, sometimes from sources closer to home, but what I hope to demonstrate throughout *The Drama of Reform* is the pivotal, if at times uneasy role that drama played in the dissemination of doctrine and practice in an era of great religious uncertainty and change.

---

[37] Haigh, *English Reformations*, p. 13.

[38] Some historians and theologians have used these terms to denote a wider group of reformers and theologians including Pietro Martire Vermigli (Peter Martyr) and John Calvin 'who created and shaped "Reformed" as opposed to Lutheran Protestantism'. I have retained the term 'Calvinist' to denominate this second group. See Wallace, *Puritans and Predestination*, p. 3.

Chapter 1

SPECTACLE AND SACRILEGE:
THE CROXTON *PLAY OF THE SACRAMENT*
AND THE PERFORMANCE OF MIRACLES

A t her trial for heresy on 5 November 1511, Alice Rowley, widow of the late William Rowley, a former mayor of Coventry, was '[a]sked whether she spoke against the sacrament of the altar or heard anyone teaching against the sacrament'.[1] The defendant, one of the leading women of the Coventry Lollard community and also, thanks to the status of her husband, one of its highest ranking, denied the charge, but did admit that 'she spoke the words, "How can the prieste make God?"'.[2] It is a question very similar to those posed by the Jewish protagonists of the Croxton *Play of the Sacrament*, who share Rowley's scepticism about the ability of the Mass-priest to transform the sacramental eucharistic bread into the real body of Christ. Expressing incredulity

---

[1] 'Interrogata preterea an verba habuit cum aliquot contra sacramentum altaris vel audivit aliquem alium contra sacramentum altaris vel audivit aliquem alium contra huiusmodi sacramentum dogmatisasse.' *Lollards of Coventry*, ed. and trans. by McSheffrey and Tanner, pp. 159, 155. Alice Rowley's trial is documented in Lichfield, Record Office, MS B/C/13, Court Book of Bishop Geoffrey Blyth of Coventry and Lichfield, 1511–1512, fols 6ᵛ–7ʳ, 5ʳ (fol. 6ᵛ). The Court Book of Bishop Blyth reveals that Rowley was tried three more times between 31 October 1511 and 24 January 1512.

[2] 'Interrogata an habuit huiusmodi verba, "How can the prieste make God?"'. *Lollards of Coventry*, ed. and trans. by McSheffrey and Tanner, pp. 159, 156. As McSheffrey and Tanner note, William Rowley, who died in 1506, had been a sheriff and Justice of the Peace as well as mayor of Coventry in a long career as civic leader. 'Introduction' in *Lollards of Coventry*, ed. and trans. by McSheffrey and Tanner, pp. 1–56 (p. 27).

at the idea that 'þe might of hys word' can effect a substantial transformation, Jonathas argues that transubstantiation is 'a conceyte' devised by the clergy to 'make vs blynd'.[3] Like the Court Book of Bishop Geoffrey Blyth of Coventry and Lichfield, which uses vernacular quotations to suggest the authenticity of Alice Rowley's recorded beliefs, the Croxton *Play* ventriloquizes the speech of its heterodox protagonists.[4] In this respect, the play, like the Lichfield Court Book, does not offer direct access to genuine heretical beliefs. Instead, both texts offer real examples of the way heterodox thought was portrayed by the orthodox majority. Moreover, just as Rowley is '[w]illing with pure hert and free will to forsake those erroures and articles [...] and to beleve from hensforth aftre the teching of all holy church', so Jonathas is 'bownd to kepe Crystys lawe | And serue þe Father, þe Son and þe Holy Gost' (962–63), swearing to amend his 'wyckyd lyuyng', 'And trust in God, of myghtys most,/Neuer to offend as we haue done befor' (965, 966–67).[5] Like the Lichfield Court Book, the Croxton *Play* defuses the threat of heresy by documenting the abjurations of its heterodox protagonists. But, where the Court Book is the original record of trials carried out in the diocese of Coventry and Lichfield between 1511 and 1512, the Croxton *Play* is the dramatic re-enactment of events reported to have taken place in Aragon in 1461. In other words, the scribes who wrote the Court Book had the clear function of recording the events of the trials that took place under the ecclesiastical authority of Bishop Blyth, but what function might the Croxton *Play* have served in late medieval English society?

In 1410, just three years after Archbishop Thomas Arundel called a convocation at Oxford that would lead to the publication of his anti-Wycliffite Constitutions, the Carthusian prior Nicholas Love composed his translation of the Pseudo-Bonaventuran *Meditationes Vitae Christi*, *The Mirror of the Blessed Life of Jesus Christ*. As the title implies, the text is offered as a vernacular alternative to the Latin gospels, a gospel harmony into which Love's own post-scriptural glosses have been interpolated. Although the Lambeth Constitutions specified 'that no one from now on should translate any text of holy scripture on his own authority into the English language or any other, by way of book, pamphlet or

---

[3] *The Croxton Play of the Sacrament*, ed. by Davis, p. 64, ll. 202, 203. All further references are to this edition with line numbers given in parentheses within the text. The play has also recently been edited by David Bevington and Greg Walker. See *The Croxton Play of the Sacrament*, ed. by Bevington; and *The Croxton Play of the Sacrament*, ed. by Walker.

[4] Alice Rowley's quip about priests being unable to make their makers is quoted in the vernacular. See footnote 2.

[5] *Lollards of Coventry*, ed. and trans. by McSheffrey and Tanner, p. 274.

tract', it is clear that the *Mirror* and Archbishop Arundel's anti-Wycliffite programme were in fact highly compatible.[6] As Love's most recent editor has commented, what the Lollards required was the naked truth of scripture without the intrusion of interpretive dogma. What Love produced 'was a set of meditations on the entire story of the life of Christ with the interpretations embedded in the narrative itself — and more, specifically anti-Lollard, arguments added to that'.[7] Implicitly, the entire text of the *Mirror*, its form, structure, and content, stands in opposition to a Wycliffite world view.[8] In Anne Hudson's words, '[t]hough the inculcation of Christian virtues through the consideration of Christ's life and passion is not, of course, inimical to Lollard thought, the whole method of this particular treatise is contrary to Lollard insistence upon the difference between scripture, on the one hand, and other teaching however pious, on the other.'[9] In this chapter I want to explore the possibility that the Croxton *Play of the Sacrament* is similarly dedicated to the promotion of orthodox doctrine and the opposition of Lollardy. This thesis was first put forward by Cecilia Cutts, who argued that '[w]here the continental tales emphasize only the doctrine of transubstantiation, and subordinate even that to the anti-Jewish and relic aspects', the Croxton Play's emphasis on 'pure doctrine' suggests that it was designed to function as counter-Lollard propaganda.[10] Hudson has argued that because the play does not overtly mention heresy it is difficult to substantiate such a claim.[11] But, resurrecting Cutt's original argument, I want to suggest that the play's treatment of obedience to the ecclesiastical hierarchy, auricular confession, and the Eucharist coincide with Love's anti-Wycliffite additions to the *Meditationes Vitae Christi* and might therefore be understood as a conscious

---

[6] '[S]tatuimus igitur et ordinamus, ut nemo deinceps aliquem textum sacrae scripturae auctoritate sua in linguam Anglicanam, vel aliam transferat, per viam libri, libelli, aut tractus.' The Latin text of the Constitutions is reproduced in full in Wilkins, *Concilia Magnae Britanniae et Hiberniae*, III, 314–19. The English translation quoted above is from Sargent, 'Introduction', p. intro 56.

[7] Sargent, 'Introduction', p. intro 57.

[8] In using the term 'world view' I don't intend to suggest that all Lollards shared the same, fixed vision of society and its need for reform. Instead I refer to those aspects of theology, ecclesiology, and politics that can be traced across a wide range of Wycliffite documents. These ideologies are discussed in Hudson, *The Premature Reformation*, pp. 278–389.

[9] Hudson, *The Premature Reformation*, p. 439.

[10] Cutts, 'The Croxton *Play*: An Anti-Lollard Piece', p. 45.

[11] Hudson, *The Premature Reformation*, p. 445.

reaction to Lollard denigration of these areas of orthodox doctrine.[12] Perhaps more crucially, the histrionic miracle at the heart of the play recalls the miracle narratives offered by Love as affective evidence of the truth of transubstantiation, suggesting that the playwright(s) evolved a spectacular dramaturgy in direct response to Wycliffite attacks on the sensory modality of eucharistic miracles and devotional imagery.

This chapter is divided into four sections. The first provides an overview of recent critical discussion about the Croxton *Play* and offers a close reading which highlights the four main ways that the play is different from its continental analogues. The second argues that these alterations suggest that the play's author(s) may have been directly influenced by the sacramental treatise which appears at the end of all but three non-atelous manuscripts of Love's *Mirror*.[13] The third suggests that the attacks by the play's Jews on the doctrine of transubstantiation, the authority of the clergy, and the efficacy of images resonate powerfully with the recorded testaments of defendants in late medieval heresy trials. Consequently, its stress on eucharistic devotion and its spectacular dramaturgy suggest that, like Love's *Mirror*, it might have been written 'for the edification of the faithful and the confutation of heretics or lollards'.[14] I conclude this chapter by considering the ways in which the play exemplifies both the anti-theatrical criticisms of the authors of the Lollard *Tretise of Miraclis Pleyinge* and the anti-papal criticisms of England's earliest reformers and propose that the play's survival in a mid-sixteenth-century manuscript suggests that it might have appealed to reformers who wished to expose the sensuality of the Roman Church.

---

[12] Love's anti-Wycliffite additions are discussed by Sargent, 'Introduction', pp. intro 54–intro 75. Recently, a number of other critics have returned to and upheld Cutts's original argument. See Nichols, 'Lollard Language in the Croxton *Play of the Sacrament*'; Hill-Vásquez, '"The Precious Body of Crist"'; and Damon, 'Enacting Liturgy: *Estote fortes* in the Croxton *Play of the Sacrament*'.

[13] Oxford, Bodl. Libr., MS Bodley 131, Oxford, Wadham College, MS 5, and Oxford, Bodl. Libr., MS Hatton 31, all lack the treatise. In Manchester, Chetham's Library, MS 6690 it is separate from the main body of the *Mirror*, appearing after other devotional works. In Longleat, The Marquis of Bath, MS 14, it has been added in another hand.

[14] '[A]d fidelium edificacionem, & hereticorum siue lollardorum confutacionem.' Sargent, 'Introduction', p. intro 37. These words conclude the 'Memorandum of Approbation' that either precedes or follows the text of the *Mirror* in twenty of the forty-two manuscripts not deficient at the appropriate juncture.

The Play of the Sacrament

The 'Play of þe Conuersyon of Ser Jonathas þe Jewe by Myracle of þe Blyssed Sacrament' has been uniformly referred to as the Croxton *Play of the Sacrament* since it was first edited by Whitely Stokes in 1860–61 (p. 60). In fact, the only reference to Croxton in the entire play is in the banns, which were presumably played in advance to advertise the play proper, and declare:

> And yt place yow, thys gaderyng þat here ys,
> At Croxston on Monday yt shall be sen;
> To see the conclusyon of þis lytell processe
> Hertely welcum shall yow bene. (73–76)

Although these words seem to suggest that the recorded text represents a touring production, the play's East Anglian provenance (there are Croxtons in Norfolk, Lincolnshire, and Cambridgeshire) is confirmed by linguistic characteristics it shares with other East Anglian texts.[15] The same banns also state the miracle performed by the play originally occurred in Eraclea, 'that famous cyté', in the Kingdom of Aragon 'Yn the yere of our Lord, a thowsand fowr hundder sixty and on' (12, 58). In fact, there is no city called Eraclea in what is now the autonomous region of Aragon, and the play survives in a single manuscript that was copied considerably later than the date the miracle is reported to have happened.[16]

The play's action revolves around a host miracle in which Jews profane the real body of Christ in the form of the host. The most popular version of this genre of libels against Jews sets the events in Paris in 1290, but numerous textual and pictorial examples from across Europe occur throughout the late Middle Ages and into the sixteenth century.[17] The Croxton *Play* represents the sole English dramatic example of this kind of host miracle, but dramatic treatments of this theme are recorded in Italy, the Netherlands, and France.[18]

---

[15] The play's language is discussed in Davis, 'Introduction to *The Croxton Play of the Sacrament*', pp. lxxvi–lxxxv.

[16] For a full discussion of the problems involved in the dating of the manuscript see my article, Atkin, 'Playbooks and Printed Drama'.

[17] Davis includes a brief discussion of the legend in Davis, 'Introduction to *The Croxton Play of the Sacrament*', pp. lxxiii–lxxv. For a fuller treatment of similar themes see *The Blood Libel Legend*, ed. by Dundes; and Rubin, *Gentile Tales*.

[18] In 1473 Florentine actors performed a host miracle play as part of a festival held in Rome in honour of Leonore of Aragon. The Florentine printer Bartolomeo de'Libri (*fl.* 1487–1500)

Although the Eucharist is tested in all surviving dramatic versions, the English play differs from these continental versions in a number of significant ways. The European versions dramatize historical events commemorated by extant sites of worship, usually in Paris or Rome. In other words, they make truth claims about the recent past that are supported by contemporary devotional practices. But the Croxton *Play* takes place in a fictional city; there are no documentary versions of the narrative it dramatizes; and there are no relic shrines dedicated to a miracle 'don in the forest of Aragon, in [...] the yere of owr Lord God M cccc.lxj' (p. 89).[19] Perhaps, as Cutts has suggested, 'the choice of a vague and foreign setting' was a deliberate attempt on the part of the writer(s) to keep the doctrinal teaching on a high and spiritual plain'.[20] Certainly the other innovations have the effect of emphasizing the play's theological message. In other versions, the host is betrayed by a poor woman who conceals it under her tongue; in the Croxton *Play* a merchant agrees to steal it for a considerable sum of money. The Croxton *Play* incorporates a comic scene involving a quack doctor and his boy that has no obvious analogues in any of the continental versions. Indeed, so different is the tone of this comic episode that at least one critic has concluded that it is a later interpolation.[21] Finally, in all other versions vengeance is taken on the Jewish ringleader, but in the Croxton *Play*, Jonathas and his men are forgiven and freely convert to Christianity. As David Lawton has commented, '[t]he ending of the Croxton play is uniquely at odds with the active intolerance that generated such stories in the first place. It is, on the face of it, a bizarre choice — to turn a Host miracle into a story of Jewish conver-

---

published a dramatic version of the miracle, *La Rappresentazione d'un miracolo* ([*c*. 1498]), which may have been identical to the play performed in Rome in 1473 and was reprinted several times in the sixteenth century. A Dutch play, roughly the same length as the Croxton *Play*, was written and performed at Breda in around 1500, and three separate editions of a French play, titled *Le mistere de la saincte hostie* ([*c*. 1512–19]), *Le mistere de la saincte hostie nouuellement imprimé* ([*c*. 1530–37]), and *Le Jeu et Mystere de la Saincte Hostie par personnages* ([*c*. 1547–66]), were printed in the sixteenth century. For further discussion of the Croxton *Play*'s relation to these continental analogues see Barns, 'The Background and Sources of the Croxton *Play of the Sacrament*'; Cutts, 'The English Background of the *Play of the Sacrament*'; and Wright, 'What's so "English" about Medieval English Drama?'.

[19] This note appears on the final folio of the manuscript, Dublin, Trinity College, MS F. 4. 20, fols 338ʳ–356ʳ (fol. 355ᵛ).

[20] Cutts, 'The Croxton *Play*: An Anti-Lollard Piece', p. 47.

[21] Craig, *English Religious Drama of the Middle Ages*, pp. 326–27. In fact, there are good reasons for believing that the episode belongs to the play's original design See pp. 27–28 below..

sion and Christian apostasy.[22] In what follows I attend more closely to these four distinct features of the English version. In doing so, I intend to sketch the contours of recent critical discussion about the play. But I also hope to demonstrate the extent to which the writer(s) of the English version worked in a context and with materials foreign to the writers of the continental versions.

The relocation of events from Paris or Rome in the late thirteenth century to Aragon in 1461 suggests that on one level the play seeks to dramatize a connection between anti-Jewish rhetoric and anti-Jewish policy. The original 1290 libel concerning a Parisian Jew provided both the context and justification for King Philip IV of France's decree of expulsion of the Jews in 1306.[23] It may be that the miracle 'don in the forest of Aragon, in the famous cite Eraclea, the yere of owr Lord God M cccc.lxj' was designed to provide a similar backdrop to the expulsion of the Jews from Spain by King Ferdinand and Queen Isabella in 1492. Although it is impossible to determine whether or not the Croxton *Play* was written before or after the expulsion, the transfer to an Iberian setting does seem to indicate an awareness of the increasingly difficult conditions for Jews in Spain in the late fifteenth century and might even be taken to illustrate the use of host libel narratives by the Spanish authorities to manipulate the diabolic Jewish stereotype in order to justify a policy of expulsion. What is more, at the play's end Jonathas and his men, like the exiled Jews of Spain, resolve to 'walke by contré and cost, | Owr wyckyd lyuyng for to restore: | And trust in God, of myghtys most, | Neuer to offend as we haue don befor' (964–67). The Croxton *Play* might conclude with their conversion, but as they leave the playing space the play's Jews persist as the wandering Jews of Christian legend.[24] Nonetheless, while recent scholarship has been eager to insist that the play's Jews represent real Jews, it has, for the most part, insisted on their real absence.[25] England

---

[22] Lawton, 'Sacrilege and Theatricality', p. 289.

[23] For further discussion of the expulsion of the Jews from France in 1306 see Chazan, *Medieval Jewry in Northern France*, esp. pp. 182–86; and Menache, 'Faith, Myth, and Politics'.

[24] For a thorough discussion of the evolution of the legend in literature see Anderson, *The Legend of the Wandering Jew*. Most medieval versions of the myth follow the 1228 entry in Roger of Wendover's *Flores historiarum* and Matthew Paris's *Chronica maiora*. On these entries and for Paris's illustration see Lewis, *The Art of Matthew Paris*.

[25] Scholarly work that has focused on the question of the play's Jews includes: Beckwith, 'Ritual, Church, and Theatre', esp. pp. 72–75; Clark and Sponsler, 'Othered Bodies'; Kruger, 'The Bodies of Jews in the Middle Ages'; Kruger, 'The Spectral Jew'; Lampert, 'The Once and Future Jew'; and Ruth Nisse, 'Into Exiled Hands: Jewish Exegesis and Urban Identity in the Croxton *Play of the Sacrament*', in Nisse, *Defining Acts*, pp. 99–124.

was the first European country to showcase a policy of expulsion, and following increasing restrictions on their work and dress, Jews were expelled in 1290.
But by situating the play in Spain, the author(s) of the Croxton *Play* go out of
their way to prevent an anachronistic Jewish presence. Moreover, '[w]ho is to
say that the play's representation of Jewish merchants passing through a local
port may not testify indirectly to the actual experience of East Anglia in the
fifteenth century'?[26] According to Lawton, 'we should be inquiring into the
possible presence of Jews, and people's perceptions of them, not their assumed
absence and fictive construction.'[27] Nonetheless, the legal absence of Jews in
England in the late Middle Ages introduces the possibility that the play's Jews
are figures for something more familiar to a late medieval East Anglian audience, and a number of critics have explored the possibility that the play's Jews
stand in for Lollards.[28]

If the removal of the action to Aragon has refocused the critical discussion
about the play's Jews, the betrayal of the host by a merchant rather than a woman
refines questions about the relationship between the competing economies of
the host and profit driven commerce. Discussion on this subject has centred on
the scene in which the host is given a market value when Jonathas buys it from
Aristorius. The negotiation begins with Jonathas's offer of 'twenti pownd' for
'Yowr God, [...] in a cake' (282, 285). Aristorius's initial response is one of out-
rage: he will not sell the host, not even 'for an hundder pownd' (288). Jonathas
increases his offer, this time suggesting a sum of forty pounds. Again, Aristorius
insists that he 'w[o]ld not for a hundder pownd' (312). Finally, Jonathas, call-
ing Aristorius's bluff, offers 'an hundder pownd' (315). The deal is sealed, and
Aristorius agrees to deliver the goods 'To-morowe betymes' (321). Sarah
Beckwith has commented that 'the point here is not so much the final price of the
host but the fact that in the process of being bargained for it is exposed to a different financial and symbolic economy.'[29] In a way she is right: the haggling between
the two merchants renders the immutable, priceless body of Christ mutable and
valuable or as Seth Lerer has put it, bargaining over its price transforms the host's

---

[26] Lawton, 'Sacrilege and Theatricality', p. 293.

[27] Lawton, 'Sacrilege and Theatricality', p. 293.

[28] See, for instance, Cutts, 'The English Background of the *Play of the Sacrament*'; Cutts,
'The Croxton *Play*: An Anti-Lollard Piece'; Gibson, *The Theater of Devotion*, pp. 34–40;
Nichols, 'The Croxton *Play of the Sacrament*: A Re-Reading'; Nichols, 'Lollard Language in
the Croxton *Play of the Sacrament*'; Hill-Vásquez, '"The Precious Body of Crist"'; and Damon,
'Enacting Liturgy: *Estote fortes* in the Croxton *Play of the Sacrament*'.

[29] Beckwith, 'Ritual, Church, and Theatre', p. 69.

'absolute and stable value as a symbol into something that may be exchanged: a thing of fluid, thus ultimately debased worth'.[30] But such observations ignore the fact that at the start of the bartering process the sum that is finally agreed on is unimaginably large. Aristorius's first response to Jonathas's bargain, 'I woll not for an hundder pownd', names a price beyond the dreams of avarice. But by the end of the negotiating process this inconceivable sum has become a tangible amount, 'an hundder pownd, neyther mor nor lasse, | Of dokettys good' (315–16). A sum without currency, one hundred pounds, has been transformed into an amount of coins, one hundred pounds in ducats.[31] What is more, the final figure that the two merchants agree on is more than just a cipher for a lot of money.[32] The Venetian ducat was one of two dominant gold coins of the later Middle Ages. First struck in 1282, it retained its original weight and purity until its last issue in 1840. Conversely, at the beginning of the sixteenth century, after many medieval debasements, the pound sterling as a money-of-account represented just over half a Tower pound of sterling silver in weight (186.7g).[33] When Jonathas offers Aristorius one hundred pounds in ducats he is offering him the sum in ducats that would be necessary to buy one hundred pounds sterling on the day of trade. It is a good deal. At the time of exchange one hundred pounds in ducats would have been equivalent to around four thousand five hundred pence. By 1526 the same number of ducats would be worth five thousand and sixty three pence. Like

---

[30] Lerer, '"Represented Now in Yower Syght"', p. 49. Other critics who have treated this topic include: Reid-Schwartz, 'Economies of Salvation'; Higginbotham, 'Impersonators in the Market'; and Ciobanu, '"City of God?"'.

[31] Pound coins have only been in circulation since 1983, when they were introduced to replace the one pound banknote. However, the predecimal sovereign, which was first minted in 1489, had the value of one pound sterling. Other late medieval plays have been dated on the basis of coins mentioned in their texts. For example, noting Nowaday's demand for 'rede reyallys', that is royals or rose nobles (originally minted 1464/5), and the conspicuous absence of the angel (first minted sometime between 1468 and 1470), Donald Baker has dated the East Anglian morality play *Mankind* to 1464–71. The currencies and coins mentioned in the Croxton *Play* are of no such use. Pound coins did not exist and ducats had been in circulation since 1284. See *Mankind*, in *The Macro Plays*, ed. by Eccles, pp. 153–184 (p. 169, l. 465). See also Baker, 'The Date of *Mankind*'; and Baker, 'The Angel in English Renaissance Literature'.

[32] Between 1360 and 1530 a master carpenter working at Oxford, Exeter, or Canterbury would have earned around six pence per day. In other words, one hundred pounds was considerably more than the annual salary of the most highly skilled craftsman of the later Middle Ages. See Brown and Hopkins, 'Seven Centuries of Building Wages'.

[33] A Tower pound is equal to 5400 grains or 349.944 g. Until 1526 the English monetary unit known as the pound was a Tower pound of sterling silver. In 1526 the standard was altered to the Troy pound (5760 grains or 373.242 g).

the host that they buy, these ducats continue in their outward appearance even while their inward value multiplies.

Arguments about 'mercantilism's absorption of the Host into its commercial economy' can clearly be extended to include the analogies that the play draws between the competing authorities of religion and trade; between mighty merchants and the Lord Almighty.[34] At the play's opening Aristorius introduces himself as 'Syr Arystory [...] A merchaunte myghty of a royall araye' (89–90). This impression of merchants invested with the power and authority of kings is heightened in the speech that follows:

> In Antyoche and in Almayn moch ys my myght,
> In Braban and in Brytayn I am full bold,
> In Calabre and in Coleyn þer rynge I full ryght,
> In Dordrede and in Denmark be þe clyffys cold;
> In Alysander I haue abundaw[n]se in the wyde world.
> In France and in Farre fresshe be my flower[ys],
> In Gyldre and in Galys haue I bowght and sold,
> In Hamborowhe and in Holond moch merchantdyse ys owrys; (97–104)

Aristorius's trading empire maps the extent of the known world. Lawton has suggested that Aristorius's alliterative map is a close relation to the Knight's portrait in Chaucer's *General Prologue*.[35] Like Aristorius's list of places in which he might buy and sell, the Knight's list of places to attack and defend is a 'wide-ranging survey of world geography [... and ...] needs to be recognized as a topos of medieval literature'.[36] Such maps, Lawton has added, explore the relationship between Christianity (the religion) and Christendom (the area on the map it controls): 'If religion is so right, and its one true God so omnipotent, how does it come about that Christendom itself is so circumscribed, and that the areas it fails to control, including its own holy places, should be so far from being "marginal" or "peripheral" by the yardstick of the map?'[37] But Aristorius's map does more than illustrate Christianity's geographical limitations; it also reveals the extent to which trade relations are not bound by such restrictions. And by alliterating from 'Antyoche' to 'Oryon', Aristorius suggests that he and not God is 'Alpha and Omega, the first and the last'.[38] To put it another way, the figure of

---

[34] Reid-Schwartz, 'Economies of Salvation', p. 2.

[35] The Knight's portrait in the *General Prologue* to *The Canterbury Tales*, in Chaucer, *The Riverside Chaucer*, ed. by Benson, p. 24, I (A), ll. 43–78.

[36] Lawton, 'Sacrilege and Theatricality', p. 286.

[37] Lawton, 'Sacrilege and Theatricality', p. 286.

[38] '[E]go sum Alpha et Omega principium et finis.' Revelation 1. 8.

the merchant and the commercial system of exchange that he represents intro-
duce a challenge to the authority of God and the salvific economy of the host.
However, although the play introduces commerce as a threat to the symbolic
construction of the Eucharist, it ends by reasserting the authority of orthodox
doctrine and practice. The reinstatement of the host on the church altar by the
Episcopus illustrates the host's reabsorption into the Christian economy of salvation. And the penance imposed on Aristorius by the Episcopus, 'neuermore
for to bye nor sell' (915), demonstrates the merchant's impotence in the face of
ecclesiastical authority.

The comic episode involving the Flemish quack, 'Mayster Brendyche of
Braban' (533), and his mocking boy, Coll, similarly represents a mundane
threat to the supremacy of orthodox Christianity by opposing human and
divine medicine, physical and spiritual health. However, it is a threat that fails
to dupe the play's Jewish protagonists; they chase the doctor and his boy out
of the playing space before either has had an opportunity to demonstrate their
so-called healing powers. Victor Scherb has argued that the Jews' recognition
of 'the imposters for what they are', their 'chasing away of the false healer' and
his boy, sets the stage for their eventual acceptance of the true healer, Christ
the doctor.[39] The topos of *Christus medicus* derives from the metaphor of
Christ as physician in Mark 2. 17, and occurs frequently in Origen, Tertullian,
Augustine, and Jerome.[40] In his sermons Augustine frequently returns to the
figure of the divine physician, and it is his work more than any other patristic or
medieval writer that seems to bear directly upon the treatment of the trope in
the Croxton *Play*. For instance, in sermon 174 Augustine describes the Passion
as an attack by insane patients against their doctor:

> Desperately ill is he who, in his delirium, strikes the Physician. Of what nature
> then must be the madness of the patient who kills the Physician? And how great,
> indeed, must be the goodness and power of the Physician who, from His blood, has
> prepared the medicine for His killer?[41]

---

[39] Scherb, *Staging Faith*, p. 78.

[40] 'Hoc audito Jesus ait illis: Non necesse habent sani medico, sed qui male habent: non
enim veni vocare justos, sed peccatores.' 'When Jesus heard it, he saith unto them, They that are
whole have no need of the physician, but they that are sick: I came not to call the righteous, but
sinners to repentance.' Mark 2. 17.

[41] '[D]esperate aegrotat, qui per insaniam medicum caedit. Qualis ergo ejus insania, qui
medicum occidit? Quanta vero bonitas et potentia medici, qui de sanguine suo, insano interfec-
tori suo medicamentum fecit?' *PL*, xxxviii (1865), col. 943.

Augustine describes the attitude of the Jews towards Christ as a form of spiritual insanity. They killed the physician, but in turn were cured by the sacrament of His blood which, in their madness, they had shed. The same train of thought is clearly found in the Croxton *Play*. Like their biblical forebears, Jonathas and his men subject Christ to 'new passyoun', 'a new turmentry' when they put the sacrament to 'dystresse' (38, 45, 72). Just as Augustine characterizes the Jews who buffeted Christ as insane or spiritually sick, so Jonathas '*renneth wood, with þe Ost in hys hond*' (503 sd). For Jonathas and his men, as for the scriptural Jews who tortured Christ, the cure for this madness is the medicinal blood that He 'b[l]edyth owt on euery syde!' (714). The success of this cure is two-fold since contrition of the heart, 'Alas, þat euer I dyd agaynst thy wyll' (786), and conversion of the spirit, 'Oh thow my Lord God and Sauyowr, osanna!' (778), precipitate the miraculous renovation of Jonathas's hand. In comparison with this all-powerful physician, Brundyche, who leaves the playing space at the first sign of trouble, seems particularly unimpressive. Consequently, I disagree with Lawton, who has suggested that the Flemish quack episode 'serves to undermine easy assumptions that the play exists as orthodox propaganda on the eucharist'.[42] To my mind the episode functions to emphasize the inadequacy of human science in direct contrast to the spiritual salve offered by Christ's real presence in the Eucharist. A more effective piece of orthodox propaganda can hardly be imagined.

Augustine's treatment of *Christus medicus* also illuminates the decision to stage the Jews' conversion rather than execution. For Augustine, Christ's medical authority is particularly evident in His healing of Saul, famous as an early persecutor of the Church. As Thomas Martin has observed, 'Augustine delighted in the opportunity to highlight the particularly remarkable transformation of *Saulus Persecutor* to *Paulus Praedicator*. It was all the work of *Christus medicus*.'[43] In sermon 175 Augustine diagnosed the Jews who buffeted Christ with a form of mental disturbance. In sermon 88, he similarly identifies Saul's cruelty as a form of spiritual madness, characterized, as before, by brutality and unbelief. And like those Jews who were amazed, did penance, and were converted and healed, so Saul is struck down and transformed from persecutor to preacher:

> Saul persecuted the members of Him [Christ] who was already sitting on His throne in heaven. Having lost his mind and being desperately ill, he persecuted them fiercely with his madness. But Christ calling from heaven: 'Saul, Saul, why

[42] Lawton, 'Sacrilege and Theatricality', p. 288.

[43] Martin, 'Paul the Patient', p. 220.

dost thou persecute me?' (Acts 9. 4), by this word alone struck him down, a raging man, and raised him up whole.[44]

The similarities between Augustine's version of Paul's conversion and the conversion of the Croxton *Play*'s Jews are worth noting. After its transformation from bleeding host, the image of the tortured Christ repeats the question asked of Saul on the road to Damascus, '[w]hy wrath ye me?' (724). In response, the Jews, like Saul, are stunned by His words and fall to their knees in prayer. And raised up, they, like Paul, commit themselves to a life of pious preaching as they 'walke by contré and cost' (964).

Scherb has suggested that

> [t]he play could have ended with Jonathas's cure if the writer meant only to show the conversion of the Jews, but the larger healing process is not yet complete. His ambitions were more expansive, and in the play's final section the action extends to and encompasses the community of the faithful involving the entire audience, as the action of the play symbolically cures them of their sickness of doubt.[45]

In this final section, Jesus's words to the contrite Jews implicitly extend His medicinal powers to the clergy, represented in the play by the figure of the Episcopus. Paraphrasing Christ's command to the ten lepers in Luke 17. 14, 'Go shew yourselves unto the priests', the image of Jesus gives the commandment '*Ite et ostendite vos sacerdotibus meis*' (765).[46] Noting the addition of the significant pronoun '*meis*', which converts the Vulgate's 'to the priests' to 'to *my* priests', Scherb has argued that Jesus's words link 'Christ's original actions with the contemporary clergy's miracles of spiritual healing, most obviously mani-

---

[44] 'Persequebatur membra ejus jam sedentis in coelo Saulus: persequebatur graviter in phrenesi, mente perdita, morbo nimio. At ille una voce de coelo clamans ei, *Saule, Saule, quid me persequeris?* percussit phreneticum, erexit sanum; occidit persecutorem, vivificavit praedicatorem.' See *PL*, XXXVIII (1865), col. 538. The use of a single word, 'membra', to refer to both Christ's body and the community of the faithful strongly recalls 1 Corinthians 12. 12–14: 'For as the body is one, and hath many members, and all members if that one body, being many, are one body: so also is Christ. For by one Spirit we are all baptized into one body, whether we be Jews or Gentiles, whether we be bond or free; and have been all made to drink into one Spirit. For the body is not one member, but many.' 'Sicut enim corpus unum est, et membra habet multa, omnia autem membra corporis cum sint multa, unum tamen corpus sunt: ita et Christus. Etenim in uno Spiritu omnes nos in unum corpus baptizati sumus, sive Judæi, sive gentiles, sive servi, sive liberi: et omnes in uno Spiritu potati sumus. Nam et corpus non est unum membrum, sed multa.'

[45] Scherb, 'The Earthly and Divine Physicians', p. 168.

[46] '[I]te ostendite vos sacerdotibus.'

fested in their ministration of the Sacraments'.[47] In fact, rather than ministering the sacraments, the most obvious display of the Episcopus's healing power is his transformation of the bloody image of Christ back to its accidental form as bread. This cure clearly recalls Christ's physical healing of Jonathas's hand. At the same time, Christ's spiritual healing, indicated by the Jews' confession of doubt and conversion of spirit, is echoed by the Episcopus's baptism of the Jews at the play's end. By replacing execution with conversion, the play dramatizes the extension of Christ's medicinal powers to the contemporary clergy. And after the comic buffoonery of the quack and his boy, the effectiveness of the Episcopus's healing powers can hardly be underestimated. Physically transforming the image of Christ back to its appearance as bread and spiritually converting the plays' Jewish persecutors to Christian preachers, the figure of the Episcopus acts as a powerful defence of the contemporary clergy as the true doctors of late medieval England.

In different ways, the Croxton *Play*'s four significant alterations to the original and commonest host libel draw attention to and defend the most contested aspects of late medieval orthodox religious practice and belief, including the religious use of images, the sacraments of baptism, penance, holy orders, and, in particular, the Eucharist. Though it might be impossible to fully uncover the play's original function, its treatment of these most controversial points of orthodox doctrine suggests that it might have served to promulgate and defend traditional religious practices and beliefs against the range of criticisms expressed by Lollards and other late medieval heretics. In the next section, I turn to Nicholas Love's *Mirror of the Blessed Life of Jesus Christ* not only as an example of the kind of vernacular works that were written in response to heretical attacks on orthodoxy, but also as a possible source for the Croxton play's idiosyncratic treatment of the original host libel.

Seeing and Believing

Although the Croxton *Play* represents the only known English dramatic version of a host miracle, between the proclamation of the doctrine of transubstantiation as dogma at the fourth Lateran Council in 1215 and the promulgation of the feast of Corpus Christi by Pope Urban IV and its official adoption at the Council of Vienne in 1311, numerous Latin accounts of host miracles appeared

---

[47] Scherb, 'The Earthly and Divine Physicians', p. 169. Rudolf Arbesmann has traced the comparison of priests with doctors to Cyprian. See Arbesmann, 'The Concept of "Christus Medicus" in St. Augustine', p. 7; Cyprian, *De lapsis*, ed. and trans. by Bévenot, pp. 21–23, ch. 14.

across Europe.[48] And, as Leah Sinanoglou has argued, '[b]y the late fourteenth and fifteenth century, veneration of the host was a cult of fanatical proportions' and was accompanied by a proliferation of vernacular narrative versions of host miracles.[49] In late medieval England, the most widely available vernacular accounts of host miracles were the eight narratives that appear in the sacramental treatise 'at þe last ende of þis boke [Nicholas Love's *Mirror*] as in a conclusion of alle'.[50] These narratives, which offer 'opune prefe' of transubstantiation (228, ll. 3–4), derive from a number of sources: Aelred of Rievaulx's *Life of Saint Edward, King and Confessor*; Adam of Eynsham's *Life of Saint Hugh of Lincoln*; Paul the Deacon of Montecassino's *Life of Gregory the Great*; and Gregory I the Great's *Dialogues, Commentary on Job*, and *Gospel Homilies*.[51] In Love's words, 'I shalle telle shortly sume merueiles & myracles þat I fynde writen, þe whech bene of so grete auctorite as to my felyng þat þere may no man aȝeyn sey hem bot he be worse þan a Jewe or a payneme' (228, ll. 5–8). Such is the authority of these miracles and their authors that to dispute them would mark the backbiter worse than a Jew or pagan. Of course this is exactly what the Croxton *Play*'s Jewish protagonists do. While the narratives are direct translations or paraphrases from other well known sources, Love's classification of them into three groups is unique. The first group consists of miracles in which 'oure lorde

---

[48] Many of the more famous examples are discussed in, Sinanoglou, 'The Christ Child as Sacrifice', esp. pp. 491–98.

[49] Sinanoglou, 'The Christ Child as Sacrifice', p. 498.

[50] Love, *The Mirror of the Blessed Life of Jesus Christ*, ed. by Sargent, pp. 3–239 (p. 154, ll. 8–9). All further references are to this edition with page and line numbers given in parentheses within the text. Sargent begins the 'Introduction' to this edition by asserting that 'to judge by the number of surviving manuscripts and early prints, it was one of the most well-read books in late-medieval England'. The text survives in sixty-four manuscripts, of which fifty-nine were originally complete, and was printed nine times before 1535. To put these figures in context, Sargent notes that the Wycliffite Bible survives in over two hundred manuscripts; the *Prick of Conscience* in 123, of which 115 were originally complete; and the *Canterbury Tales* in eighty-two, of which fifty-five were originally complete. Sargent, 'Introduction', p. intro 1.

[51] The relevant passages are: p. 228, l. 17 to p. 229, l. 37, a translation from Aelred's *Vita sancti Edwardi regis et confessoris*, in *PL*, cxcv (1855), cols 760–61; p. 230, ll. 1–30, a translation from Adam of Eynsham, *The Life of Saint Hugh of Lincoln*, ed. and trans. by Douie and Farmer, i, 85–92; p. 230, l. 36 to p. 231, l. 13, a translation from *Vita, auctore Paulo Diacono Monacho Cassinensi*, in *PL*, lxxv (1862), cols 52–53; p. 233, l. 11 to p. 234, l. 23, a translation from Gregory's *Dialogorum Libri IV*, in *PL*, lxxvii (1862), cols 424–25, and from his *Homiliae in Evangelia XXXVII*, in *PL*, lxxvi (1857), cols 1274–81; p. 233, ll. 28–35, a translation from *Dialogorum Libri IV*, in *PL*, lxxvii (1862), cols 420–21; p. 234, l. 39 to p. 235, l. 12, a paraphrase from *Dialogorum Libri IV*, in *PL*, lxxvii (1862), col. 425; and p. 235, l. 35 to p. 236, l. 10, a translation from Gregory's *Moralia in Job*, in *PL*, lxxvi (1857), col. 659.

sumtyme sheweþ opunly [...] to confort hem þat bene in trewe byleue & kyndle
hir hertes in to þe more feruent loue of god' (228, ll. 9–12). In other words,
miracles in which the person of Jesus, 'in likenes of a passyng faire litel childe'
perhaps (230, ll. 10–11), is made visible to inspire the faithful. Love recounts
two exempla to illustrate this type of miracle. The first, drawn from Aelred's
Life of Edward the Confessor, records a vision of Christ in the elevated host as
seen by King Edward the Confessor and Earl Leofric of Mercia (228–29). In
the second, translated from Adam of Eynsham's *Life of Saint Hugh*, a clerk is
reported to have seen a vision of a beautiful child in the host (229–30). The
second group of miracles are those 'shewede in þis blessede sacrament of goddes
body' to 'conuerte hem þat bene of misbyleue in to þe trewe byleue' (230, ll. 32,
33). Here too Love offers two examples (230–33). In the first, derived from the
Life of Gregory the Great, a Roman matron who scoffed at the Eucharist since
she had herself baked the bread for the offertory witnesses and is converted by

a vision of the host in 'þe likenes of a fynger in flesh & blode' (231, ll. 7–8).
After her conversion, 'þe self sacrament by praiere of seynt gregour turrnede in
to þe likenes of brede as it was before' (231, ll. 9–10). In the second example,
also from the *Life of Saint Hugh*, a priest describes how he was converted from
his former dissolute life by the sight of the host turned flesh and blood when it
was broken before the second elevation. The third type are miracles that offer
'opune prefe of þe grete vertue þerof in delyuerance of peynes & sauynge fro
bodily meschefe & gostly' (233, ll. 7–9). These are all drawn from Gregory, and
include the story of a prisoner whose 'bondes were lowsede & vndone' by
the power of the Eucharist (233, l. 20), and the tale of a lost shipman nour-
ished by 'one' that 'aperede to him in middes [of] þe see & ȝafe him brede
to ete, þe which also sone as he hade eten, he toke strengþe, & sone after in a
shippe, þat came þereby he was taken & brouht to lande safe' (234, ll. 15–18).

In all extant dramatic versions of host desecration narratives, the violence
inflicted on the host produces two miracles. The torture sequence in the French
play, *Le mistere de la saincte hostie*, offers a representative example. First Jacob
the Jew 'takes the host and nails it with a nail to a column and blood runs out
upon the ground'.[52] Then 'he casts it into the fire, where it will not stay'.[53] Next

[52] '[P]rent l'hostie et la cloue d'un clou en une coulompne et le sang en coule a terre.' *Le mistere de la saincte hostie*, sigs A1ʳ–L4ᵛ (sig. C2ʳ), in *Le Mistere de la Saincte Hostie*, ed. by Petryszcze. Although the second edition, *Le mistere de la saincte hostie nouuellement imprimé* was reissued in Aix in 1817, there are no modern, critical editions of the play. However, Petryszcze's online text provides a parallel transcription of all three sixteenth-century imprints. All further references are to her transcription of the first, *c.* 1512–19 Paris imprint.

[53] 'Il le gecte au feu et il ne se vault tenir.' *Le mistere de la saincte hostie*, sig. C2ᵛ.

'the Jew takes a lance and hits the host against the fireplace', before 'he takes a kitchen knife and hacks up the host'.[54] In response to this last insult, the host turns into 'a crucifix in the cauldron against the fireplace'.[55] In simple terms the bleeding host is transformed into a crucifix. Unlike the continental versions, the Croxton *Play* contains three miracles, and I would like to suggest that they correspond to the groups outlined by Love in his sacramental treatise. The first, like the first miracle in *Le mistere de la saincte hostie*, is the graphic outpouring of blood from the tortured host. As Jonathas pricks 'Þe mydle part', the host begins to bleed (478). But the second and third miracles are unique to the Croxton *Play*. These are the appearance of the image of Jesus '*with woundys bledyng*' (713 sd) and the making '*hole agayn*' of Jonathas's hand (777 sd). Like the miracles which Love classifies as caused to convert those who do not believe in Christ's real presence in the Eucharist, in the Croxton *Play*'s first miracle the host appears as bloody flesh to the unbelieving Jews. The second miracle corresponds with the miracles that Love groups as caused to edify the faithful: the Jews' nascent belief is confirmed by the vision of an image of Christ. In the third, like the miracles narrated to illustrate Love's third category, physical salvation is granted by the strength of the sacrament. And just as Gregory was able to transform the finger of flesh that appeared to the Roman baker back to its accidental form as bread by praying, so the Croxton *Play*'s Episcopus effects the change of the image of Jesus back to bread with his supplication '*miserere mei*' (816).

In his recent consideration of the function of the sacrament of the altar in the making of orthodox Christianity, David Aers has said of Love's first two categories of miracles that they 'exemplify the closure of the gap between sign and referent, the termination of any play between Christ's presence and absence in their model of the presence of Christ's body'.[56] To put it another way, by making the sign (bleeding host, image of Christ) identical with the referent (Christ's bodily presence), the production of symbolic meaning is precisely the opposite of that in the miracle of transubstantiation, in which inward change is accomplished without alteration of outward appearance.[57] In Love's own words, the

[54] 'Le Juif prent une lance et frappe l'hostie contre la cheminee'; 'Il prent un costeau de cuisine et hache l'hostie.' *Le mistere de la saincte hostie*, sig. C2ᵛ.

[55] '[U]ng [sic] crucifix en la chaudiere contre la cheminee.' *Le mistere de la saincte hostie*, sig. C4ʳ.

[56] Aers, *Sanctifying Signs*, p. 26.

[57] This chain of signification in transubstantiation is clearly expressed by the conservative theologian Roger Dymmok who writes, 'I ask, what sensible change do you see in a boy newly baptised, in a man who has confessed, in a body or a man who has been confirmed, in consecrated bread, in a man ordained into the priesthood, in marriageable persons betrothed

distinction is between the inward miracle of the turning of bread and wine into the body and blood of Christ, which occurs 'euery day priuely, whereof we haue knowyng onely by byleue withinforþ' (226, ll. 27–28), and the occasional out-ward miracles done in evidence of real presence 'whereof we haue knowyng by trewe tellyng of myracles shewede wiþoutforþ' (226, ll. 29–30). These miracles done 'sumtyme opunly' (226) reflect one characteristic of late medieval piety that challenged 'the claims of historical veracity with the claims of the eye' by transforming 'the abstract and theological to the personal and concrete'.[58] As Gail McMurray Gibson has argued, the affective piety that 'began for the Franciscan preachers as an incarnational aesthetic sustaining their vision of the world, had by the fifteenth century turned itself outward and transformed that world'.[59] This transformation is witnessed not just in late medieval mira-cle narratives, but in all aspects of fifteenth-century devotion, from the liturgy to the visual and mechanical arts. So, as Gibson has noted, '[i]nstead of God the Pantocreator with his book of mysteries, the relevant central image for the late Middle Ages is the suffering human body racked on a cross; the book has become His body, its secrets red, fresh, and bleeding if still mysterious to the minds of man.'[60] Gibson's choice of words is insightful since, from the time of Gregory I the Great, the primary justification for Christian art was the argu-ment that images functioned as *bibliae pauperum*: books for the illiterate, lay majority.[61] In two letters admonishing Bishop Quintus Serenus of Marseille

or joined? [...] all receive a new virtue, except the bread, which simply ceases to exist without any kind of sensible change, and is transubstantiated into the body of Christ.' 'Qualem, rogo, uides mucacionem sensibilem in puero nouiter baptizato, in homine confessato, in puero uel homine confirmato uirtutem nouam, in pane consecrato, in homine in presbiterum ordinate, in sponsis nouiter desponsatis aut in infirmis inunctis? [...] omnia iam recitata | uirtutam nouam spiritualem recipient, pane excepto, qui simpliciter desinit esse sine quacunque sensibili muta-cione, et in corpus Christi transubstanciatur.' As Strohm has commented, the ultimate efficacy of the explanation offered by Dymmok 'is located in a single, irrational point: in the eucharis-tic bread, which is not only symbolically transformed but obliterated, to assume a completely new substance. *And* to assume this identity without external or visible change (change in its "accidents").' Dymmok, *Liber contra XII errores et hereses Lollardorum*, ed. by Cronin, p. 130; Strohm, 'The Croxton *Play of the Sacrament*', p. 34. On the Dymmok passage see also Aers, *Sanctifying Signs*, pp. 7–10; Stanbury, *The Visual Object of Desire*, p. 138; and Strohm, *England's Empty Throne*, p. 61.

[58] Gibson, *The Theater of Devotion*, pp. 10, 6.

[59] Gibson, *The Theater of Devotion*, p. 8.

[60] Gibson, *The Theater of Devotion*, p. 6.

[61] In fact, although the use of images in religious worship seems to be at odds with the

for the destruction of paintings and statues in his diocese, Gregory explains that 'pictures are used in churches so that those who are ignorant of letters may at least read by seeing on the walls, what they cannot read in books'. [62] This emphasis on the pedagogic use of images is carried through to later defences of visual art. For instance, in the fifteenth-century prose dialogue *Dives and Pauper*, Pauper responds to Dives's accusatory question, 'Querof seruyn þese ymagys? I wolde þey weryn brent euerychon', as follows:[63]

> Þe seruyn of thre thynggys. For þey been ordeynyd to steryn manys mende to thynkyn of Cristys incarnacioun and of his passioun and of holy seyntes lyuys. Also þey been ordeynyd to steryn mannys affeccioun and his herte to deuocioun, for often man is more steryd be syghte þan heryng or redyngge. Also þey been ordeynyd to been a tokene and a book to þe lewyd peple, þat þey moun redyn in ymagerye and peynture þat clerkys redyn in boke.[64]

The third of Pauper's arguments in support of visual art is clearly indebted to the case made by Gregory in his letters to Bishop Serenus. Indeed, Pauper goes on to cite Gregory directly, stating that 'as þe lawe seyȝt, [...] a bysshop [...] was accusyd to þe [pope], Seynt Gregory, quiche blamyd hym gretly for þat he hadde so dystroyid þe ymagys'.[65] Gibson has suggested that the oft-repeated *biblia pauperum* justification is here accorded with the remoteness of ancient law.[66] Certainly its position at the end of Pauper's tripartite defence of religious images does seem to reflect a shift in the emphasis in the theoretical justification of art. But I disagree with Gibson's view that the first of Pauper's

---

First Commandment against 'any graven image, or any likeness of any thing that is in heaven above, or that is in earth beneath, or that is in the water under the earth', any potential conflict was resolved on the grounds that the biblical injunction had been given to the Jews when the Incarnation had not yet sanctified human form. 'Non facies tibi sculptile, neque omnem similitudinem quae est in caelo desuper, et quae in terra deorsum, nec eorum quae sunt in aquis sub terra.' Exodus 20. 4.

[62] 'Idcirco enim pictura in Ecclesiis adhibetur, ut hi qui litteras nesciunt, saltem in parietibus videndo legant quae legere in Codicibus non valent.' For the English text see *A Select Library of Nicene and Post-Nicene Fathers of the Christian Church*, ed. by Schaff and Wace, XIII: *Gregory the Great, Ephraim Syrus, Aphrahat*, ed. and trans. by James Barmby (1898), pp. 53–54, (XI.13, p. 54). For the Latin see *Sancti Gregorii Magni Registri Epistolarum Lib. IX, Epist. 105*, in *PL*, LXXVII (1862), cols 1027b–28a (1027c–1028a).

[63] *Dives and Pauper*, ed. by Barnum, I, 82.

[64] *Dives and Pauper*, ed. by Barnum, I, 82.

[65] *Dives and Pauper*, ed. by Barnum, I, 82–83.

[66] Gibson, *The Theater of Devotion*, p. 16.

arguments, that images provoke thoughts of Christ's incarnation and passion,
is the 'most fundamental for an understanding of fifteenth-century religious
arts'.[67] Clearly, Christ's humanity, '[t]he sanctifying presence of God's image
in the world', was central to late medieval arguments against idolatry.[68] But it
is Pauper's second argument, that man is stirred more readily by sight than he
is by hearing or reading, that represents the defence offered most frequently
throughout the fifteenth century; consequently it provides a unique insight
into late medieval iconodulia. As W. R. Jones has noted, from Roger Dymmok
to Reginald Pecock, English iconodules 'argued on behalf of the superiority of
the visual to the audial and literary methods of Christian education'.[69] To give
just one example, from Pecock's *Repressor of Over Much Blaming of the Clergy*,
completed and published between 1449 and 1455, 'the iȝe siȝt schewith and
bringith into the ymaginacioun and into the mynde withynne in the heed of a
man myche mater and long mater sooner, and with lasse labour and traueil and
peine, than the heering of the eere dooth.'[70]

Showing and bringing forth Christ's carnal presence in the Eucharist, the
miracle narratives that Love includes in his sacramental treatise similarly testify
to the priority of sight in the transmission of late medieval religious thought.
However, while they seem to prove that man is more stirred by sight, their
form, miracle *narratives*, ensures that their consumption relies on an audience
capable of hearing or reading. In contrast, the Croxton *Play*, by dramatizing
the kind of miracle narrative recounted in Love's sacramental treatise, enacts
rather than merely reports a miracle to its audience. To put it another way, by
performing the 'myracle [...] don in the forest of Aragon', the play collapses the
distinction between the occurrence of the miracle as a historical event and its
transmission as an aesthetic one. So how is the staged miracle in the Croxton
Play different from the historical miracle it seeks to make present? What status
did medieval theologians accord eucharistic miracles that made Christ's real
presence a sacramental sign visibly accessible to those who witnessed them?
And how are these widely proclaimed miracles distinct from the hidden miracle of transubstantiation?

---

[67] Gibson, *The Theater of Devotion*, p. 15.

[68] Gibson, *The Theater of Devotion*, p. 15.

[69] Jones, 'Lollards and Images', p. 46. In addition to Dymmok and Pecock, Jones lists examples from works by Walter Hilton, Robert Rypon, Robert Alyngton, William Woodford, and
Thomas Netter. See Jones, 'Lollards and Images', pp. 37–48.

[70] Pecock, *The Repressor of Over Much Blaming of the Clergy*, ed. by Babington, I, 212–13.
This quotation is treated at greater length in the Conclusion. See pp. 153–56 below.

Love writes that in the sacrament Christ is made present 'bodily vnder þe forme & liknes of brede, & his verrey blode vndur likenes of wyne substancially & holely, without any feynyng or deceit, & not onely in figure as þe fals heritike seiþ' (151–52, ll. 41–42). In Aquinas's words, '[a]s a result of the sacramental sign, we have under this sacrament — under the appearances of the bread — not only the flesh, but the whole body of Christ, that is, the bones and nerves and the rest.'[71] However, '[s]ome people did not pay attention to these points and they declared that Christ's body and blood were only symbolically in this sacrament' (iiia. 75. 1).[72] In these formulations, Christ's real rather than figurative presence in the sacrament remains invisible to the human eye and is perceived by faith alone. Clearly, by setting Christ's presence before His communicants 'under the appearances of things in common human use, namely bread and wine', the 'merit of [...] faith' may be redounded (iiia. 75. 5).[73] But there is a further reason for the accidents, or outward appearance, of the bread and wine remaining after consecration. 'Divine providence very wisely arranged for this', says Aquinas, because 'men have not the custom of eating human flesh and drinking human blood; indeed the thought revolts them' (iiia. 75. 5).[74] A similar argument is made by William of Shoreham in his long poem on the sacrament, which was written around 1320:

> For ȝef he schewed hym in flesch,
> Oþer ine blody þynge,
> Hydous hyȝt were to þe syȝte,
> And to þe tast wlatynge
> And pyne.
> Þanne hys hyt betere in fourme of brede,
> And eke in forme of wyne.[75]

[71] 'Ad secundum dicendum quod ex vi sacramenti sub hoc sacramento continetur, quantum ad species panis, non solum caro, sed totum corpus Christi, id est ossa et nervi et alia hujusmodi.' Aquinas, *Summa theologica*, ed. and trans. by Gilby and others, lviii: *The Eucharistic Presence (3a. 73–78)* (1965), pp. 94–95, iiia. 76. 1. All further references are to this edition with part, question, and article number given in parentheses within the text.

[72] 'Quæ quidam non attendentes, posuerunt corpus est sanguinem Christi non esse in hoc sacramento nisi sicut in signo.'

[73] '[S]ub speciebus illorum quæ frequentius in usum hominis veniunt, scilicet panis et vini'; 'meritum fidei.'

[74] 'Quod quidem rationabiliter per divinam providentiam fit [...] quia non est consuetum hominibus, sed horribile, carnem hominis comedere sanguinem bibere.'

[75] William of Shoreham, *The Poems*, ed. by Konrath, p. 25, ll. 694–700, cited in Aers, *Sanctifying Signs*, p. 6.

The real, physical presence of Christ in the consecrated bread remains invisible in order to conceal the horror of cannibalism from those receiving the sacrament. The point is reiterated by Thomas Brinton, bishop of Rochester (d. 1389), who explains that Christ's sacramental presence is hidden so as to prevent us from hating the act of eating flesh and blood.[76] Given the potential for shock and revulsion, it is perhaps no surprise that Christ's tendency to show his usually invisible carnal presence is limited, for the most part, to those who reject orthodox doctrine. What is more, as Miri Rubin has noted, '[e]ffective as the tales of miraculous events were for teaching eucharistic symbolism, medieval intellectuals were obliged to analyse the nature of miraculous phenomena as part of their preoccupation with sacramental action.'[77] Indeed, many medieval commentators were eager to preserve a distinction between the divine gift of transubstantiation, by which Christ's body is made totally present in the substance of the sacrament, and miracles of the host, which merely move the viewer to perceive Christ's natural form:

> Why should we gape at a sensory image of this divine gift, when every day we behold
> by faith this heavenly sacrifice whole and entire? Let that man look with his bodily
> eyes on the minute fragment, who cannot by faith internally behold the whole.[78]

Here, in his *Life of Saint Hugh*, Adam of Eynsham distinguishes between the greater miracle of transubstantiation which is perceived by faith and lesser miracles of the host that are perceived by sight. Love translates these words of Adam of Eynsham in his sacramental treatise:

> Wheþere we þat euery day seene with þe trewest innere siht of oure soule alle holy
> & fully þis heuenly sacrifice hauen in merueile þe particleres ymages of þis ȝift of
> godde? As who seiþ naye. Bot let him go see þe litel small porciones þerof wiþ his
> bodily eye þat seeþ not alle þe hole wiþ his innere gostly eye. (232)

---

[76] Brinton, *The Sermons*, ed. by Devlin, I, 162, cited in Aers, *Sanctifying Signs*, p. 4. Note the revisionary observations in Richardson, 'Review of Devlin'. The view that the invisibility of Christ's body is providentially granted is also expressed in Dymmok, *Liber contra XII errores et hereses Lollardorum*, ed. by Cronin, pp. 95, 97, 98–99, 100–102, 106, cited in Aers, *Sanctifying Signs*, pp. 7, 184. For further arguments about disguise and cannibalism see Fitzpatrick, *In Breaking of Bread*, pp. 167–73.

[77] Rubin, *Corpus Christi*, p. 113.

[78] 'Num miramur particulares ymagines huius diuini muneris, qui totum integrum hoc celeste sacrificium cotidie intuemur fidelissimo aspectu mentis? Intueatur illius exiguas portiunculas uisu cororeo, qui totum non intuetur fidei conspectus interno.' Adam of Eynsham, *The Life of Saint Hugh of Lincoln*, ed. and trans. by Douie and Farmer, I, 95.

This distinction between bodily and ghostly or spiritual sight is also evident in Aquinas's discussion of the difference between miracles of perception and miracles of faith. For, as Aers has noted, Aquinas insists 'that the body of Christ cannot be seen by any bodily eye as it exists in the consecrated host. While the body is totally present, it is present not dimensionally but in the mode of substance, hence invisibly, unimaginably, and open only to intellectual apprehension.'[79] In contrast, although a 'miraculous change' occurs in the 'accidental qualities' when bloody flesh or an image of Christ is perceived in the host, 'Christ's natural form is not seen, but a form [is] miraculously produced either in the eyes of the beholders or even in the dimensions themselves of the sacrament' (IIIa. 76. 8).[80] By downgrading eucharistic miracles to accidental miraculous apparitions, orthodox theologians were able to preserve the integrity and uniqueness of the substantial but invisible transubstantiation of the eucharistic wafer into the real body of Christ. But by defining miracles of the host as accidental rather than substantial, visible rather than invisible, and external rather than internal, orthodox discourse transformed the appearance of the host as blood, flesh, or image of Christ into a dramatic event.

Spectacular Proof

By making sensible the invisible transformation of the eucharistic bread into the body of Christ, miracles of the host highlight the centrality of the Eucharist to orthodox devotional practice and illustrate the priority of sight in late medieval religious culture.[81] I have already suggested that such narratives functioned to affirm the doctrine of transubstantiation. But to what extent might their elevation of sight, their use of concrete imagery, and their proof of orthodox eucharistic doctrine be considered as a conscious reaction to Lollard or other heretical attacks on images and the sacrament of the Eucharist? The anti-Wycliffite status of the miracle narratives that Love translates in his sacramental treatise is confirmed in the 'Memorandum of Approbation' that, by Michael Sargent's

[79] Aers, *Sanctifying Signs*, p. 11. See Aquinas, *Summa theologica*, ed. and trans. by Gilby and others, LVIII: *The Eucharistic Presence (3a. 73–78)* (1965), pp. 114–19, IIIa. 76. 7.

[80] '[F]it miraculose quædam immutatio circa alia accidentia'; 'non videtur propria species Christi: sed species miraculosa formata vel in oculis intuentium, vel etiam in ipsis sacramentalibus dimensionibus.'

[81] A different view about centrality of sight to pre-Reformation religious practice is proposed by Matthew Milner in Milner, *The Senses and the English Reformation*. For his assessment of role of the senses in late medieval experiences of the Eucharist see pp. 144–62.

estimation, either precedes or follows the text of the *Mirror* in twenty of the
forty-two manuscripts not deficient at the appropriate place:[82]

> Memorandum: that about the year 1410, the original copy of this book, that is,
> *The Mirror of the Life of Christ* in English, was presented in London by its com-
> piler, N, to the Most Reverend Father and Lord in Christ, Lord Thomas Arundel,
> Archbishop of Canterbury, for inspection and due examination before it was freely
> communicated. Who after examining it for several days, returning it to the above-
> mentioned author, commended and approved it personally, and further decreed
> and commanded by his metropolitan authority that it be published universally for
> the edification of the faithful and the confutation of heretics or Lollards. Amen.[83]

Aside from Love's *Mirror*, only one other work describes itself as having been
submitted to the relevant authorities in order to conform with the stipula-
tions of the Lambeth Constitutions: an explication of the Brigittine office
composed in the first half of the fifteenth century known as *The Mirror of Our
Lady*. Nicholas Watson has argued that Love's *Mirror*, 'which was the first
work to take advantage of the protection offered by the Constitutions, seems to
embody their ideology so well that it is tempting to speculate (with Jonathan
Hughes) that it was written in part to order'.[84] Although this argument needs
to be treated with some caution — the 'Memorandum' does not occur in any
manuscripts produced during Arundel's lifetime — it is certainly true that
Love's *Mirror* and Archbishop Arundel's anti-Wycliffite serve similar agendas.
So while it is plausible that Arundel's approbation was given to a completed
version of the work that may, as Anne Hudson has noted 'have had some currency before the licence was procured', Ian Doyle's conclusion that the submission of the text to Arundel could reflect some challenge to the work's original

---

[82] Sargent, 'Introduction', pp. intro 36, intro 147–intro 148.

[83] 'Memorandum quod circa annum domini Millesimum quadringentesimum decimum, originalis copia huius libris, scilicet Speculi vite Christi in Anglicis presentabatur Londoniis per compilatorem eiusdem .N. Reuerendissimo in Christo patri & domino, Domino Thome Arundell, Cantuarie Archiepiscopo, ad inspiciendum & debite examinandum antequam fuerat libere communicate. Qui post inspeccionem eiusdem per dies aliquot retradens ipsum librum memorato eiusdem auctori proprie vocis oraculo ipsum in singulis commendauit & approbauit, necnon & auctoritate sua metropolitica, vt pote catholicum, pulpice communicandum fore decreuit & mandauit, ad fidelium edificacionem, & hereticorum siue lollardorum confuta-cionem. Amen.' Sargent, 'Introduction', pp. intro 36–intro 37. For the Latin original see Love, *The Mirror of the Blessed Life of Jesus Christ*, ed. by Sargent, p. 7, ll. 9–21.

[84] Watson, 'Censorship and Cultural Change in Late-Medieval England', pp. 852–53. See also Hughes, *Pastors and Visionaries*, pp. 230–31.

circulation seems unlikely.[85] More plausible is Sargent's view, that Love made some significant revisions to his text when he was preparing it for submission to Arundel.[86] Following Hudson, he has further proposed that the entire sacramental treatise is an addition to Love's original conception of the work, 'made before the final, "official" version of the *Mirror* [...] was put into circulation'.[87] To put it another way, Love's treatise on the sacrament, including the eight miracle narratives contained within it, was intended 'to confort [...] hem þat treuly byleuen, & to [confuse] alle fals lollardes & heritykes' (221).[88]

Love's miracle narratives' status as anti-Wycliffite propaganda could not be clearer. But the same cannot be said of the miracles in the Croxton *Play*. In the *Mirror*, a series of marginal notes identify original passages on the subjects of the legitimacy of the ecclesiastical hierarchy, confession, and the Eucharist as 'Contra lollardos'.[89] In the Croxton *Play* there are no references to Lollards or heretics of any kind, either within the play text itself or its supporting apparatus. So, unlike Love, who makes clear his intention to counter Wycliffite claims in the *Mirror*, the Croxton *Play* nowhere advertises a commitment to the refutation of Lollard ideas. Moreover, while there is irrefutable evidence of a link between Love's text and Archbishop Arundel, there is no surviving proof to suggest that the Croxton *Play* was ever associated with any real clerical figure, archbishop or otherwise. Nonetheless, a number of critics have argued that the play served an active role in the ongoing battle against heresy. For instance, Cutts has argued that the play seems 'to be a thoroughly English product written (or revised) not long after 1461 by some devout member of the clergy for presentation in a district (or districts) disturbed by Lollard dissent'.[90] Gibson has advanced a similar view, suggesting that 'what is certain about the Croxton *Play* is that [...] it is a careful, polemical answer to Lollard heresy, staunchly if somewhat ingeniously affirming the miracle of Real Presence and the importance of

[85] Hudson, *The Premature Reformation*, p. 438; Doyle, 'Reflections on Some Manuscripts', pp. 82–83, 86–87.

[86] Sargent, 'Introduction', pp. intro 74–intro 76, intro 147–intro 150.

[87] Sargent, 'Introduction', p. intro 67. See Hudson, *The Premature Reformation*, pp. 438–39.

[88] The remarkable verbal echo between this, the closing phrase of the 'Transition' paragraph, which appears at the end of Love's translation of the *Meditationes*, before the beginning of his eucharistic treatise, and the closing words of Arundel's 'Memorandum' are discussed in Sargent, 'Introduction', pp. intro 66–intro 67, intro 148–intro 150.

[89] See, for instance, Love, *The Mirror of the Blessed Life of Jesus Christ*, ed. by Sargent, pp. 25, 90, 132, 138, 142, 151.

[90] Cutts, 'The Croxton Play: An Anti-Lollard Piece', p. 60.

the sacraments and defending the efficacy of the priesthood'.[91] Given the play's
tidy treatment of orthodox sacramental doctrine and its defence of the clerical
hierarchy in response to the Lollard like challenges of its Jews, I am inclined to
tentatively agree with these conclusions. But there are some significant objections that need to be answered before turning to the play's anti-Lollard bias.

The most frequently cited objection to the argument that the play functioned as a weapon against Lollardy is that its protagonists are Jews and not
Christian heretics. As Lawton has put it, '[t]he play works with stereotypes of
Jews as Jews, not with the notion that the Jews represent some other group
entirely.'[92] To put it another way, if the play's Jews 'are supposed to be Lollards,
they're curiously *Jewish* Lollards'.[93] Or another: 'whatever the possibility of
reading the Jews as Christian dissenters, the play itself stresses Jews as Jews.'[94]
What all these arguments fail to address is that the Jews do not need to stand
for Lollards for the play's miracle to serve an anti-Lollard purpose. Indeed, I
am not aware of a single miracle narrative with proven anti-Lollard links in
which Lollards feature as chief witnesses to the miracle. On the other hand,
by the late Middle Ages there was already a well established tradition of Jews
as witnesses to host miracles. In what Sinanoglou has described as the earliest recorded example from the *Vitae Patrum*, a Jew seeking to test Christ's real
presence in the sacrament sees 'an infant torn limb from limb in the hands of
St. Basil'.[95] Later medieval examples of Jewish witnesses given by Sinanoglou
include the tale recounted by John Bromyard (d. *c.* 1352) in his *Summa predicantium* (first printed 1485) of a Jewish convert who complains to his priest
that he is no longer able to see the Christ child at the elevation as he had done
before his conversion and the story, as told in the late fourteenth-century
Vernon Manuscript, of a Jew who converts after witnessing the Christ child
cannibalized by a priest and his congregants.[96] Although none of Love's eight
miracle narratives feature a Jew as witness, his prefatory remark that he 'shalle
telle shortly sume merueiles & myracles [...] þe whech bene of so grete auctorite

---

[91] Gibson, The Theater of Devotion, p. 35.

[92] Lawton, 'Sacrilege and Theatricality', p. 290.

[93] Nisse, *Defining Acts*, p. 101.

[94] Clark and Sponsler, 'Othered Bodies', p. 69.

[95] Sinanoglou, 'The Christ Child as Sacrifice', p. 493; 'infantulum membratim incidi in manibus Basilii.' See *Vita sancti Basilii*, in *PL*, LXXVIII (1862), cols 295a–313a (col. 301d).

[96] Sinanoglou, 'The Christ Child as Sacrifice', p. 493. See also Bromyard, *Summa predican-tium* (1485), unpaginated, E.vi ('eucharistica'), article 24; and 'De festo corporis Christi', in *The Minor Poems of the Vernon Manuscript*, ed. by Horstmann and Furnivall, I (1892), 174–77.

[...] þat þere may no man aȝeyn sey them bot he be worse þan a Jewe' (228, ll. 5–8), implicates Jews as apt witnesses to eucharistic miracles. In the context of this tradition I see no reason why the Jews in the Croxton *Play* cannot function as Jewish witnesses to a host miracle designed to counter heretical views on the sacrament of the Eucharist.

Further, more serious objections to the Croxton *Play*'s anti-Lollard status turn about its late date and unknown auspices. As I have already indicated, a terminus a quo is provided by a note on fol. 356ʳ, consistent with the hand of one of the play's three scribes:

> Thus endyth the Play of the Blyssyd Sacrament, whyche myracle was don in the forest of Aragon, in the famous cité Eraclea, the yere of owr Lord God M cccc. lxj, to whom be honowr, Amen.

A terminus ad quem is harder to establish, but the manuscript points towards a mid-sixteenth-century copying date.[97] However, as Norman Davis has cautioned, 'the extent of scribal interference suggests a considerable time separated the original text from the surviving copy.'[98] Clearly all conclusions must necessarily be speculative, but it seems likely that the play was written in the final third of the fifteenth century, perhaps during the 1480s and survives in a manuscript copied towards the middle of the sixteenth century. But to what extent did Lollardy survive through the late fifteenth and into the sixteenth centuries? And if the play is indeed an anti-Lollard piece is it best read as a response to a generalized anxiety about the spread of heresy, or can surviving documentary and textual evidence situate it within a specific context?

The various attempts to determine where the play was composed and performed have, on the whole, been thwarted by the lack of evidence preserved by the sole surviving manuscript. The play's association with Croxton arises from the Second Vexillator's prefatory remark that 'thys gaderyng þat here is, | At Croxston on Monday yt shall be sen' (73–74). As E. K. Chambers noted long ago, 'the name Croxton is common to places in Norfolk, Cambridgeshire,

---

[97] The arguments in support of this late copying date are outlined in my article, Atkin, 'Playbooks and Printed Drama'. On the basis of Davis's watermark dating, Michael Jones has situated his discussion of the play's sixteenth-century reception in the religious controversy of the 1530s. Davis, 'Introduction to *The Croxton Play of the Sacrament*', p. lxxi; Jones, 'Theatrical History in the Croxton *Play of the Sacrament*', pp. 240–49. On the need for caution in using watermark dating on its own as a criterion for dating see Irigoin, 'La Datation par les filigranes du papier'.

[98] Davis, 'Introduction to *The Croxton Play of the Sacrament*', p. lxxxiv.

Leicestershire, and other counties', so theoretically, at least, the Second Vexillator could be referring to any of these.[99] However, as David Bevington has written, 'local allusions to "colkote [the "Tolcote" or tollhouse just opposite the friary near the North Gate of Bury] a lytyll besyde Babwell Mill" make it clear that the play was performed near Bury St. Edmunds in Suffolk.'[100] Still, since both of these allusions appear in passages that some critics have argued are later interpolations, it might be that Croxton, fourteen miles directly north of Bury on the Thetford road, represents *a* site, but not necessarily *the original* site of performance. Records of payments in 1506/7 and 1524/5 to 'the gylde of Crokeston' and 'the Gildam de croxston' by the Cluniac priory at Thetford might indicate that productions of the play were mounted in or around Croxton during those years, but there is no surviving documentary evidence of any earlier productions in this location.[101] It may be that the same priory at Thetford not only sponsored its occasional performance, but was also responsible for the play's composition. Gibson has offered an alternative view, proposing that the play originated in Bury and was produced by one of the numerous guilds of the town, possibly one whose members included clergy.[102] One point that critics have generally agreed on is that the presence of banns (i.e. the prologue spoken by the First and Second Vexillators, ll. 1–80) testifies to the play's status as a touring production at least at some point in its performance history. But there has been disagreement about the relationship of the banns to the original state of production. Some critics, Michael Jones for example, have suggested that the play always travelled. '[I]t seems', he has argued, 'designed to have been performed by a professional troupe of actors invited into the community.'[103] Other scholars, for instance Gibson, have argued that the banns can only reflect the performance conditions at the time the manuscript was copied in the sixteenth century. 'In the early sixteenth century', she has written, 'a copy of the play was made for a performance at the small [...] Norfolk village of Croxton.'[104] Further disagreement has arisen over whether the play text or the players travelled.

[99] Chambers, *The Mediæval Stage*, ii, 427.

[100] Bevington, *Tudor Drama and Politics*, p. 756. The quotation is from his edition. In 'The Croxton *Play of the Sacrament*', ed. by Davis the same quotation reads, 'colkote [...] A lytyll besyde Babwell Myll' (ll. 620–21).

[101] *Records of Plays and Players*, ed. by Galloway and Wasson, pp. 106, 111. For the original records see Cambridge, CUL, MS Additional 6969, fols 76ʳ, 173ᵛ.

[102] Gibson, *The Theater of Devotion*, p. 38.

[103] Jones, 'Theatrical History in the Croxton *Play of the Sacrament*', p. 232.

[104] Gibson, *The Theater of Devotion*, p. 40.

Jones has staunchly advocated the 'travelling troupe' theory.[105] But Scherb has disagreed, arguing that 'a more likely interpretation of the banns is suggested by evidence from counties adjacent to East Anglia like Kent and Lincolnshire. These records imply that while banns criers did travel [...], the plays usually did not.'[106] Scherb's argument is supported by the presence of doubling instructions on the final folio. For, as John Wasson has noted, if the play 'were the play written *at* Croxton *for* Croxton players' the note that 'XI may play yt at ease' would probably have been unnecessary (p. 89).[107]

The material evidence of the surviving manuscript has been interpreted to support arguments on the one hand about the play's original state of performance and on the other about its performance at the time of copying. But instead of aligning the manuscript with one or other of these moments from its performance history, it makes more sense to think of it as a palimpsest, shedding light on a range of different auspices from its composition to its transcription. So it may be that the play was originally intended for performance by one group of actors, professional or otherwise, but that when it came to be copied in the sixteenth century the scribe who wrote the note on fol. 356ʳ thought it profitable to advertise the text to a wider acting audience. Or it might be that the play was originally performed in a location no longer mentioned in the manuscript, and that the surviving text preserves the place of performance when the play was written down in the sixteenth century. Indeed, until more evidence is brought to light the most that can be said about the play's auspices and date is that internal references and 'the language as a whole' situate the play in the region of Thetford sometime at the end of the fifteenth century.[108] At the same time, its survival in a post-medieval manuscript and the possible references to its performance in Thetford indicate that it continued to be read and perhaps performed in Norfolk well into the sixteenth century. How does this information tally with contemporary heretical practice, both at large and more specifically in East Anglia?

Given the dramatic decline in the number of Lollard texts copied and composed after about 1440, the episcopal records, though hostile and often incomplete, provide the clearest picture of late medieval Wycliffite activity.[109] John

---

[105] Jones, 'Theatrical History in the Croxton *Play of the Sacrament*', p. 232.

[106] Scherb, *Staging Faith*, pp. 31–32.

[107] John Wasson, 'Letter to Gail McMurray Gibson' (19 November 1981), cited in Gibson, *The Theater of Devotion*, p. 34.

[108] Davis, 'Introduction to *The Croxton Play of the Sacrament*', p. lxxxiv.

[109] Hudson has noted that the copying of Wyclif's own writing effectively, although per-

Thomson has argued that in the period immediately following the Oldcastle rebellion '[a]lthough Lollardy continued to be widespread it was now more concerned with self-preservation than with revolution, conforming to the normal practices of the Church to avoid detection rather than spreading bills against the establishment'.[110] Certainly, this is one explanation for the reduced number of heresy trials between 1430 and 1480. In his table of 'Major Heresy Prosecutions Recorded 1414–1522', Thomson records just five series between 1438 and 1476 as opposed to seventeen between 1486 and 1522.[111] Although Hudson is, I think, right to caution that the concentration upon serious sequences of enquiry may distort the evidence, Patrick Hornbeck's inventory of all known and dateable cases for these periods produces a similar picture: trial records survive for around eighty defendants between 1433 and 1477; this number jumps to around 290 for the period between 1481 and 1522.[112] In East Anglia, following the cessation of Bishop Alnwick's 1431 proceedings, much time was to lapse before further trials took place, and when they did they occurred on a greatly diminished scale.[113] The register of Bishop Grey of Ely records proceedings against three Lollards in 1457 that resulted in them being put to penance in the market places of Ely and Cambridge and in their respective parish churches.[114] After these cases there is a gap in the records of some forty-five years until 1501, when a certain Thomas Cutting of Moulton

---

haps unsurprisingly, ceased after the early fifteenth century. *Wycklyffes Wycket* (*c.* 1470s) is the only text known to have been composed in this latter half of the Lollard era, but no medieval manuscript survives and the text is preserved in two 1546 imprints (STCs 25590 and 25590.5) and two 1548? imprints (STCs 25591 and 25591a). Other texts that first appear during this period include *Epistula Sathanae ad cleros* (in a single early sixteenth-century copy, Cambridge, CUL, MS Ff. 6. 2, fols 81ʳ–84ᵛ), *The praierand [sic] complaynte of the ploweman* ([1531?]; STC 20036), and *The ploughman's tale* ([*c.* 1535]; STC 5099.5). But as Hudson has noted, the origins of all three are probably substantially earlier. Hudson, *The Premature Reformation*, pp. 451–52.

[110] Thomson, *The Later Lollards, 1414–1520*, p. 19.

[111] Hudson has usefully noted that for two of the 'major' prosecutions the surviving evidence is incomplete, and in one case is only found in the secular sources. Hudson, *The Premature Reformation*, p. 447.

[112] Hudson, *The Premature Reformation*, p. 447; J. Patrick Hornbeck, Personal letter to the author (7 March 2008), typescript.

[113] Under Alnwick, Thomson has counted three burnings, at least forty abjurations, and ten purgations. Hornbeck has counted one execution, forty-five abjurations, fourteen purgations, and two cases for which the outcome is uncertain. Thomson, *The Later Lollards, 1414–1520*, pp. 120–31, 237; J. Patrick Hornbeck, Personal letter to the author (7 March 2008), typescript.

[114] *Ely Episcopal Records*, ed. by Gibbons, pp. 144–45.

was arrested for hindering the citation of Thomas Harward on a charge of heresy.[115] The *Norwich Consistory Court Depositions* records the 1511 case of one Richard Loose of Wisset, Suffolk, who 'coude not broke the vicar of Bramfield, nor he coude not be content with hym, saieng further that he had as leve see an oester shell betwix the vicar's handes at the sacring of the masse as the blessed sacrament'.[116] Further cases in 1499 and 1507 are recorded and illustrated by John Foxe, the Protestant martyrologist.[117] Although Foxe's reliability is at times questionable, his account of the burning of Thomas Norice of Norwich in 1507 is at least corroborated by John Bale's eyewitness testimony.[118] Clearly, in comparison to the levels of recorded Lollard activity throughout the rest of England in this later period, the evidence of the ecclesiastical and secular records suggests that heretical action in East Anglia was relatively light. Does this reflect a genuine decline in East Anglian Lollard practice and belief? Or did superficial conformity to the normal practices of orthodoxy convince the authorities that Lollardy had been stamped out? Moreover, what precisely did it mean to accuse someone of Lollardy in the late fifteenth and early sixteenth centuries? Did these later suspects share a framework of ideas with their earlier predecessors? Since accounts of heresy trials represent a major source for later Lollard practices and beliefs, it is perhaps unsurprising that Wycliffite views are so often expressed in negative terms. Nevertheless, from the time of Wyclif to the dawn of the Reformation, Lollard books and testimonies commonly feature the denigration of orthodox teaching on the sacraments, of the ecclesiastical hierarchy, and of the external signs of faith. In what follows I would like to explore the overlap between these views and the views repudiated by the Croxton *Play*.

James Simpson has argued that 'Eucharistic belief became a key litmus test of faith in post-Arundelian England'.[119] Certainly, with more than two hundred cases in which defendants' eucharistic beliefs were judged to be heretical, the Eucharist was undoubtedly the theologoumenon most frequently contested in English heresy trials before 1522.[120] It may be that the Eucharist appears so frequently in trial records because the intricacies of eucharistic discourse provided

---

[115] *Norwich Consistory Court Depositions*, ed. by Stone and Cozens-Hardy, fol. 28ʳ, no. 16.

[116] *Norwich Consistory Court Depositions*, ed. by Stone and Cozens-Hardy, fol. 170ᵛ, no. 117.

[117] Foxe, *TAMO (1563 Edition)*, III, 425; and Foxe, *TAMO (1570 Edition)*, VI, 887.

[118] Bale, *Scriptorum [...] catalogus* ([1557]), I, 644.

[119] Simpson, *Reform and Cultural Revolution, 1350–1547*, p. 557.

[120] Hornbeck, *What is a Lollard?*, p. 90.

ample ground for inquisitors to ensnare less able defendants. As Paul Strohm has commented, 'the uneven terrain of eucharistic discussion, riddled with theological pitfalls and places of potential doctrinal entrapment, rendered a perfect ground for the analysis and discovery of error.'[121] On the other hand, as Hornbeck has argued, 'the centrality of the mass in popular religious practice made the sacrament of the altar a likely site for dissent.'[122] Still, whether in incomprehension, confusion, or conviction, heresy trial defendants express a variety of different views on the sacrament. Wyclif's own final view was a version of consubstantiation; the bread and wine remain substantially present, but with the words of institution they coexist with the spiritual presence of Christ's body and blood.[123] In his own words, 'Þe breed of þe sacrid oost is verry breed in his kynde, and is eten bodili; but it is Goddis bodi in figure. And it is þe same bodi þat is Goddis bodi in his kynde [...] þis oost is eten bodili and goostli of sum men, but Cristis body in his kynde is not eten bodili.'[124] The sacrament might not involve any substantial transformation, but it is nonetheless a true sign of Christ's being. Although space does not permit further consideration of Wyclif's own views, given their subtlety and complexity it is perhaps no surprise that his followers often simplified or modified them, with a tendency to stress either the substantial remanence of the bread and wine or the figurative power of the sacrament as a true sign of Christ's salvific authority.[125]

The view that the original substances of bread and wine persist after the consecration recurs frequently in trial records from the period 1450 to 1522. So, for instance, in May 1457, two brothers, William and Richard Sparke of Somersham, appeared before Bishop Chedworth of Lincoln and confessed

---

[121] Strohm, *England's Empty Throne*, p. 49.

[122] Hornbeck, *What is a Lollard?*, p. 145. McSheffrey and Tanner have used the same argument to support the obverse position. 'The emphasis on the cult of the eucharist', they have suggested, 'may have been placed, not by the Lollards, but by the prosecutors precisely because of the centrality of the eucharist to late medieval orthodox practice.' See 'Introduction' in *Lollards of Coventry*, ed. and trans. by McSheffrey and Tanner, pp. 1–56 (p. 15).

[123] Recent treatment of Wyclif's eucharistic theology includes: Leff, 'Ockham and Wyclif on the Eucharist'; Phillips, 'John Wyclif's *De eucharistia*'; Catto, 'John Wycliff and the Cult of the Eucharist'; Aers, *Sanctifying Signs*, ch. 3; Denery, 'From Sacred Mystery to Divine Deception'; and Hornbeck, *What is a Lollard?*, pp. 71–6.

[124] Wycliffe, *Select English Works*, ed. by Arnold, II: *Sermons on the Ferial Gospels and Sunday Epistles: Treatises* (1871), p. 112.

[125] Only three studies have focused on the eucharistic theologies of individual Wycliffites as testified by their recorded views: Hudson, 'The Mouse in the Pyx'; Aers, *Sanctifying Signs*, ch. 4; and Hornbeck, *What is a Lollard?*, pp. 90–100.

their belief that the host remains true bread.[126] In the same month their father Robert Sparke was apprehended by Bishop Grey of Ely and argued at his trial that the priest has no more power to produce the body of God than straw.[127] Indeed belief in remanence remained so popular among early sixteenth-century Lollards, that Archbishop Warham of Canterbury included it in the formulaic abjurations of over forty heresy trial defendents signed in 1511 and 1512.[128] A number of late fifteenth- and early sixteenth-century defendants expressed the related view that the sacrament is an efficacious sign of Christ's suffering and/or eucharistic presence. Typical are the statements of Thomas Branbrooke, 'that the hoste consecrate was not the very body of our Lorde but a figur', and John Bull that the sacrament of the altar is 'a sign of Christ's passion', which are together recorded in the records of the 1511/12 heresy trial proceedings under Bishop Blyth of Coventry.[129] Both men seem to have been influenced by one John Blumston, Bull's uncle, 'otherwise called Master John Physician'.[130] The different but related position of the sacrament as a commemoration of Christ's suffering is found in a growing number of testimonies in the late fifteenth and early sixteenth centuries. John Qwyrk, who was tried in Lincoln diocese in 1463, seems to have been the first dissenter in this period to describe the sacrament as a memorial.[131] In the sixteenth century similar views are expressed by Agnes Corby of Coventry, who in 1512 said she would accept the sacrament only 'in memory of Christ's passion', and Christopher Shoemaker, a parishioner of Great Missenden in Suffolk recorded by Foxe as believing the sacrament to be 'in substaunce bread, bearing the remembraunce of Christ'.[132]

[126] *Lincoln Diocese Documents*, ed. by Clark, pp. 90–93.

[127] *Ely Episcopal Records*, ed. by Gibbons, pp. 144–45.

[128] See for instance the abjurations of Christopher Grebill; William Riche; John Grebill Sr; John Grebill Jr; William Olberd Sr; Agnes Ive; Agnes Chetynden; Thomas Mannyng; Robert Hilles; Thomas, Joan, and Philip Harwode; Stephen Castelyn; William Baker; William Olberde Jr; Robert Reignold; and Thomas Feld, in *Kent Heresy Proceedings, 1511–12*, ed. by Tanner, pp. 27–37, 41–42, 61–69.

[129] '[S]ignum passionis Christi.', *Lollards of Coventry*, ed. and trans. by McSheffrey and Tanner, pp. 195–96, 215–16.

[130] '[A]lias vocatus magister John Phisicion', *Lollards of Coventry*, ed. and trans. by McSheffrey and Tanner, pp. 215–16.

[131] Hornbeck, *What is a Lollard?*, p. 99. See also the register of John Chedworth, bishop of Lincoln (r. 1452–71), Lincoln, Archive Office, Episcopal Register XX, fols 59ᵛ–60ʳ.

[132] '[Q]uod acciperet illud in memoriam passionis Christi.', *Lollards of Coventry*, ed. and trans. by McSheffrey and Tanner, p. 235; Foxe, *TAMO (1570 Edition)*, VII, 984.

One way of understanding commemorative views on the sacrament is to recognize that for some Lollards and other late medieval nonconformists Christ's sacrifice was both unrepeatable and entirely sufficient.[133] In contrast, traditional religion argued for the reiteration of Christ's sacrifice on the cross in and through the sacrifice of the Eucharist. So where some heretics focused on the Eucharist as a commemorative act, orthodox doctrine understood the sacrament as a repetition of Christ's redemptive passion. The Croxton *Play* is particular in its rejection of commemorative eucharistic theologies and staunchly defends the orthodox position on the sacrament. In the banns, the Second Vexillator stresses the repeatability of Christ's passion, describing the Jews' desecration of the host as 'a new turmentry' (45). The truth of this interpretation of the sacrament is then revealed to the audience in the play's central sequence, in which the host's susceptibility to repetition causes it to bleed. At the climax of the desecration sequence, this position is restated when the image of the bleeding Christ likens the Jews to their historical forbears who buffeted Jesus:

> Why blaspheme yow me? Why do ye thus?
> Why put yow me to a *newe tormentry*,
> And I dyed for yow on the crosse? (731–33; my emphasis)

The words of Christ inspire hope and faith in His salvific blood, which bleeds now as it did on the cross. Jonathas responds by echoing the first verse of Psalm 26, traditionally sung by David before he was anointed, '*Tu es protector vite mee; a quo trepidabo?*' (741).[134] Like the Second Vexillator's address to the audience in the play's banns, Jesus's words to Jonathas and his men focus on the sacrament as a new passion, providing a gloss on the desecration sequence as a demonstration of the repeated and repeatable power of the consecrated host. It has become commonplace to argue that memorial interpretations of the sacrament became more popular in the late fifteenth and early sixteenth centuries, and this may explain why the Croxton *Play*'s polemic is largely directed towards the repudiation of such views. Nonetheless, the play's desecration sequence also clearly checks Lollard theologies of remanence. For instance, the heretical view of William Baker of Cranbook in Kent, 'that the blissed sacrament of the aulter ys not Crists very body, flesshe and bloode, but oonly materiall bred', is powerfully refuted by the first two of the play's three miracles.[135] The bleeding host

---

[133] This is a view shared by later reformers. See Chapter 4, pp. 135–46.

[134] '[T]he Lord is the strength of my life; of whom shall I be afraid?'; 'Dominus protector vitæ meae: a quo trepidabo?' Psalms 27. 1.

[135] *Kent Heresy Proceedings, 1511–12*, ed. by Tanner, p. 65.

demonstrates its substantial conversion from bread to the flesh and blood of Christ, and its transformation into an image of Jesus indicates both the integrity of Christ's true body in the sacrament and the extent to which material bread has ceased to exist. What is more, it is only when the entire company has accepted and given thanks for Christ's substantial presence in the host that '*þe im[a]ge change*[s] *agayn*' into its accidental appearance as bread (825 sd).

Hudson has commented that, '[w]hatever the discussion over the position of the episcopacy, there is complete unanimity amongst Lollards about the primary function of all the clergy: this is the preaching of the gospel to all and, in so far as it contributes to that and nothing further, the study of the bible and of aids to its understanding.'[136] Given this drastic limitation of the powers traditionally ascribed to the clergy, it is perhaps no surprise that many late medieval heresy trial defendants denigrate the role of the clergy in the administration of the sacraments, in particular auricular confession, the Eucharist, and baptism. The role of the clergy in the sacrament of penance was questioned by no less than twenty defendents between 1450 and 1522.[137] For instance, in 1511 a parishioner of Tenterden in the diocese of Canterbury complained 'that a prest was not sufficient to here a mannys confession and absoile hym of his synnes, for suche absolution of a prest was nothing profitable for a mannys soule', arguing instead 'that confession was to be made oonly to God by mynde'.[138] Lollard disparagement of the clerical role in the Mass is clearly behind the quip that priests cannot make their maker that Hornbeck has noted in at least a dozen heresy trials between 1429 and 1514.[139] In one particularly memorable example, Thomas Abell of Coventry commented to Bishop Blyth '[t]hat God made man and not man God, as the carpenter doith make the howse and not the howse the carpenter'.[140] Here, the basic message is fairly straightforward: traditional eucharistic doctrine is blasphemous since it requires the Mass-priest to possess Godlike powers. The refutation of the priest's function in baptism is less well documented in the period, but there are isolated cases where such a stance is evident. For instance, at her trial in 1511 Agnes Grebill's son insisted that she 'held, belyved, taught and defendid [...] that baptisme was nothing worth, for a childe putt into the founte was no more the better than if he had been putt

---

[136] Hudson, *The Premature Reformation*, p. 353.

[137] J. Patrick Hornbeck, Personal letter to the author (7 March 2008), typescript.

[138] *Kent Heresy Proceedings, 1511–12*, ed. by Tanner, p. 63.

[139] Hornbeck, *What is a Lollard?*, p. 98.

[140] *Lollards of Coventry*, ed. and trans. by McSheffrey and Tanner, p. 183.

into other water'.[141] Yet more explicit are the views of one Thomas Goston from London who, in 1499, declared that he could baptize as well as any priest.[142]

At the beginning of this chapter I indicated that Jonathas argues that ortho-dox teaching on the sacrament is 'a conceyte' devised by the clergy to 'make vs blynd' (203). Accusing the clergy of duplicity, he expresses incredulity at the idea that 'þe prest dothe yt bynd, | And by þe myght of hys word make yt flessh and blode' (201–02). I have already suggested that the miraculous outpour-ing of Christ's salvific blood from the tortured host visibly challenges his belief that the sacrament does not involve any substantial change of matter. The play's end complements this proof by reinstating confidence in the clerical powers so clearly undermined by Jonathas at the start of the play. Moreover, since the miracle of the bleeding host acts as a cautionary tale against negligent priests who perhaps, like the play's Presbiter, have unwittingly exposed the host to volatile forces beyond the church's walls, the end of the play also emphasizes the need for 'worthy' priests that will keep 'pyxys lockyd' and 'be ware of the key of Goddys temple' (922, 926, 927).[143] These ends are achieved in a series of interrelated actions: the transformation of the image of Jesus back into a piece of bread at the Episcopus's words, 'Thowgh we haue be vnrygh[t]full, forgyf vs owr rygore, | And of owr lamentable hartys, good Lord, take hed' (824–25); the formal procession, led by the Episcopus, of the host back into the church and on to the altar (865 sd); and the Episcopus's admonition to 'þou preste, for thy neclygens' (920). With the Eucharist returned to its accidental form and interned safely in the locked pyx, the play concludes by restoring the host to clerical control. The Croxton *Play*'s final sequence also serves to defend the orthodox position on the clerical role in the sacraments of confession and bap-tism. However, as Cutts has already written about these issues at some length, I will say nothing further here except that their treatment suggests a familiarity with orthodox anti-Lollard literature rather than with actual Lollards.[144]

[141] *Kent Heresy Proceedings, 1511–12*, ed. by Tanner, p. 20.

[142] 'Et ulterius idem Georgius deposuit manum suam in fontem baptismalem, sic dicendo, This may I doo, as well as the preste.' Hale, *A Series of Precedents and Proceedings*, p. 67.

[143] Conversely, Ethan Campbell has recently argued that far from shoring up the institu-tional authority of the clergy, the play's treatment of Isoder the Presbiter suggests it should be treated as an example of late medieval anticlerical satire. However, these ends need not be at odds. There is no reason why the play cannot stand as both a staunch defence of orthodox doc-trine and a critique of clerical corruption. See Campbell, '"Be Ware of the Key"'.

[144] Cutts, 'The Croxton *Play*: An Anti-Lollard Piece'; and Cutts, 'The English Background of the *Play of the Sacrament*', esp. pp. 47–51. Ann Eljenholm Nichols has similarly suggested

Before I move on to the final section of this chapter, I want to say something about the play's defence of images. By the end of the fourteenth century, arguments against images were frequently associated with Lollardy, and between 1461 and 1522 the evidence of an overwhelming number of suspected Lollards reflects varying degrees of iconomachy. Indeed, Lollards were so frequently linked with arguments against images that in 1547 the conservative Bishop of Winchester, Stephen Gardiner wrote that 'in England they are called Lollards, who denying images, thought therwith, al the crafts of painting, grauing to be generally superfluous and naught, and against Gods lawes'.[145] As Hudson has noted, the severe position of practical iconoclasm had been reached as early as 1382 when William Smith and his friends 'used an image of St Katherine as fuel to cook their supper, a second martyrdom on which they wryly commented'.[146] But not all Lollards occupied so extreme a stance. Far more common was to deny that images should be worshipped or that oblations be offered to them. For instance, the author(s) of the 'Twelve Conclusions of the Lollards' state:

Þis conclusion God openly schewith, commanding to don almesse dede to men þat ben nedy, for þei ben þe ymage of God in a more likenesse þan þe stok or ston.[147]

The position expressed here, that offerings are better made to poor men than dead images recurs in the testimonies of heresy trial defendants throughout the fifteenth and into the sixteenth centuries. For example, when Robert Bartlet was tried for heresy by John Longland, bishop of Lincoln, in 1521 he admitted that he had taught his brother Richard that 'Images of saintes were but stockes and stones & dead thinges'.[148] However, in some quarters there does seem to have been partial support for the well worn Gregorian argument which permitted images on the grounds that they functioned as books for those unable to read. As one early fifteenth-century polemicist puts it, although 'veyn glorie þat is hangid on hem [is] an opyn errour aȝenus Christis gospel', images nonethe-

that the play's Lollard language reflects an awareness of anti-Wycliffite material rather than real life Lollards. See Nichols, 'Lollard Language in the Croxton *Play of the Sacrament*'; and Nichols, 'The Croxton *Play of the Sacrament*: A Re-Reading'.

[145] 'Examples and copies of certayne letters written by Steuen Gardiner Bishop of Winchester', in Foxe, *TAMO (1563 Edition)*, IV, 784–810 (p. 785).

[146] Hudson, *The Premature Reformation*, p. 303.

[147] 'Twelve Conclusions of the Lollards', in *Selections from English Wycliffite Writings*, ed. by Hudson, pp. 24–29 (p. 27).

[148] Foxe, *TAMO (1570 Edition)*, VII, 986.

less 'ben bokis of lewid men to sture þem on þe mynde of Cristis passion'.[149] But
here as elsewhere this view was commonly attended by the anxiety that ignorant
men might mistake the sign (i.e. images and statues of Christ and His saints)
for the referent (i.e. the spiritual reality of Christ and His saints): 'For summe
lewid folc wenen þat þe ymagis doun verreyly þe myraclis of hemsilf, and þat
þis ymage of þe crucifix be Crist hymsilf, or þe seynt þat þe ymage is þere sett
for lickenesse.'[150] Chopping up or burning an image was one way of disproving
its alleged miraculous qualities; witness the views of one Elizabeth Sampson,
cited for heresy before Bishop FitzJames of London in 1509. Inveighing against
images of Our Lady at

> Wyllesdone, at Staninges, at Crome, at Walsinghame, & the image of saint Sauiour,
> of Barmonseye [...] she had spoken these or lyke words. That our Ladie of Wildes-
> done, was a burnt ars elfe, and a burnt ars stocke, and if she might haue holpen men
> and women whiche go to her on pygrymage, she would not haue suffred her taile
> to haue bene brent, and what should folke worship our lady of Willesdone [for she
> is but] a burnt ars stocke.[151]

Behind these words is the clear suggestion that fire offers the ultimate disproof
of an image's alleged miraculous powers, the strongest argument 'for the lack of
relationship between lifeless representation and actual saint'.[152] In the Croxton
Play, fire does not destroy but rather proves the image's power. At the climax of
the play's miraculous action, the fiery furnace rives '*asunder and blede*[s] *owt at
þe cranys, and an image appere*[s] *owt with woundys bledyng*' (712 sd). Cast into
the oven, the flames do not destroy the host; rather they effect its transformation into an image of Christ. And in the action that follows it is not Christ but
'*þe image*' that speaks '*to the Juys*' (716 sd). This speaking image has a powerful effect on Jonathas. Falling to his knees, he meekly asks 'mercy, amendys to
make' (745). In contrast to the effect of the sight of the bleeding host, which
had provoked horror, alarm, and even madness, the vision of the image of
Christ inspires faith. So, far from disproving its supposed powers, the chopping up of the host actually proves its miraculous properties. And rather than
exposing the perceived relationship between His lifeless image and the histori-

---

[149] 'Images and Pilgrimages', in *Selections from English Wycliffite Writings*, ed. by Hudson,
pp. 83–88 (p. 83).

[150] 'Images and Pilgrimages', in *Selections from English Wycliffite Writings*, ed. by Hudson,
p. 87.

[151] Foxe, *TAMO (1563 Edition)*, III, 425.

[152] Aston, *England's Iconoclasts*, p. 136.

cal Christ as false, the desecration sequence collapses the distinction between the image as a sign of Christ and His reality as its referent. To put it another way, the play not only refutes verbal assaults on images, it also suggests that iconoclastic attacks prove rather than disprove the miraculous power of images.

The denial of the miraculous attributes of certain images and shrines is often linked to the suggestion that relics and sometimes even miracles might be faked. In one example, William Wynch of Salisbury claimed that 'among the reliques that be worshipped in churches is many shippes bone'.[153] In the Croxton *Play*, the miracles the audience witness are not real miracles but things made by a cast of actors. '[Þ]e *Ost must blede*' (480 sd), but it bleeds animal blood or blood col-oured liquid rather than the real blood of Christ. Later, when 'All thys oyle wax-yth redde as blood, | And owt of the cawdron yt begynnyth to rin' (674–75), the cauldron boils what appears to be blood. As the stage directions note, '*Here shall þe cawdron byle*, apperyng *to be as blood*' (672 sd, my emphasis). Perhaps, as Daryll Grantley has speculated, a fountain was used: '[i]t would [...] have brought about the overflow of liquid from the cauldron and, if the incoming liquid contained red dye, give the impression that the liquid in the cauldron was turning to blood.'[154] Later still, at the play's climax, '*þe image*' that speaks '*to the Juys*' is not Christ, or even an image of Christ, but most likely an actor playing Christ (716 sd).[155] To put it another way, the Croxton *Play* defines the miraculous as theatrical. In the final part of this chapter I would like to explore these phenomenal pressures more fully, first in the context of late medieval anti-theatricalism, and then within the framework of Henrician iconoclasm.

Playing Miracles

A Tretise of Miraclis Pleyinge, which is contained in a single early fifteenth-cen-tury manuscript, is frequently described as the longest and most significant piece of surviving medieval dramatic criticism in English.[156] As its editor has

---

[153] The register of Edmund Audley, bishop of Salisbury, Chippenham, Wiltshire and Swin-don History Centre, D1/2/14, fol. 147ʳ, cited in Hudson, *The Premature Reformation*, p. 305.

[154] Grantley, 'Producing Miracles', pp. 83–84.

[155] Although Grantley has argued that a picture or small model would have been used in original productions, William Tydeman has suggested that the image of Christ was in fact played by an actor. See Grantley, 'Producing Miracles', p. 85; Tydeman, *English Medieval Theatre, 1400–1500*, p. 67.

[156] For instance, Jonas Barish has described it as 'chief surviving antitheatrical document from the Middle Ages'. See Barish, *The Antitheatrical Prejudice*, p. 67.

noted, it is '[m]ost often identified as the product of a hostile Wycliffite [...] author or authors'.[157] The scope of the *Tretise*'s attack is broad and seems to refer to more than one type of play. So, in addition to the miracle plays identified in the *Tretise*'s *incipit* ('Here beginnis a tretise of miraclis pleyinge'), it may be that some of the text's criticism is directed at the large-scale Corpus Christi cycles that were performed regularly in the north of England throughout the later Middle Ages. However, in the course of attacking drama, the *Tretise*'s writer or writers present a set of propositions that offer a fairly coherent argument in favour of religious plays and dramatic representation more generally.[158] Although this argument is offered as a false defence of drama (in fact, much of the *Tretise* is preoccupied with its refutation), it seems to present what might, in another context, have served as a genuine case in support of religious drama. Briefly summarized, the points in favour of dramatic presentation are: that plays turn men to belief;[159] that drama moves people to compassion and devotion (98, ll. 162–65); that through games and play men are encouraged to leave sin and are drawn towards virtue (98, ll. 166–74); and that played miracles are better than any other sort of recreational activity (98, ll. 176–78). Although the Gregorian argument of images as *bibliae pauperum* is here excluded, it is clear that all these points are indebted to standard medieval defences of artistic representation. So, just as pictures 'steryn manys mende to thynkyn of Cristys incarnacioun and of his passioun and of holy seyntes lyuys', so plays encourage men to 'leeven ther pride and taken to hem afterward the meke conversacion of Crist and hise seintis' (97, ll. 158–60).[160] And just as images 'steryn mannys affeccioun and his herte to deuocioun', so drama moves men 'to compassion and devocion' (98, l. 164).[161] In fact this debt to the traditional argument in defence of art is pretty well acknowledged in the final point in favour of dramatic representation:

> Also sithin it is leveful to han the miraclis of God peintid, why is it not as wel leveful to han the miraclis of God pleyed, sithin men mowen bettere reden the wille of

[157] Davidson, 'Introduction', p. 1.

[158] Rosemary Woolf has even suggested that the author(s) may have been replying to some corresponding Latin treatise in defence of mystery plays. See Woolf, *The English Mystery Plays*, p. 85.

[159] *A Tretise of Miraclis Pleyinge*, ed. by Davidson, pp. 93–115 (p. 97, ll. 150–61). All further references are to this edition with page and line numbers given in parentheses within the text.

[160] *Dives and Pauper*, ed. by Barnum, i, 82.

[161] *Dives and Pauper*, ed. by Barnum, i, 82.

God and his mervelous werkis in the pleyinge of hem than in the peintinge? And betere they ben holden in mennes minde and ofere rehersid by the pleyinge of hem than by the peintinge, for this is a deed bok, the tother a quick. (98, ll. 179–85)[162]

Extending the conventional argument that 'man is more steryd be syghte þan heryng or redyngge', the defence here proposes that man is more often stirred by moving or 'quick' images than he is by still or 'deed' ones.[163] What is more, by asking why plays of God's miracles are not permissible when paintings of God's miracles are, the defence recognizes that representational art and drama rely on similar iconic systems of signification in which one thing is used to represent another. However, in acknowledging the iconicity of drama, this defence is open to the same kinds of criticisms that were levelled at devotional imagery, and it is to these that I would now like to turn.

Central to the *Tretise*'s attack on drama is the distinction between the 'efectuel' miracles of Christ and His saints and theatrical miracles performed 'in bourde and pleye' (93, ll. 23, 24). Performing miracles is tantamount to taking God's name 'in idil' and is indistinguishable from blasphemy (93, ll. 28–29). This argument — that plays and actors 'reversith Crist' by making game of earnest — is reworked in various ways throughout the *Tretise* (94, l. 57). For instance, God is scorned when His words and acts are taken in vain: 'miraclis pleying is scorning of God, for [...] bourdfully taking Goddis biddingis or wordis or werkis is scorning of him' (97, ll. 129–32). And actors turn away from God and undermine and scorn His works: 'thes miraclis pleyeris taken in bourde the ernestful werkis of God, no doute that ne they scornen God' (97, ll. 133–34); 'Men thane pleyinge the name of Goddis miraclis as plesingly, they leeve to do that God biddith hem so they scornen his name and so scornyn him' (97, ll. 144–46). As Davidson has noted, 'the *Tretise*'s attitude towards *play*, particularly when religious matters are involved, remains harsh and lacking in sympathy.'[164] Indeed, the *Tretise* sees no difference between the actors who play miracles and the 'Jewis that bobbiden Crist' (97, l. 133):

Right therfore as men by feinyd tokenes bygilen and in dede dispisen ther neighboris, so by siche feinyd miraclis men bygilen hemsilf and dispisen God, as the tormentours that bobbiden Crist. (99–100, ll. 226–29)

---

[162] For a further discussion of this, the capstone argument of the defence of drama, see Woolf, *The English Mystery Plays*, pp. 86–95.

[163] Woolf, *The English Mystery Plays*, p. 82

[164] Davidson, 'Introduction', p. 6.

By playing miracles actors both beguile themselves and disrespect God in just the same way that Christ's tormentors did when they spat 'in his face, and buffeted him'.[165] To put it another way, by identifying drama with the game 'which the soldiers played with Christ at His Passion' the *Tretise* 'specifically associates play-acting with the cruel sport' of Christ's torturers.[166] Seen from this perspective, the Croxton *Play* is a genuine affront to God because it feigns the miraculous transformation of the eucharistic wafer into an image of Jesus. What is more, because it is played and performed the Jews' desecration of the host is a genuine act of torture, no different from the actions of Christ's historical tormentors. To a dissenting observer in sympathy with the *Tretise*'s attack on drama, the play's analogy between Jonathas and his men and the biblical Jews who tortured Christ could not be more real.

Aston has argued that 'not all illusions were to be equated with delusion'; that those who watched a play 'could both revere the miraculous and respect the limitations of physical enactment'.[167] As Pecock puts it, viewers might say '"Here at this autir is the Trinitye, and there at thilk auter is Iesus"', but that does not mean that they actually think 'this ymage is the Trinyte, or that thilk ymage is verily Iesus'.[168] Instead they recognize that 'these ymagis ben the liknessis or the ymagis of hem'.[169] In actuality, the fact that drama is like but not the same as reality is integral to the *Tretise*'s attack on dramatic representation as feigned, as fake, and as *play*. As V. A. Kolve has noted, the *Tretise* fears that drama 'teaches men that hell is only a *locus* on a pageant stage, and that the wrath of God is merely a dramatic attitude, for it is obvious to any spectator that the damned souls are not really punished in any Judgment Day pageant'.[170] Since drama *re*presents reality, the *Tretise* supposes that the viewer will discredit not only the truth of the actions unfolding before him, but also the truth of the reality they represent:

> For Crist seith that folc of avoutrie sechen siche singnys as a lecchour sechith signes of verrey love but no dedis of verrey love. So sithen this miraclis pleyinge ben

---

[165] '[T]unc expuerunt in faciem eius colphis eum ceciderunt.' Matthew 26. 67.

[166] This definition of the 'bobbid' game is from Oxford, Bodl. Libr., MS Bodley 649, as quoted by Owst, *Literature and Pulpit in Medieval England*, p. 510; and Davidson, 'Introduction', p. 27.

[167] Aston, 'Iconoclasm in England: Official and Clandestine', p. 61.

[168] Pecock, *The Repressor of Over Much Blaming of the Clergy*, ed. by Babington, pp. 151–52.

[169] Pecock, *The Repressor of Over Much Blaming of the Clergy*, ed. by Babington, p. 152.

[170] Kolve, *The Play Called Corpus Christi*, p. 21.

onely singnis, love withoute dedis, [...] these miraclis pleyinge been verrey leesing as they ben signis withoute dede. (99, ll. 197–207)

Just as the lecher's signs of true love resemble but are not the same as deeds of true love, so played miracles are only signs; love without deeds. Reliant on actors and props that stand for things which they are like but not the same as, religious plays detach the signs of faith from true belief. The *Tretise's* recognition of and anxiety about drama's dependence on an epistemology of deceit recurs in later attacks on drama, but it is particularly pertinent to plays like the Croxton *Play* that are engaged with eucharistic theologies of presence. In the previous section I argued that the Croxton *Play* may have intervened in contemporary controversy to defend, amongst other things, the orthodox doctrine of transubstantiation. By showing the miraculous outpouring of blood from the host and its transformation into an image of Christ, the play uses spectacle to confirm the veracity of orthodox teaching on the Eucharist. But, as Beckwith has argued, the miracles in the Croxton *Play* are 'overtly, explicitly and outrageously theatrical'.[171] Christ is not made substantially present, but appears as a figure, a dramatic sign played by an actor or represented by a small image or model. Consequently it is possible that to those who believed the sacrament was a figure, a sign without substance, plays like the Croxton *Play* both proved the error of orthodox doctrine and exposed the rituals and ceremonies of the Roman Church as 'onely singnis, love without dedis' (99, ll. 200–01). In the final part of this chapter I would like to suggest that this desire to reveal the fraudulent theatricality of the Roman Church may provide one context to explain the play's survival in a Tudor manuscript.

Aston has commented that, '[t]he story of iconoclasm was always a complex interaction between government and people, between the official and the unofficial, the legal and the illegal; and what believers learnt to believe was not the same as what they were authorized to believe.'[172] Nonetheless, imagery appeared on the official agenda of reform as early as 1536 with the publication of the Ten Articles in July and the first of Henry VIII's royal Injunctions in August. Both of these documents sought to limit the abuse of images and prevent idolatry by banning the setting forth or extolling of 'any ymages, relyques, or myracles, for any superstytion or lucre'.[173] While these decrees still permitted certain prac-

---

[171] Beckwith, 'Ritual, Church, and Theatre', p. 68.

[172] Aston, *England's Iconoclasts*, p. 220.

[173] England and Wales Sovereign, *Iniunctions gyuen [by the auc]toritie*, ([1536]; STC 10084.7), sig. 1ᵛ (no pagination).

tices – veneration, adornment, pilgrimages, and offerings — by 1538 orders were given for the wholesale removal of any images which attracted these practices:

> [S]uche Images as ye knowe in any of your cures to be so abused with pilgrimages or offerings of any thing made thervnto, ye shal for auodyng of that moste detestable offence of Idolatrie, furthwyth take down and deleye.[174]

Here, it is unclear exactly what is meant by the word 'delaye'. Were the clergy being instructed to 'put down or repress', to 'quell or put down' abused images?[175] Or were they being asked to 'lay [them] down, lay [them] aside'?[176] Were images to be destroyed or simply removed? For some of the more zealous reformers, this item provided the perfect pretext, not only for the removal of misused images, but also for testing them, proving them false, and finally destroying them. Following the publication of the 1538 Injunctions, unveilings of abused images took place with some regularity, often accompanied with great pomp and ceremony. The exposure of two such images helped to create a context for the transcription of the Croxton *Play* in the late 1530s: the showing of the Blood of Hailes at Paul's Cross in November 1538; and the exposure of the Boxley Rood of Grace in February of the same year. I will return to the showing of the Boxley Rood in Chapter 3, so will say nothing further here except that accounts of the exhibition of the Rood's 'certain engines and old wire [...] which caused the eyes to move and stir the head thereof' are clearly dramatic critical in their lexis.[177] For instance, John Hoker of Maidstone writes to Heinrich Bullinger, the Swiss Reformer that the Rood 'was made to act amid the jeers of the courtiers', and that a few days later 'it performed again'.[178]

[174] Church of England, *Iniunctions for the clerge (1538); STC 10086)*, fol. 1ʳ (no pagination).

[175] 'allay, *v.*¹, II., 8, 9', *The Oxford English Dictionary*, 2nd edn, <http://dictionary.oed.com/cgi/entry/50005864> [accessed 5 June 2013].

[176] 'allay, *v.*¹, I., 1', *The Oxford English Dictionary*, 2nd edn, <http://dictionary.oed.com/cgi/entry/50005864> [accessed 5 June 2013].

[177] *Letters and Papers of the Reign of Henry VIII*, XIII, 1, ed. by James Gairdner (1892), p. 79, no. 231 (Jeffray Chamber to Cromwell). Further accounts of the showing and destruction of the Boxley Rood can be found in pp. 283–84, no. 754 (Nicholas Partridge to Bullinger); p. 120, no. 348 (John Hoker, of Maidstone, to Bullinger); p. 239, no. 643 (John Finch to Conrad Humpard); p. 239, no. 644 (William Peterson to Conrad Pulbert); and Wriothesley, *A Chronicle of England during the Reigns of the Tudors*, ed. by Hamilton, I (1875), 75–76. For a fuller discussion of the performativity of the Boxley Rood see Groeneveld, 'A Theatrical Miracle'.

[178] *Letters and Papers of the Reign of Henry VIII*, XIII, 1, ed. by James Gairdner (1892), p. 120, no. 348 (John Hoker, of Maidstone, to Bullinger). The original Latin text is edited in Burnet, *The History of the Reformation of the Church of England*, VI, 194–95, no. 55.

Similarly, in another letter to Bullinger, Nicholas Partridge describes how the 'formerly immoveable' Boxley Rood was now 'ridden up to London and performed miracles in public'.[179] The analogies to the Croxton *Play* are quite obvious. Like the play that 'At Croxston on Monday [...] shall be sen' (74), the Boxley Rood performs its 'miracles' to order. Its mobility and susceptibility to repetition echo the performance conditions of the Croxton *Play*, which was probably played over and again at a number of different locations. And its contrivances are not so different from the devices required to effect the bleeding of the host, the splitting apart of the oven, and the boiling of the cauldron in the Croxton *Play*. Indeed, recalling the Rood's 'graces and engines', the miracles in the Croxton *Play*, like their counterparts in *Le Mistere de la Saincte Hostie*, may have 'been accomplished by devices and hidden places'.[180]

The parallels between the exposure of the Blood of Hailes and the dramaturgy of the Croxton *Play* are equally telling. The Cistercian abbey at Hailes had held a relic of Christ's sacred blood since 1270, and the abbey had long been a popular site for pilgrimage. In February 1538 the Abbot of Hailes wrote to Thomas Cromwell, Lord Privy Seal, confessing that the Blood was not Christ's but in fact drake's blood which required changing on a regular basis.[181] The first public denunciation of the Blood occurred not long after. During a sermon at Paul's Cross, John Hilsey, bishop of Rochester recounted the confession of a miller's wife that he had heard some twenty years earlier. According to the Tudor chronicler, Charles Wriothesley,

> she shewed him how the abott of the same place had given her manye jewells that had bene offred ther at the holie bloud, and how he would have geaven her one jewell [... but ...] she was afraid because it hanged by the holie bloud, and the abbott said tush! thou thou art a foole, it is but duckes bloode.[182]

---

[179] *Letters and Papers of the Reign of Henry VIII*, XIII, 1, ed. by James Gairdner (1892), pp. 283–84, no. 754 (Nicholas Partridge to Bullinger).

[180] Wriothesley, *A Chronicle of England during the Reigns of the Tudors*, ed. by Hamilton, I (1875), 75. Hamilton suggests that 'graces' is 'probably a clerical error for vices'. See editorial note c on the same page. '[S]e faisoit [...] par engiens et secrets.' The quotation is taken from Philippe de Vigneulles's eyewitness account of the 1513 performance of the French play. The text is reproduced in de Julleville, *Histoire du théâtre en France: les mystères*, II, 103–04 (p. 104), quoted, with the English translation, in Enders, 'Dramatic Memories and Tortured Spaces', pp. 213–14.

[181] *Letters and Papers of the Reign of Henry VIII*, XIII, 1, ed. by James Gairdner (1892), p. 119, no. 347 ([Abbot of Hailes to Cromwell]).

[182] Wriothesley, *A Chronicle of England during the Reigns of the Tudors*, ed. by Hamilton, I

Concluding his sermon by suggesting these facts 'should be known more open-
lie afterward' (1, 76), it would only be a matter of time before the Blood was
brought to London for its public exhibition. In October, during a Visitation of
the abbey, Hugh Latimer, bishop of Worcester, wrote to Cromwell to explain
that the Blood 'seems to be an unctuous gum and compound of many things.
It has a certain unctuous moistness, and though it seems somewhat like blood
while it is in the glass, yet when any parcel of the same is taken out it turneth
to a yellowness and is cleaving like glue.'[183] In November, Bishop Hilsey once
again preached at Paul's Cross and, refuting his earlier statement about duck's
blood, confirmed Latimer's observation that it was 'but hony clarified and coloured with saffron, and lyinge lyke a goume' (1, 90). He also 'did let every man
behould yt there at Paules Crosse, and all the way as he went to dinner to the
mayres, to loke on yt, so that every person might well perceive the abuse of the
sayd thinge' (1, 90). By 1550 more extreme claims were being made about the
Blood of Hailes. In his tract, *The Pilgrim* (*c.* 1546), the scholar William Thomas
claims the monks of Hailes could make the blood seem to appear or disappear
to extort money from unsuspecting pilgrims.[184] Again, the similarities to the

(1875), 75–76. All further references in this chapter are to this edition with page numbers given
in parentheses within the text.

[183] *Letters and Papers of the Reign of Henry VIII*, XIII, 2, ed. by James Gairdner (1893),
pp. 272–73, no. 709 (Latimer to Cromwell).

[184] The work is preserved in a number of contemporary manuscripts: BL, MS Cotton
Vespasian D. xviii; BL, Addit. MS 33383; BL, MS Harley 353; and Oxford, Bodl. Libr., MS
Bodley 53. A fifth copy was made in 1861 by Thomas James and is preserved as London, Lambeth
Palace, MS 464. The tract was first printed in Italian in 1552 and later in two English editions
(Thomas, *The Pilgrim*, ed. by Froude, pp. 3–81, and Thomas, *The Works*, ed. by D'Aubant,
pp. 3–127). The relevant passage, here transcribed from BL, Addit. MS 33383, which may be
the original copy, is as follows:
     In a certein monasterie called hailes, there was a great offering vnto the bloudde of Christ,
brought thither many yeres agoon out of the holy lande of Jerusaleme. And this bloudde had
such virtue, that as longe as the pilgryme were in dedely synne his sight wolde not serue him
to regarde it. But incontinentlie as he were in the state of grace he shulde cleerelie beholde it.
See here the crafte of these develish sowle qwellers. It behoved eche person that came thither
to see it, first to confesse himself, and then paieng a certein to the comon of that monasterie to
enter into a Chapell, vpon the aulter whereof this blessed bloudde shulde be shewed him. Ther
meane while by a secret waye behinde the aulter came the moonke that had confessed him, and
presented vpon the aulter a pixe of Christall great and thicke as a bawle on thone [sic] side,
and thynne as a glasse on the other side, in which this bloudde on the thinne side was cleere
and oapen to the sight, and on the thicke side impossible to be discerned. Nowe if this holy
confessor thought by the confession that he had hearde that the qualitie of the partie confessed

Croxton *Play* are abundantly clear. Like the Blood of Hailes, the blood in the Croxton *Play* is *not* the blood of Christ, but instead animal blood or blood coloured liquid. And just like the monks who made the Blood seem to appear and then disappear again, the actors in the Croxton *Play* make the host bleed by placing 'a tightly filled bladder inside the sacramental loaf' and squeezing it to produce 'a fountain of blood'.[185]

What I have been trying to propose is that the reasons behind the reformers' exposure of the machines and devices of certain much loved Catholic icons may also be behind the transcription of the Croxton *Play* into a sixteenth-century manuscript. In other words, by exhibiting the tricks 'by which the simple were imposed upon by the priests [...] the ignorant people [can] now call them mere conjurors, and despise their contrivances, objecting the deceits they practices against them'.[186] To put it another way, by revealing the artifice involved in an array of different Catholic devotional practices, the reformers were able to prove the error of those practices and the deceitfulness of those who perpetuated them. What is more, they demonstrated that this duplicity was akin to a kind of artfulness; an exaggerated sense of show. In the next chapter, I explore this nexus of ideas about Catholicism — its falseness, deceptiveness, and theatricality — in the plays of John Bale. In the 1530s, was it possible for reformed playwrights to distinguish their stagecraft from the Catholic histrionics they sought to condemn?

wolde yelde him more mooney, then shewed he foorthe the thicke side of the pixe, thorough the which the bloudde was invisible: so that the person seing himself remaigneng in deadely synne, must torne and retorne vnto his confessor, till by paieng for masses and other such almes he had purchased the sight of the thynne side of the Christall, and then was he sauf in the favor of God vntill he fell in synne agein. (BL, Addit. MS 33383, fols 1ʳ–65ʳ (fols 30ʳ–31ʳ))

On the publication history of Thomas's tract including the case for BL, Addit. MS 33383 as an autograph copy, see Martin, 'The Manuscript and Editorial Traditions'.

[185] Grantley, 'Producing Miracles', p. 84.

[186] *Original Letters Relative to the English Reformation*, ed. and trans. by Robinson, II (1847), 607, no. 278 (John Finch to Conrad Humpard). An extract from this letter is printed in *Letters and Papers of the Reign of Henry VIII*, XIII, 1, ed. by James Gairdner (1892), p. 239, no. 643.

Chapter 2

Performance and Polemic:
John Bale and the Poetics of Propaganda

O n 25 January 1537 John Stokesley, bishop of London, ordered the arrest of the parish priest of Thorndon in Suffolk on a charge of heresy. The priest was John Bale, former prior of the Carmelites at Ipswich and a recent convert to the reformed cause. In his defence Bale produced an answer 'vnto serten artycles vnjustlye gadred vpon hys prechyng', addressing seventeen different accusations of error, among them rejection of the Henry VIII's approved catechism, the doctrine of the harrowing of hell, and auricular confession.[1] The document offers a wealth of information both about Bale's confessional stance, and more generally about the nature of contemporary doctrine. However, for our purposes, what is perhaps more interesting is what it reveals about Bale's attitude towards representational art. Responding to the charge that he had 'denyed, descendit ad inferna', Christ's descent into hell, 'to be an artycle of ye crede', Bale insists that he 'neuer denyed':

> but desyred ye peple reuerentlye so to receue yt [...] I requyred them also to be very cyrcumspect in receyuyng the seyd artycle. And not to beleue yt as yei se yt sett forth in peynted clothes, or in glasse wyndowes, or lyke as my self had befor tyme sett yt forth in ye cuntre yer in a serten playe. for thowgh ye sowle of crist soch tyme as hys corse laye in ye graue, ded vysytt hell, yet can we not iustlye suppose yt he

XXIX

---

[1] The single, autograph copy is preserved in Kew, NA, SP 1/111, fols 183ʳ–187ʳ (fol. 183ʳ). It is reprinted in full in McCusker, *John Bale, Dramatist and Antiquary*, pp. 6–11.

check fancashire? where would Bale have seen this play? works of art injunctions? check Nichols

✗ ✗   fawgt vyolentlye with ye deuyls, for ye sowles of ye faythfull sort, and so toke them
        owte of yer possessyon.[2]

Bale's position on Christ's harrowing of hell follows the first of the King's
Lutheran inspired Ten Articles (1536), which asserts the binding authority
of the Bible, the three Ecumenical creeds, and the first four Ecumenical coun-
cils. Two of the Ecumenical creeds, the Apostles' and the Athanasian, state
respectively that Christ 'suffered under Pontius Pilate, was crucified, died,
and was buried; He descended into hell', and that He 'suffered for our salvation: He descended into hell: on the third day He rose again from death'.[3]
Neither creed treats the exact nature of Christ's descent into hell, but Bale
follows the orthodox view expressed by Aquinas that Christ's body remained
entombed while His soul harrowed hell.[4] However, orthodox theology also
taught that 'the fact of Christ's body not being in hell does not prevent the
whole Christ from being there: but proves that not everything appertaining to
human nature was there'.[5] Conversely, Bale's view that we cannot 'iustlye suppose yt he fawgt vyolentlye with ye deuyls', draws a keen distinction between
the redemption bought by Christ's body (on the Cross) and His soul (in hell)
and is therefore closer to the Calvinist line that the descent into hell represents
the spiritual suffering that Christ underwent for mankind.[6] Unlike orthodox
theologians who attempted to reconcile the separation of Christ's body from
His soul after His death, Bale's interpretation of the descent as part of the price
of man's redemption relies on a strict division of Christ's corporality from his
spirituality.

---

    [2] McCusker, *John Bale, Dramatist and Antiquary*, p. 7.

    [3] '[P]assus sub Pontio Pilato, crucifixus, mortuus, et sepultus; descendit ad inferna'; '[q]
ui passus est pro nostra salute: descendit ad inferos: tertia die resurrexit a mortuis.' Schaff,
The History of the Creeds, ed. by Schaff, II: *The Creeds of the Greek and Latin Churches, with
Translations* (1878), pp. 45, 69.

    [4] Aquinas, *Summa theologica*, ed. and trans. by Gilby and others, LIV: *The Passion of Christ
(3a. 46–52)* (1965), pp. 160–65, IIIa. 52. 3.

    [5] 'Et ideo per hoc quod corpus Christi non fuit in inferno, non excluditur quin totus
Christus fuerit, sed ostenditur quod non fuit ibi totum quod pertinet ad humanam naturam.'
Aquinas, *Summa theologica*, ed. and trans. by Gilby and others, LIV: *The Passion of Christ (3a.
46–52)* (1965), pp. 162, IIIa. 52. 3.

    [6] Calvin addressed Christ's descent into hell as early as 1534 in both the Latin and French
editions of *Psychopannychia*. An English translation of the French version of this tract was
printed in 1581 as Calvin, *An excellent treatise of the immortalytie of the soule*, trans. by Stocker
(STC 4409). See also Calvin, *Institutes of the Christian Religion*, ed. by McNeill, I, 512–520.

Bale's interpretation, which argues against Christ's bodily presence in hell, goes some way to explain his position on artistic representations of the subject, in particular his retraction of a 'certen playe' on the subject written in his youth. All religious art and drama uses human signs to represent divine referents. But while apologists for religious iconography might have argued that in translating the spiritual and mysterious referents of Christianity into a series of human and familiar signs, sacred truths are made accessible to an otherwise uncomprehending audience, for Bale, and other reformers like him, the use of earthly signs to represent spiritual realities was equivalent to a gross and dangerously seductive falsification of the truth. Expressing heavenly truths in human terms, medieval plays about the descent of Christ into hell necessarily depict the spiritual suffering endured by Christ's soul as a bodily encounter between Christ and the devils of hell. So, Jesus's claim in the Towneley *Extraccio animarum* that his 'body shall abyde in graue' while His soul harrows hell is clearly undermined when the actor playing Jesus physically descends to the hell represented in and by the playing space.[7] Likewise, Christ's words in the N-Town pageant on the harrowing of hell, 'I am þe sowle of Cryst Jesu', are contradicted by the dramatic necessity of the actor's bodily presence.[8] In both of these pageants actors are a phenomenal requirement; they are the material signs through which the audience are referred to a series of sacred truths. But for Bale the danger of this kind of representational practice is that by lavishing attention on the human image divine truth can easily be forgotten or, worse still, the carnal sign might be mistaken for sacred referent.

Although he might have rejected the subject matter and mode of performance typified by his 'serten playe' as ill-suited to the reformed stage, Bale went on to write a number of plays in the service of the reformed cause, and in this chapter I want to explore the terms of Bale's dramatic polemic. In the previous chapter I argued that the Croxton *Play of the Sacrament* fulfils its homiletic task in terms that are primarily positive. In other words, every aspect of the play's action and dialogue is designed to affirm the veracity of orthodox doctrine and ritual. Conversely, Bale's extant plays are less concerned with the instruction of religious truth than they are with the exposure of erroneous belief and custom. And for Bale, a recent convert to radical reform, false theology and corrupt practice are always associated with the Roman Church. In the first part of this chapter I examine what Paul Whitfield White has called the

---

[7] *Extraccio animarum*, in *The Towneley Plays*, ed. by England, pp. 293–306 (p. 293, l. 23).

[8] *The Harrowing of Hell (Part 1)*, in *The N-Town Play*, ed. by Spector, I, 336–37 (p. 336, l. 9).

ꭓ 'dramatic inversion of the Old Virtues as new Vices'; the ways Bale reinvents virtuous characters like the Croxton *Play*'s Episcopus as the vicious characters of his own morality plays.[9] By branding his Vices as proponents of the Roman Church, Bale also draws on an earlier dramatic tradition which associated the Vice with jokes, jests, and games to imply that Catholic clerics are little more than imposters and players and their rituals mere stagecraft. In the second part of this chapter I explore this designation of the Roman Church as theatrical, arguing that characters like Infidelitas in *Three Laws* ([*c.* 1547]; STC 1287) and Sedicyon in *King Johan* (*c.* 1538) bolster the equation of Catholicism with playing established by the early reformer William Tyndale. But, as Greg Walker has noted, this 'conscious use of theatricality to parody what Bale saw as the abuses of catholic observance masks a deeper anxiety about the use of drama for theological ends'.[10] Bale's plays might strengthen the spectacular equation between Catholicism, theatricality, and vice, but they also come dangerously close to condemning all drama as idolatry. In the final part of this chapter I examine the efforts Bale makes to distinguish his own pious stagecraft from the impious theatricality of his Catholic Vices.

King Johan *and* Three Laws

Sometime in the late 1530s, Sir Richard Morison, propagandist for Henry VIII, produced a treatise entitled, *A Discourse Touching the Reformation of the Lawes of England*.[11] Although the treatise begins as a discourse on English law, Morison soon turns his attention towards the evils of the Roman Church. In a lengthy digression he argues that the evils of popery need to be recalled regularly and in the strongest possible terms lest the people forget the miseries from which they have been freed:

> Playes, songes and books are to be born withal, thowghe they payne and vexe some, specyally whan they declare eyther the abhominacion of the bisshop of rome and his adherenttes, or the benefittes browght to thys realme by your graces tornyng hym and hys out of it, they are to be borne with all, thowghe som thyng in them be to be misliked.[12]

[9] White, *Theatre and Reformation*, p. 35.

[10] Walker, *Plays of Persuasion*, p. 191. These tensions have also been productively discussed in Simpson, 'Three Laws'.

[11] For a recent and full assessment of Morison as propagandist, scholar, politician, theologian, and diplomat, see Sowerby, *Renaissance and Reform in Tudor England*.

[12] BL, MS Cotton Faustina C. ii, fols 5ʳ–22ʳ (fol. 16ʳ). An extract of the text is edited as

White has argued that, 'the fact that Morison's proposals were implemented across the realm indicates the extent to which the Cromwellian regime recognized drama, processions, ceremonies, and other religious or quasi-religious practices as a means of legitimating and internalising its vision of a politically and religiously reformed England.'[13] But while the Privy Council did promote a programme of spectacular propaganda that included processions, feasts, sermons, and pamphlets, drama does not seem to have been part of this campaign.[14] However, it is clear that Thomas Cromwell, Lord Privy Seal, did take a personal interest in the writing and performance of the plays of at least one virulent anti-Catholic: John Bale.

John Bale was born at Cove in Suffolk in 1495.[15] At the age of twelve he was sent to the Carmelite friary at Norwich where he spent the next five years before going up to Cambridge in 1514. He remained at Cambridge until 1529, when he was admitted to the degree of Bachelor of Divinity, and although there is no record of his attaining further degrees, by 1534 he was using the title Doctor of Divinity. In 1530 he became prior of the Carmelite convent at Maldon in Essex. Three years later he was promoted to the convent at Ipswich, and in July 1534 he became prior at Doncaster. His conversion to the reformed faith clearly occurred around this time; licensed to preach throughout the diocese of York, probably in support of the royal supremacy, Bale came under the investigation of Archbishop Lee of York for his unorthodox beliefs.[16] Two years later, as I

'Extract from "A Discourse Touching the Reformation of the Lawes of England"', in Anglo, 'An Early Tudor Programme for Plays', pp. 177–79. All further references are to this edition. Morison's defence of drama is also considered in the Conclusion to this volume, see pp. 154–57.

[13] White, *Theatre and Reformation*, p. 14.

[14] See Great Britain Record Commission, *State Papers [...]: Henry the Eighth*, 1 (1830), 411–14; Lancashire, *Dramatic Texts and Records of Britain*, pp. 66, 99, 202; and Anglo, *Spectacle, Pageantry, and Early Tudor Policy*, pp. 269–70.

[15] Bale writes about his own life in four autobiographical accounts. See Oxford, Bodl. Libr., MS Selden Supra 41, fol. 195ʳ; BL, MS Harley 3838, fols 111ᵛ–112ᵛ; Bale, *Illustrium [...] scriptorum [...] summariu[m]* (1548; STC 1295), fols 242ᵛ–244ᵛ, and Bale, *Scriptorum [...] catalogus*, 1, 702–05. He also wrote and published a detailed narrative of his appointment to the bishopric of Ossory, including details of his escape from there in Bale, *The vocacyon [...] to the bishoprick of Ossorie* (1553; STC 1307). All of Bale's autobiographical accounts are historically inconsistent, and his embellished hindsights, as Happé has noted, 'may be part of a deliberate process of reconstructing the past to fit with later polemical needs, but they may alternatively, be due to lapses in memory'. See Happé, *John Bale*, p. 2.

[16] The accusation of heresy originated with Thomas Kirby, a conservative Franciscan, who claimed that Bale had criticized the honouring of saints. See Dickens, *Lollards and Protestants*

indicated at the opening of this chapter, Bale was again charged with heresy, this time by Bishop Stokesley. It was during this period of incarceration that Bale produced his 'answer'. In his *Scriptorum illustriu[m] maioris Brytannie quam nunc Angliam & Scotiam uocant catalogus* ([1557]), Bale claims that on both occasions it was his association with Cromwell that saved him from conviction. He says, 'deprived of all possessions I was soon dragged from the pulpit to the courts of justice, first under Lee at York, and then under Stokesley at London: but the pious Cromwell who was in the confidence of King Henry always set me free on account of the comedies I had published.'[17] Although there is no evidence to confirm Cromwell's intervention during the first heresy trial, there are two letters to him, one from Bale himself, another from John Leland, the King's Antiquary, on Bale's behalf, which indicate that by 1537 Bale was under Cromwell's protection.[18] And although neither of these letters repeats the assertion, made in the *Catalogus*, that Cromwell had a particular interest in Bale on account of the comedies he produced, it seems that by 1538 Bale was writing and revising plays that promoted the political and religious views of the Lord Privy Seal.

Two such plays are *King Johan* and *Three Laws*. That these plays were linked to other propaganda materials produced by and for Cromwell has been the subject of critical discussion by Alan Stewart and Paul Whitfield White who have both argued that from early 1537 to early 1540 Bale was under Cromwell's direct patronage.[19] It seems that Bale's association with Cromwell came about as a result of his relationship with Leland, well known as one of Cromwell's print propagandists, for whom he produced the first of his bibliographical works, the *Anglorum Heliades* (1536). However, within two years, the association existed in its own right; Bale's name appears twice in Cromwell's financial accounts for payments made to 'Balle and his felowes' for performances attended by the Lord Privy Seal at St Stephen's Church, near Canterbury in September 1538

---

in the *Diocese of York*, pp. 141–43; Fairfield, *John Bale: Mythmaker for the English Reformation*, p. 36; Happé, *John Bale*, p. 7; and Elton, *Policy and Police*, p. 233.

[17] 'Exutus fortunis omnibus, ex concione ad tribunalia mox trahebar, Eboraci primum sub Læo, Londini postea sub Stokisleyo: sed pius Cromvuelus, qui regi Henrico ab intimis erat, ob editas comœdias me semper liberauit.' For the English translation see the second appendix in Bale, *The Complete Plays*, ed. by Happé, I (1985), 147–48 (p. 147). For the Latin original see Bale, *Scriptorum [...] catalogus*, I, 702. Bale's chronology seems a little fanciful since there is no evidence to suggest that any of his plays were printed before 1547/8.

[18] BL, MS Cotton Cleopatra E. iv, fol. 167[r]; *Letters and Papers of the Reign of Henry VIII*, XII, 1, ed. by James Gairdner (1890), p. 112, no. 230 (John Leyland [sic] to Cromwell).

[19] Stewart, '"Ydolatricall Sodometrye"'; White, *Theatre and Reformation*, pp. 12–41.

and in January 1539 at an unspecified location.[20] A third performance is indicated by the depositions of John Alforde and Thomas Brown against Henry
Totehill, a shipman of St Katherine's, Tower Hill for speaking out in support of
the pope, which were included in a letter from Thomas Cranmer, archbishop
of Canterbury, to Cromwell dated January 1539 and speak of a performance
at Cranmer's Canterbury residence of an 'enterlude concernyng King Johan'.[21]
Given the unlikelihood of two King John plays circulating simultaneously, the
most likely conclusion is that the play performed at Cranmer's house was Bale's
King Johan.[22] Though we may never know for certain exactly which of Bale's
plays were performed on these three occasions, if *Three Laws* and *King Johan*
were performed by 'Balle and his felowes', the texts as they survive today bear
the marks of substantial revision that must have been made after any performances in the 1530s.

King Johan was never printed and survives in a single manuscript, San
Marino, Huntington Library, MS HM 3. There are two sections of text which
were clearly written at different times. The first occupies eighteen folios and is
written in a single hand, Scribe A. Reference at line 1229 to 'Darvell Gathyron',
a Welsh saint whose image was burnt at Smithfield on 30 May 1538 suggest it
was copied around this time.[23] Sometime afterwards, it was amended and cor-

---

[20] *Letters and Papers of the Reign of Henry VIII*, XIV, 2, ed. by James Gairdner and R. H. Brodie
(1895) pp. 317–45, no. 781 (Cromwell's Accounts, from AD 1537). Some critics have identi-
fied the company under Bale's leadership as Cromwell's own. Reference to the Lord Cromwell's
Players and the Lord Privy Seal's Men in municipal, monastic, and collegiate records between
1536 and 1540 certainly make this a possibility. See Blatt, *The Plays of John Bale*, pp. 30–31;
Harris, *John Bale*, pp. 101–03; Lancashire, *Dramatic Texts and Records of Britain*, p. 380;
McCusker, *John Bale, Dramatist and Antiquary*, p. 75; Pafford, 'Introduction', pp. xvii–xviii; and
Walker, *Plays of Persuasion*, p. 173. For the various payments made to the Lord Privy Seal's Men
and Lord Cromwell's Players see Beadle, 'Plays and Playing at Thetford and Nearby'; and Nelson,
Cambridge, I, 114–15. For a possible itinerary see White, *Theatre and Reformation*, pp. 15–27.

[21] Cranmer, *Works*, ed. by Cox, I: *Miscellaneous Writings and Letters* (1844), p. 388.

[22] Critics have treated the evidence with varying degrees of scepticism. At one end of the
spectrum, Pafford has suggested that the remuneration made to Bale's troupe in January 1539
might have been for this performance at Cranmer's residence. Occupying the middle ground,
White accepts as a given that the play performed at Cranmer's house was Bale's *King Johan* but
distinguishes it from the performance paid for by Cromwell in January 1539. Sydney Anglo
questions whether the play mentioned in Alforde and Brown's depositions need have been Bale's
King Johan. See Pafford, 'Introduction', p. xviii; White, *Theatre and Reformation*, p. 17; and
Anglo, *Spectacle, Pageantry, and Early Tudor Policy*, p. 269.

[23] See Happé, 'Notes to *King Johan*', p. 124. Accounts of the destruction of this image can
be found in Foxe, *TAMO (1563 Edition)*, III, 627–28; and Wriothesley, *A Chronicle of England*

rected by both Scribe A and a second hand, Scribe B, usually identified with Bale. Later still, four sheets were removed from the gathering, of which two have been recovered.[24] The second section, written and corrected entirely by Scribe B, takes up the play at the point at which the A text is cancelled and continues to its conclusion. The watermark date for the stock of paper on which the B text was written suggests that Bale returned to the play some time after 1558 and began to revise it to fit the altered circumstances of the first years of the reign of Elizabeth I. In short, the text preserves traces of Bale's initial project to write a play in support of Cromwell's programme of reform alongside his later efforts to reshape his play in order to reflect the political and religious situation of the early 1560s.

Three Laws similarly bears the marks of revision. It survives in two editions, the first printed on the continent by Derick van der Straten around 1547, the second in London by Thomas Colwell in November 1562 (STC 1288).[25] The title page to the first edition announces that Bale 'compyled' the play in 1538, but a version of the play must have existed in 1536 when it appears in the list of his works in the *Angolorum Heliades*. The case for a still earlier date was made some seventy years ago when Jesse W. Harris noted some striking, if ultimately inconclusive, points of correspondence between William Broman's 1535 account of heretical activities in the diocese of York and some lines in Bale's play.[26] Broman claims that 'one Bale, a White Friar, sometime prior of Doncaster, taught him about four years ago that Christ would dwell in no church made of lime and stone by man's hands, but only in heaven above, and in man's heart in earth'.[27] The sentiment, which amounts to a denial of Christ's real presence in the sacrament of the Eucharist, is partly echoed in Bale's play when Evangelium explains to Infidelitas that the true church is not 'a temple of lyme and stone, | But a lyvysh buyldynge, grounded in fayth alone'.[28] While

---

during the Reigns of the Tudors, ed. by Hamilton, I (1875), 80.

[24] These were rediscovered in the Ipswich Corporation records and found their way into the hands of John Payne Collier. See Pafford, 'Introduction', pp. v–vi.

[25] The STC suggests a publication date of [1548?] for the first edition of *Three Laws*. I suggest and adopt an earlier date of *c.* 1547 since it seems most likely the text was printed during Bale's first exile on the Continent, which came to an end on the accession of Edward VI in 1547.

[26] Harris, *John Bale*, pp. 68–69.

[27] *Letters and Papers of the Reign of Henry VIII*, IX, ed. by James Gairdner (1886), p. 276, no. 230 (New Theology).

[28] *Three Laws*, in Bale, *The Complete Plays*, ed. by Happé, II, 65–124 (p. 103, ll. 1329–30).

such scant evidence by no means proves that Bale was writing *Three Laws* as early as 1531, Broman's testament does suggest that Bale was an early proponent of reformed teaching on the Eucharist and that his conversion might have occurred earlier than has previously been thought. However, there is further evidence that points to an original date of composition sometime in the early 1530s. William Tyndale's influence on Bale has been long noted and often discussed. With regard to *Three Laws* the most common observation, first made by T. W. Craik, is that the play's title and plot must have been suggested by Tyndale's *An exposicion vppon the. v. vi. vii. chapters of Mathew, which thre chapters are the key and the dore of the scripture, and the restoring agayne of Moses lawe corrupte by the scribes and Pharises. And the exposicion is the restoring agayne of Christes lawe corrupte by the papists* ([1533?]; STC 24440).[29] But beyond this, Bale's debt to Tyndale has been treated in general rather than specific terms. For instance, though Happé does note that 'Bale follows Tyndale's language in a number of places in *Three Laws*', he goes on to argue that 'no one passage in Tyndale's work [...] has emerged as a specific source'.[30] But there is at least one passage for which a specific source can be identified:

> AMBITIO: Why, what dost thu thynke   my mytar to sygnyfy?
> INFIDELITAS: The mouth of a wolfe,   and that shall I prove by and by —
>   If thu stoupe downewarde,   loo, se how the wolfe doth gape.
>   Redye to devoure   the lambes, least any escape.
>   But thy wolvyshnesse   by thre crownes wyll I hyde,
>   Makynge the a Pope,   and a captayne of all pryde. (*TL* 1183–88)

In this passage, the Vice Infidelitas, prompts the Catholic Bishop Ambitio to bend forward so that the pointed horns of his mitre take on the appearance of a wolf's gaping mouth. It is a passage that has been beautifully treated by White:

> This stunning visual pun must have amused even Bale's Catholic spectators. But its purpose is much more than to evoke laughter. The incident satirizes the tropological significance which Catholicism ascribes to visual images, in this case clerical dress. And by applying an entirely different 'trope' to Ambition's elaborate headwear, one that identifies the bishop with the ravenous wolves of Matthew 7:15 and John 10:12

All further references to this edition are given as *TL* with line numbers given in parentheses within the text.

[29] Craik, *The Tudor Interlude*, p. 74.

[30] Happé, *John Bale*, pp. 83–85.

who deceive and devour the innocent sheep (i.e. 'the Byble readers' of the Reformation), he attacks the cruelty of Catholic authorities in persecuting Protestants.[31]

However, by reading the passage as an example of Bale's clever but general use of visual satire, White misses the topical allusion to Cardinal Wolsey that Bale lifts directly from Tyndale's *Practyse of Prelates* (1530; STC 24465).[32] Though the identification of Wolsey with 'wolvyshnesse' (*TL* 1187) can be traced back at least as far as Skelton's 1522 poem 'Why Come Ye Not to Court?', the pun was not widespread until it was popularized by Tyndale in his *Practyce of Prelates* where it appears no less than ten times.[33] Given the tract's recurrent pun on 'Thomas wolfsee' it is possible that its comparison of the pope to a 'wolf in lambes skynne' was intended to recall Wolsey's own pretensions to the Holy See after the death of Leo X in 1521.[34] Infidelitas's equation of the clergy with wolves and his suggestion that the pope wears a triple crown to disguise his lupine nature clearly echo the allusions to Wolsey's wolfishness in Tyndale's tract and therefore not only serve as general satire on the rapaciousness, covetousness, and pride of the clergy, but may also have been intended as a specific attack on Cardinal Wolsey.[35] For such topical satire to be effective Bale must have been working on an early draft of *Three Laws* before Wolsey's death in 1530.[36]

[31] White, *Theatre and Reformation*, p. 1.

[32] Bale's longstanding interest in and use of this text is evident in the revisions and additions he made to a no longer extant edition printed around 1554. One early edition of the English translation of Gardiner's *De vera obedientia* (1553; STC 11587), instructs readers to 'Loke shortly to have from me the practices of prelates | compiled by Willyam Tyndale the true martyr of God with the augmentacions of Joan Bale' (sig. H4r).

[33] In the Latin 'Descastrichon virulentum' appended to the poem Wolsey is described as 'eccemaris lupus'. The poem was first printed in 1545. See Skelton, *why come ye nat to courte* ([1545?]; STC 22615), sig. D6r.

[34] Tyndale, *The practyse of prelates*, sig. A8v.

[35] It is of course possible that the composition of *Three Laws* need not be coterminous with the first edition of *The practyse of prelates*. Indeed, the fact that Tyndale's tract was reprinted twice during Edward VI's reign (in 1548; STC 24467 and [1549?]; STC 24466) is testament to its enduring popularity long after the fall and death of its original target. To put it another way, Bale's own reading of *The practyde of prelates*, and its influence on his writing of *Three Laws* might have occurred long after its topical allusions to Wolsey had ceased to have any currency.

[36] At least one other contemporary play alludes to Wolsey in these terms. Although *A new enterlude drawen oute of the holy scripture of godly queene Hester* (STC 13251) was not printed until *c.* 1561, it was most likely composed around the time of Wolsey's downfall in 1529. In the play, a dramatization of the biblical story of Esther, the character Aman, adviser to the King Assewerus, is clearly intended as an allegorical representation of Wolsey. The similarities

The text that was finally printed in *c.* 1547 bears marks of revision that suggest Bale continued to update the play through the 1540s. References to 'Rugge', 'Corbet', and 'Wharton' point to figures that would have been obvious targets for Bale's abuse in the 1540s. William Rugg was consecrated Bishop of Norfolk in 1536, and although he upheld the king's policy towards the papacy, he was in all other matters a staunch conservative.[37] In 1539 he was listed as one of the six conservatives maintaining transubstantiation and auricular confession, and in the same year he supported the Six Articles openly. Cranmer was vociferous in his condemnation, declaring that Rugg 'doth approve none to preach [in his diocese] that be of right judgment'.[38] Wharton of Bungay was an informer who served both Cromwell and the more reactionary administration that followed. Like Rugg, he was an obvious target for Bale's abuse. In his *Yet a course at the Romyshe foxe* (1543; STC 1309), Bale describes him as 'a greatvp holder of trayterose prestes'.[39] The allusion to Corbet is more obscure, although Happé has noted a reference in *The actes of the Englysh votaryes* ([1551]; STC 1273.5) in which Corbet is described as 'a cruel iustyce'.[40] If these references point to a revision in the mid-1540s, the final three stanzas must have been written very close to the time of publication. They refer to the 'late [...] Kynge

between the text and the political charges laid against Wolsey are covered in detail in Walker, *Plays of Persuasion*, pp. 102–32.

[37] Happé's suggestion that the Rugge referred to is Robert Rugge, mayor of Norwich in 1545, seems doubtful given the greater likelihood of Bale's antipathy towards the conservative Bishop. Robert was in fact William's brother and both were members of a prominent Norfolk family with lands close to Northelham. Around 1593 Robert's granddaughter, Elizabeth, married Cromwell's great-grandson, Edward. See Happé, 'Notes to *Three Laws*', p. 175; and Happé, *John Bale*, p. 74.

[38] *Letters and Papers of the Reign of Henry VIII*, XII, 1, ed. by James Gairdner (1890), p. 584, no. 1281 (Cranmer to Cromwell).

[39] Bale, *Yet a course at the romyshe fox* (1543; STC 1309), sig. A5ᵛ. He goes on, 'I trowe master Vvharton of bongaye in soth folke will not be behynde wyth hys part now, nomore than he hath bene a fore tyme, wyth his colege of calkers that calked so longe for Cromwell, and for other more yf the worlde had not changed to ther myndes.'

[40] Happé, 'Notes to *Three Laws*', p. 175; and Happé, *John Bale*, p. 74. Bale, *The actes of the Englysh votaryes* ([1551]; STC 1273.5), II: *The second part or contynuacyon of the English votaries*, fol. 83ʳ. Although the second part of the text did not appear in the two earliest editions (1546; STC 1270, and 1548; STC 1271), Happé cites the 1546 edition as the source for this description of Corbet. The same passage in the second part of *Englysh votaryes* also describes Rugge as a 'wycked [...] mayre', which presumably accounts for Happé's equation of the Rugge mentioned in the play with the Rugge who was mayor of Norwich in the 1540s. See Happé, 'Notes to *Three Laws*', p. 175.

Henrye', champion 'Hys noble sonne Edwarde', and offer a prayer 'for Quene Kateryne' (*TL* 2022, 2033, 2040). The coincidence of the second edition with the revisions made by Bale to the *Johan* manuscript, highlights the extent to which the Elizabethan Settlement provided a suitable context for the second-ary reception of Bale's dramatic polemic and further emphasizes his appetite for revision; in the 1562 edition the concluding prayer has been amended to address 'Quene Elizabeth [...] And [...] her noble Counsellours' (sig. K5ᵛ).

Although the revisions made by Bale to both texts suggest an awareness of and a desire to respond to the shifting political and religious situation, in the most general terms both plays might be summarized as deploying a morality scheme to dramatize the reformed struggle against Catholic corruption and oppression. *King Johan* does this by imagining King Johan's attempts to free England from papal tyranny as a kind of premature reformation. Though his intention to restore Widow England to her former and proper glory is derailed by the words and actions of the play's Catholic Vices, the triumphant appear-ance of Imperyall Majestye at the play's end hints that Henry VIII will succeed where Johan has failed. *Three Laws* also concludes by banishing the corrup-tive influence of the Catholic Church and her agents. But where *King Johan* dramatizes a specific historical moment, *Three Laws* enacts the whole of human history as a pattern of conflict between the forces of the good and evil. The play's full title gives the clearest account of this narrative structure: *A comedy concernynge thre lawes, of nature Moses, & Christ, corrupted by the sodomytes. Pharysees and Papystes.* In this scheme the corruption of the laws of nature and Moses by the sodomites and the Pharisees are seen to prefigure the corruption of the law of Christ by the Catholic Church.

In his analysis of the relationship between pre- and post-Reformation morality drama, Rainer Pineas has argued:

> The main controversial technique of the polemical morality play is the establishing of the Vice (or the character dominated by the Vice) as adhering to Catholicism and his condemnation through his own words and actions. For in the figure of the old morality Vice, the Protestant polemicist found a ready-made tool for his purpose of vilifying his opponents. The evilness of the Vice was an established tradition; the audience was trained to mistrust and condemn anyone playing that role. And so there remained only one task: to demonstrate that the Vice was a Catholic and then to illustrate the evil nature of Catholicism by having its proponent, the Vice play the evil part convention had already established for him in the old morality.[41]

---

[41] Pineas, 'The English Morality Play', pp. 168–69.

Since relatively few texts and no performance records of morality plays survive from the Middle Ages it seems likely that morality play was a good deal less prevalent and certainly less archetypically medieval than Pineas's analysis assumes. However, though the surviving evidence seems to point to a less popular or significant role for the morality genre in the history of medieval drama, *King Johan* and *Three Laws* do seem to be indebted to an earlier indigenous moral dramatic tradition, particularly in their use of Vice characters.[42] In the discussion that follows I am interested in the ways Bale adapts the Vice to promote the reformed cause.

The first and most obvious way Bale adapts the Vice is to make him a Catholic. This he demonstrates in a number of ways, but most immediately by appearance. Costuming instructions are appended to the character list that appears on sig. G1ᵛ of the *c.* 1547 edition of *Three Laws* for '*the six vyces, or frutes of Infydelyte*' (*TL*, p. 121), the three pairs of Vices charged with bringing down Naturae lex (Avaricia and Pseudodoctrina), Moseh lex (Idololatria and Hypocrisis), and Christi lex (Ambitio and Sodomismus):

> *Lete Idolatry be decked lyke an olde wytche, Sodomy lyke a monke of all sectes, Ambycyon lyke a byshop, Covetousnesse lyke a Pharyse or spyrituall lawer, False Doctryne lyke a popysh doctour, and Hypocresy lyke a graye fryre.* (*TL*, p. 121)

With perhaps the exception of Idololatria, all of these characters are encouraged to dress, anachronisms notwithstanding, as adherents of the Catholic faith. In contrast, Bale offers no instructions for the costuming of the play's virtuous characters; these, he tells us '*are easye ynough to conjecture*' (*TL*, p. 121). In other words, the practical and polemical function of the costuming list is to ensure the visual association between Catholicism and vice. Though *King Johan* contains no such list, a similar effect is achieved through a series of stage directions that instruct Usurpid Powre to '*drese for the Pope, Privat Welth for a Cardynall, and Sedycyon for a monke*' (*KJ* 983 sd).[43] Sedicyon, it seems, is particularly fond of

---

[42] Brian Gourley has also argued that Bale draws on medieval dramatic practice in *King Johan* and *Three Laws*. However, where I argue that his adaptation of the Vice complements his polemical purpose to expose the theatricality of Catholicism, Gourley suggests that Bale incorporates medieval dramatic and exegetical practices in order 'to argue that the Henrician Reformation is a pre-destined outcome of medieval struggles between England and the Papacy'. See Gourley, 'Carnavalising Apocalyptic History', p. 169.

[43] *King Johan*, in Bale, *The Complete Plays*, ed. by Happé, I (1985), 29–99 (p. 54, l. 983 sd). All further references are to this edition are given as *KJ* with line numbers given in parentheses within the text.

dressing-up: much earlier in the play he confesses that he sometimes dresses like 'a monke in a long syd cowle' (*KJ* 195), sometimes like 'a channon in a syrples fayer and whyght' (*KJ* 197), and 'Sumtyme the bysshoppe with a myter and a cope; | A graye fryer sumtyme with cutt shoes and a rope' (*KJ* 201–02). The effect not only confirms the visual equation between Catholicism and vice, it also points to the theatricality of Catholicism by suggesting the vestments of its clerics are excessively elaborate and susceptible to change. If costumes offer the most immediate way of signalling the Catholicism of his Vices, Bale strengthens the association by having them declare, repeatedly, their religious affiliation. Strikingly, such declarations are often accompanied by statements of moral corruption. So, in *Three Laws* Sodomismus's claim to 'become all spyrytuall, | For the clergye at Rome' (*TL* 575–76) follows hard on the heels of his open admission to be 'so vyle a knave | As nature doth deprave' (*TL* 556–57). Similarly, in *King Johan* Sedicyon's declaration of allegiance to Rome is immediately followed by the suggestion of his moral and sexual corruption, 'I am Sedycyon that with the Pope wyll hold | So long as I have a hole with in my breche' (*KJ* 90–1). Such statements of moral corruption are not new; pre-Reformation morality Vices frequently make similar claims. But what is new is to pair such statements with declarations of adherence to Catholicism. The effect is to signal the cross-fertilization between moral and theological error.

These bragging admissions of moral corruption are just one of a number of ways Bale points to the evil nature of Catholicism. A similar kind of ill placed bravado is evident when Bale's Vices admit to their use of theological deception. For instance, in *King Johan* Dissymulacyon boasts how he uses mummings, processions, masses, saints' images, miracles, rings, and candles 'To wynne the peple' (*KJ* 698, see also 699–713). Similarly, in *Three Laws* Infidelitas encourages Idololatria to use 'brouches, beades and pynnes', 'beades, rynges, and other gere' to win people 'Unto ydolatrye' and suggests Sodomismus mix the Roman liturgy with relics, 'Ragges, rotten bones, and stykes, | A taper with other tryckes' to pervert men 'with buggerage' (660, 664, 662, 680–81, 674). The sexual corruption of the Roman Church is a charge to which Bale repeatedly turns, and sexual impurity is frequently and openly admitted by his Vices. In *Three Laws* Sodomismus exposes the hypocrisy of 'monkysh sectes' and 'popysh prestes' who cannot uphold their vows of celibacy, offering the shocking example of 'Pope Julye, | Whych sought to have in hys furye | Two laddes, and to use them beastlye, | From the Cardynall of Nantes' (*TL* 631, 632, 647–50).[44]

---

[44] These accusations also appear in Bale, *A mysterye of inyquyte* (1545; STC 1303) and Happé has noted that 'in the Cambridge University Library (Syn. 8. 54. 16⁴), the paragraph

A little later in the play, Infidelitas explains that 'Detestynge matrymonye', the pope, cardinals, priests, nuns, canons, monks, and friars 'lyve abhomyna-blye' (*TL* 734, 735, see also 730–31). Conspiratorially he then offers to 'tell ye farther newes', informing, 'At Rome for prelates are stewes | Of both kyndes' (*TL* 737, 738–39). However, the neatest expression of sexual corruption can be found in *King Johan* when Sedicyon claims birth 'under the Pope in the holy cyte of Rome' (*KJ* 183). Developing an idea seen over and again in earlier plays — that bad morals can be passed down from generation to generation — Sedicyon's statement both confirms his Catholicism and exposes the emptiness of the vow of celibacy taken by all Catholic clerics.

Inappropriate and overactive sexuality is not always so openly admitted to, and in both plays there are numerous instances where it is alluded to inadvert-ently. For example, in *King Johan*, Sedicyon unintentionally reveals his sexual depravity:

> I have great mynd   to be a lecherous man —
> A wengonce take yt —   I wold saye a relygyous man. (*KJ* 304–05)

As Happé has suggested, Bale deploys 'this conventional verbal slip by the Vice for the information and the amusement of the audience'.[45] However, the slip not only makes the association between sedition and lechery explicit, it also implies that lechers and holy men are literally bedfellows. Sexual corruption is also central to the satire of Catholic ritual in both plays. In *Three Laws* the sex-ual laxity of the Catholic clergy is suggested when Infidelitas parodies the Mass held for the dedication of a church. Infidelitas describes the dedication of the church at the Minories, a Franciscan friary in East London, including the sing-ing of the Antiphon *Lapides preciosi* by 'An olde fryre', and the recital of Psalm 128 by 'Dame Isbell, an olde nonne' (*TL* 812, 817). When Moseh lex asks, 'what includeth thys mysterye', what this rite means, he responds (*TL* 820):

> A symple probleme of bytcherye.
> Whan the fryre begonne, afore the nonne,
> To synge of precyouse stones,
> 'From my youth', sayt she, 'they have confort me,' –
> As it had bene for the nones. (*TL* 821–25)

In his version of the rite of consecration, the antiphon *Lapides preciosi*, which celebrates the precious stones that adorn the walls of the newly dedicated

---

containing it [...] is partly underlined and marked in the margin in Bale's hand'. See Happé, 'Notes to *Three Laws*', pp. 165–66.

[45] Happé, 'Notes to *King Johan*', p. 107.

church, is invoked as a crude euphemism for the friar's testicles. And Psalm 128, which unlike the *Lapides preciosi* is not traditionally part of the Mass for dedication, is mistranslated so that Israel's cry that '[ma]ny a tyme haue they fought agaynst me fro my youth' is reconstructed as the nun's boast that "'From youth [...] they have confort me"'.[46] The result is that the play on stones/testicles is extended to suggest that Catholic ritual is little more than a front for rampant sexual misbehaviour.

The most sustained of all the parodies of Catholic ritual within any of Bale's polemical moralities is *King Johan*'s parodic representation of the sacrament of penance (*KJ* 848–64, 1028–30, 1145–88, 1213–35, 1372–77, 1600).[47] As Edwin Miller has noted, 'the parody must have seemed sharp, because only a few incongruities project from a background typical of a real confessional.'[48] For example, at the beginning of the second act, Nobylyte laments the exile of 'prystes and bysshoppes' from England (*KJ* 1124).[49] When offered 'clene remyssyon to take the Chyrches parte' (*KJ* 1143), he asks Sedicyon to hear his confession:

NOBYLYTE: *Benedicite.*
SEDICYON: *Dominus. In nomini domini pape, amen.* Saye forth yowre mynd in Godes name.
NOBYLYTE: I have synnyd agaynst God;   I knowlege my selfe to blame.
In the sevyn dedly synnys   I have offendyd sore;
Godes ten commaundymentes   I have brokyn ever more;
My five boddyly wytes   I have ongodly kepte;
The workes of charyte   in maner I have owtslepte.
SEDICYON: I trust ye beleve   as Holy Chyrch doth teache ye?
And from the new lernyng   ye are wyllyng for to fle?

[46] *The byble in Englyshe* (1539; STC 2068), III: *The psalter. The prouerbes Ecclesiastes. Cantica canticorum The prophetes.*, sig. DD3ʳ.

[47] By attacking the sacrament of penance and objecting to auricular confession, Bale's position was considerably more radical than that held by King Henry and promulgated by the official pronouncements of his government. The Ten Articles of 1536 instructed that 'in no wise' bishops and preachers 'contemne this auricular confession, which is made vnto the ministers of the church'. And in the Six Articles (1539), the official stance was even clearer, declaring definitively that 'Auricular confession is expedient and necessary to be reteyned and continued vsed and frequented in the church of God'. See Church of England, *Articles deuised by the kynges* ([1536]; STC 10033), sig. B4ʳ; England, *Anno tricesimo primo Henrici Octaui* (1539; STC 9397), fol. 25ʳ.

[48] Miller, 'The Roman Rite in Bale's *King John*' (1539; STC 9397), p. 810.

[49] The division of the play into two parts is one of Bale's earliest revisions and has been dated to the early 1540s. The change is made in Bale's own hand. See Happé, 'Introduction', p. 11; Happé, 'Notes to *King Johan*', pp. 121–22; and Happé, *John Bale*, p. 90.

NOBYLYTE: From the new lernyng?   Mary, God of hevyn save me!
                    I never lovyd yt   of a chyld, so mote I the.
SEDICYON: Ye can saye yowre crede?   And yowre Laten *Ave Mary*?
NOBYLYTE: Yea, and dyrge also,   with sevyn psalmes and letteny.
SEDICYON: Do ye not beleve   in purgatory and holy bred?
NOBYLYTE: Yes, and that good prayers   shall stand my soule in stede.
SEDICYON: Well, than, good inowgh;   I warant my soulle for yowre. (*KJ* 1148–64)

The conventional details in this parodic representation of the sacrament of penance include: the use of the stole and the seating of the confessor; the Latin
call and response; the sinner's offence in the deadly sins, his breaking of the ten
commandments, his ungodly use of his bodily wits, and his neglect of works
of charity; the confessor's questions about the creed and the Ave; and the sinner's response that, in addition to these, he is also familiar with the dirige, the
penitential psalms, and the litany. As Miller has noted, the main points comply
with John Mirk's recommendations for parish priests.[50] Like Sedicyon, Mirk's
priest asks the penitent, "'Const þow þy pater and þyn aue | And þy crede, now
telle þow me'".[51] He also enquires whether the penitent has 'I-borste' any of 'þe
x. cummawndementes of god almy3t', committed any of the 'dedly synnes', and
'spende þy wytt*us* fyue | To godd*us* worshype'.[52] However, unlike Mirk, Sedicyon
does not prescribe penance to counter the sins confessed. Instead, he successfully attempts to barter indulgence for treason, 'Ye know that Kyng Johan ys a
very wycked man | [...] The Pope wyllyth yow to do the best ye canne | To his
subduyng for his cruell tyranny; | And for that purpose this prevylege gracyously
| Of clene remyssyon he hath sent yow' (*KJ* 1169–74). This confession sequence
thus substantiates Sedicyon's earlier admission that confession is used to gain
information for treasonous purpose, 'by confessyon the Holy Father knoweth
| Throw owt all Christendom what to his holynes growyth' (*KJ* 272–73).

   Further incongruities in Nobylyte's confession include: Sedicyon's questions
about 'the new lernyng', purgatory, and the sacrament of the Eucharist; and his
prayer in the name of the pope. The prayer, 'In nomini domini pape, amen', is
clearly a parody of the Trinitarian formula and suggests that the pope's authority has usurped that of God.[53] What is more, the oath 'in Godes name' two lines
above and one line below seems punningly juxtaposed to emphasize the impro-

[50] Miller, 'The Roman Rite in Bale's *King John*', p. 810.

[51] Myrc, *Instructions for Parish Priests*, ed. by Peacock, pp. 25, ll. 805–06.

[52] Myrc, *Instructions for Parish Priests*, ed. by Peacock, pp. 27, 30, 40, ll. 851, 849, 973, 1305–06.

[53] The formula also appears at ll. 1188, 1231, A59, and A79. Infidelitas makes a similar
substitution at ll. 702–04 of *Three Laws*.

priety of Sedicyon's prayer. Miller has attempted to explain the presence of questions about 'purgatory and holy bred' and prayers for the soul by suggesting that 'they may have either seemed typical or, like the question and answer and about "the new lernyng", pointedly topical'.[54] However, it seems more likely that Bale intended these and the other questions of the parodic confession to highlight areas of doctrinal conflict between the Roman and reformed faiths. For instance, although Walker has argued that Bale fails 'to mention anywhere in the play the violent controversy concerning the Sacrament of the Altar', the question about 'holy bred' not only alludes to the controversy, it also implies the fraudulence of the orthodox interpretation of the Sacrament.[55] Given Henry VIII's ongoing belief in transubstantiation and his unwillingness to tolerate dissent on this point, it is a stance that is at once radical and necessarily subtle. For a playwright more famous for biliousness than delicacy, it is a deliciously understated move.[56]

Nobylyte is not the only character to be made a traitor by Sedicyon. Clergye and Cyvyle Order are similarly corrupted when Sedicyon tells them to 'Sytt downe on yowre kneys and ye shall have absolucyon | *A pena et culpa*, with a thowsand dayes of pardon' (*KJ* 1213–14). As in the earlier confession, Sedicyon grants absolution without prescribing penance. And, in giving absolution *a culpa*, Sedicyon usurps the power of God, who alone has the authority to grant remission from guilt. The bankruptcy of the ritual is confirmed by the exhibition of dubious relics that follows:

> Here ys fyrst a bone   of the blyssyd Trynyte,
> A dram of the tord   of swete Seynt Barnabe;
> Here ys a feddere   of good Seynt Myhelles wyng,
> A toth of Seynt Twyde,   a pece of Davyds harpe stryng,
> The good blood of Haylys,   and owre blyssyd ladys mylke,
> A lowse of Seynt Fraunces   in this same crymsen sylke,
> A scabbe of Saynt Job,   a nayle of Adams too,
> A maggott of Moyses,   with a fart of Saynt Fandigo;
> Here is a fygge leafe,   and a grape of Noes vyneyearde,
> A bede of Saynt Blythe   with the bracelet of a berewarde,
> The Devyll that was hatcht   in maistre Johan Shornes bote,
> That the tree of Jesse   ded plucke up by the roote;
> Here ys the lachett   of swett Seynt Thomas shewe,

[54] Miller, 'The Roman Rite in Bale's *King John*', p. 810.

[55] Walker, *Plays of Persuasion*, p. 219.

[56] '[B]iliosus Baleus', in Fuller, *The History of the Worthies of England*, ed. by Nuttall, III, 170.

> A rybbe of Seynt Rabart   with the huckyll bone of a Jewe;
> Here is a joynt   of Darvell Gathyron,
> Be sydes other bonys   and relyckes many one. (*KJ* 1215–30)

Composed largely of spurious relics, the list is designed to expose what reformers regarded as the absurd literalism of Catholicism and to suggest the emptiness of its rituals by condemning, in particular, the cult of the saints and the veneration of relics. The relics listed are either objects of fantasy, like the bone of the Trinity (as Happé has dryly remarked, 'since the Trinity had no substance, a bone would be hard to find'); objects of ridicule, like Abbot Fantinus's fart; irrelevant objects, like the tooth of St Twide, a made-up saint; contested objects, like the image of Darvell Gathyron; or fraudulent objects, like the blood of Hailes.[57] Like the post-Reformation parody of transubstantiation as hocus-pocus, the overall impression is of a conjuror's spell designed to both deceive and entertain. And in this equation Sedicyon, the Vice, is both sorcerer and cleric; player and priest. To put it another way, in parodying its rituals just as he had parodied its ritual dress, Bale points not only to Catholicism's evils but also to its theatricality.

Playing Prelates

Bale's attack on Catholicism as theatrical is nothing new. Like so much of his polemical rhetoric it derives from Tyndale. For instance, his parody of Catholic vestments might have been suggested by a passage in *The practyse of prelates*:

> [I]f a man axe you [i.e. the Catholic clergy], what youre meruelous fassioned play-engecotes and youre other popatrye meane, and what youre disfigured heedes and all youre apesplaye meane, ye knowe not: and yet are they but signes of things which ye haue professed.[58]

---

[57] Happé, 'Notes to *King Johan*', p. 124. In April/May 1538 the image of Darvell Gadarn, a man of arms in harness, holding a little spear in his hand, and a casket of iron about his neck, was dismantled. In October of the same year the blood of Hailes was revealed as duck's blood or wax or gum. On Darvell Gardarn see *Letters and Papers of the Reign of Henry VIII*, xiii, 1, ed. by James Gairdner (1892), p. 264, no. 694 (Elis Price to [Cromwell]); and Wriothesley, *A Chronicle of England during the Reigns of the Tudors*, ed. by Hamilton, i (1875), 80. On Hailes see Chapter 1, pp. 60–63. See also *Letters and Papers of the Reign of Henry VIII*, xiii, 2, ed. by James Gairdner (1893), pp. 347, 409, nos 709, 710 (Latimer to Cromwell, and The Bp. of Worcester and Others to Cromwell); and Wriothesley, *A Chronicle of England during the Reigns of the Tudors*, ed. by Hamilton, i (1875), 75–76, 90.

[58] Tyndale, *The practyse of prelates*, sig. A3ᵛ–A4ʳ. This passage is also treated in the Intro-

Catholic vestments, argues Tyndale, resemble nothing quite so much as costumes worn by actors in a play. They might signify truths, but they are just
signs. Worse still, the truths they are intended to signify risk being forgotten
in the face of their gorgeousness and splendour. In *The obedie[n]ce of a Christen
man and how Christe[n] rulers ought to governe* (1528; STC 24446), Tyndale
extends this brief meditation on the interactions between Catholic and dramatic representational practices to suggest that all aspects of Catholic worship
are theatrical:

> Gods signes or sacramentes signifie Gods worde also and put vs in Christe. Con-
> trary wise Antichristes [i.e. Roman Catholic] Bisshopes preach not and their sac-
> ramentes speake not, but as the disgysed Bisshopes mum, so are their supersticious
> sacramentes doume.[59]

As Jonas Barish has commented, 'without the all-important adjunct of the
word, the administering of the sacrament becomes a scene of theater, in which a
pantomime actor, "disguised" — heavily made up and pretending to be a bishop
— plays an elaborate charade, "mumming" it in a dumb-show'.[60] Divorced from
the word of God, the acts of Catholic worship become empty signifiers, not
unlike the vestments of the clerics who preside over them:

> And hereby maist thou know the difference betwene Christes signes or sacramentes
> and Antichristes signes or ceremonies, that Christes signes speake & antichristes be
> dome. Here by seist thou what is to be thought of all other ceremonies, as holowed
> water, bred, salt, bowes, belles, wax, asshes and so forth, and all other disgisinges
> and apesplaye [...][61]

Distinguishing between sacraments and ceremonies, Tyndale sets out to invali-
date the sacraments of the Catholic Church by labelling them as anti-Christian
ceremonies.[62] This categorization of Catholic sacraments as ceremonial theatre
is sustained throughout *The obedie[n]ce*:

duction to this volume at p. 6.

[59] Tyndale, *The obedie[n]ce of a Christen man*, fol. 105r.

[60] Barish, *The Antitheatrical Prejudice*, p. 8.

[61] Tyndale, *The obedie[n]ce of a Christen man*, fol. 113r.

[62] It is worth noting the Antichrist's signs — holy water, bread, salt, etc. — are all closely
associated with the seven sacraments of the Roman Church. The use of holy water in the sacrament of baptism is well known, as is the centrality of bread to the sacrament of the Eucharist.
Baptismal salt is given to the catechumen before entering the church for baptism. Genuflection
is enjoined for the receiving of confirmation, the Eucharist, penance, and holy orders. From the

BAptim hath also his worde and promise which the prest ought to teach the people and Christen them in the english tonge, and not to playe the popengay with Credo saye ye, volo saye ye and baptis mum saye ye, for there ought to be no mummynge in soch a mater.[63]

Speaking in English, the reformed priest both teaches and christens his congregants. In contrast the Latinate cleric is strangely impotent. Mumming rather than speaking, he is cast as an actor whose role as popinjay punningly links his 'mechanical repetition of words and phrases' to the authority conferred on him by the pope.[64] Tyndale condemns the Mass-priest presiding over the sacrament of the Eucharist in the same terms:

What helpeth it also that the prest when he goeth to masse disgiseth him selfe with a great parte of the passion of Christe and pleyeth out the rest vnder silence with signes and profers, with noddinge, beckinge and mowinge, as it were Iacke a napes, when nether he him selfe nether any man else woteth what he meaneth?[65]

Like a tame ape or monkey in his tricks, airs, and behaviour, the Mass-priest plays with signs he is unable to understand.[66] Tyndale is quick to point out the dangers of such a cleric to his parishioners:

For as moch as it not only destroyeth the fayth and quencheth the love that shulde be geven vnto the commaundemente, and maketh the people vnthankefull, in that it bringeth them into soch supersticion, that they thinke that they haue done abundauntly ynough for God, yee and deserued aboue measure, yf they be present once in a daye at soch mummynge.[67]

introduction of the elevation of the host in the Mass at the beginning of the thirteenth century it has been customary to ring a bell. With the exception of penance, wax candles are associated with the conferring of all Catholic sacraments. And references to use of ashes as a symbol of penance in works by a number of the Church fathers indicate the liturgical use of ashes can be traced to the early church; ashes are also associated with extreme unction.

[63] Tyndale, *The obedie[n]ce of a Christen man*, fol. 89ᵛ.

[64] 'popinjay, n., 2. b', in *The Oxford English Dictionary*, 2nd edn, <http://dictionary.oed.com/cgi/entry/50184126> [accessed 5 June 2013]. The *OED*'s etymological entry for 'popinjay' suggests that 'Middle English forms with *pop-* for *pap-* (compare and forms) may perhaps be folk etymological alterations after POPE *n.*¹'.

[65] Tyndale, *The obedie[n]ce of a Christen man*, fol. 69ʳ.

[66] 'jackanapes, 2. c', in *The Oxford English Dictionary*, 2nd edn, <http://dictionary.oed.com/cgi/entry/50188241> [accessed 5 June 2013].

[67] Tyndale, *The obedie[n]ce of a Christen man*, fols 69ʳ–69ᵛ.

The communicants of a Catholic Mass are likened to spectators at a pageant; seduced by the spectacle of the Mass, their faith in the underlying reality of its signs is destroyed.

Dramatically corrupting their parishioners, Roman clerics resemble nothing so much as Antichrist as described by Tyndale in his letter to the reader that prefaces his translation of *That fayth the mother of all good workes iustifieth vs* (1528; STC 24454), later published as *The parable of the wicked mammon*, whose nature is 'to go out of the Playe for a season and to disgyse him selfe and then to come in agayne with a new name and new raymente'.[68] Insisting that 'ther is difference in the names betwene a pope, a Cardinall, a Bisshope, and so forth, and to say a scribe, a pharisey, a seniour and so forth: but the thinge is all one', Tyndale identifies the Catholic clergy with the scribes and Pharisees of the gospels, suggesting they all represent types of the Antichrist.[69] In contrast, he equates all the proponents of Christ with the reformed cause. The result is a typology in which the representatives of the true Church of Christ and the false Church of Anti-Christ are sharply polarized along the lines of contemporary religious controversy.[70]

In Bale's morality plays the Catholic Vices frequently advertise their theatricality in terms that recall and reinforce the condemnation of Catholicism in a number of Tyndale's works, particularly in *The obedie[n]ce*.[71] The Vices' reveal their true nature in three different but related ways: by disclosing their duplicitous behaviour, as when Infidelitas professes his recourse to 'sutyle polycye' (*TL* 378); by revealing their ability to shift shape, as when Idololatria confesses 'now ych am a she' (*TL* 426); and, perhaps most strikingly, by directly acknowledging that they are playing a part, as when Infidelitas declares he will 'contryve

---

[68] Tyndale, *That fayth the mother of all good works iustifieth us*, sig. A4ʳ.

[69] Tyndale, *That fayth the mother of all good works iustifieth us*, sig. A4ʳ.

[70] This typology is typical of Tyndale's polemic and is also evident in Tyndale, *An exposicion vppon the. v. vi. vii. chapters of Mathew* ([1533?]; STC 24440). The case for this work as a source for *Three Laws* is discussed above. See p. 73.

[71] The importance of Tyndale's *Obedience* as one of four sources for the plot of *King Johan* has already been established. However, its influence on the phrasing of individual speeches has not widely been acknowledged. The other sources for *King Johan* are: the expanded, second edition of Barnes, *A supplicacion vnto the most gracyous prynce* (1534; STC 1471); Fish, *A supplicacyon for the beggers* ([1529?]; STC 10883); and a poem on King John written out by Bale and preserved in Cambridge, CCCC, MS 152, fol. 48ᵛ. The relevant passages are reproduced in 'Appendix III', in Bale, *The Complete Plays*, ed. by Happé, I (1985), 149–51.

the dryft of another playe' (*TL* 1422).[72] Most examples that fall into this third category are found in *King Johan*. At the opening of the play, Englande explains her sad predicament:

> For they take from me   my cattell, howse and land,
> My wodes and pasturs   with other commodyteys;
> Lyke as Christ ded saye   to the wyckyd Pharyseys,
> 'Pore wydowys howsys   ye grosse up by long prayers',
> In syde cotys wandryng   lyke most dysgysed players. (*KJ* 62–66)

Paraphrasing Tyndale, 'for ye devoure poure wedowes howses under the color of longe prayer', Englande emphasizes the typological relationship between the Pharisees of the New Testament and modern Roman prelates. But she also makes explicit the analogy between priests and players in her condemnation of the theatrical trickery used by Catholic clerics to exploit poor widows and other vulnerable innocents.[73] Englande's condemnation of the clergy as financially corrupt and physically deceptive reinforces a similar accusation made only thirty lines earlier, that clerics, disguising their 'heades in ther hoodes', idly 'lyve by other menns goodes' (*KJ* 36, 37). In both instances, Bale undermines the authority of the Catholic clergy by suggesting that Catholicism and drama share an epistemology of deceit.

Deciding to pursue Englande's complaint, King Johan reviles Catholicism's 'Latyne howres, serymonyes and popetly playes' (*KJ* 415). As Janette Dillon has commented, 'King John's sneering at "popetly plays" of the clergy [...] uses wordplay to link Catholicism with entertainment: the word "popetly" condemns the church's shows by equating puppets or dolls with the pope and sneering simultaneously at both.'[74] This equation is reinforced by the list of Catholic practices and ceremonies that follows:

> In her more and more   Godes holy worde decayes,
> And them to maynteyn   unresonable ys the spoyle
> Of her londes, her goodes,   and of her pore chylderes toyle.
> Rekyn fyrst yowre tythis,   yowre devocyons and yowre offrynges,
> Mortuaryes, pardons,   bequestes and other thynges,

[72] These lines have led a number of critics to conclude that Bale portrays Infidelitas as a playwright. See Kendall, *The Drama of Dissent*, pp. 108–09; and Hermen, *The Squitter-Wits and Muse-Haters*, pp. 54–55.

[73] Tyndale, *The obedie[n]ce of a Christen man*, fol. 69ʳ.

[74] Dillon, *Language and Stage in Medieval and Renaissance England*, p. 91.

> Besydes that ye cache   for halowed belles and purgatorye,
> For iwelles, for relyckes,   confessyon and cowrtes of baudrye,
> For legacyes, trentalles   with scalacely messys,   ?
> Wherby ye have made   the people very assys:
> And over all this   ye have browght in a rabyll
> Of Latyn mummers   and sectes desseyvabyll
> Evyn to dewore her   and eat her upp attonnys. (*KJ* 416–27)

King Johan argues that Englande, 'her londes, her goodes, and her pore chyl-
deres toyle', have been exploited to maintain the hours, ceremonies, and games
of Catholic worship, which were the subject of reformed abuse by the late
1530s. In a move that was not welcomed by the clergy, the fees to be charged for
mortuary or the customary oblation paid out of the estate of the deceased to his
church were limited by the Probate and Mortuaries Act of 1529. While the doctrine of purgatory was not outlawed during Henry's reign, it was condemned
by the group of bishops headed by Cranmer who published *The institution of
a Christen man* in 1537 (STC 5164).[75] In particular, *The institution*, or the
Bishop's Book as it came to be known, called for the abolition of those abuses,

> whiche vnder the name of purgatorie, hath ben aduaunced: as to make men beleue,
> that through the bysshop of Romes pardons soules might clerely be delyuered out
> of purgatorie, and all the peynes of it: or the masses sayd at *Scala celi*, or other
> where, in any other place, or before any ymage, myght lykewyse delyuer them from
> all theyr peyne, & sende them streyghte to heuen, and other lyke abuses.[76]

This formulation is almost identical to King Johan's; he similarly argues that
the rites and practices associated with the doctrine of purgatory, 'legacyes, tren-
talles with scalacely messys', make 'the people very assys'. What is more, his suggestion that 'halowed belles and purgatorye' provide the pretext for clerical
extortion strongly echoes Tyndale's view that, 'The Pope for money can empty
purgatory when he will [...] His fatherhode sendeth them to heuen with scala
celi: þat is, with a ladder, to scale þe walles. For by the dore Christ, will they not
let them come in. That dore haue they stopped vp, and that by cause ye shulde
bye laders.'[77] Tyndale's influence is also felt in Johan's characterization of the
priests who preside over these ceremonies as 'Latyne mummers'. Like the dumb

---

[75] The STC counts five imprints produced in the same year, of which it estimates STC 5164
to be the earliest.

[76] *The institution of a Christen man* (1537; STC 5164), fol. 97ʳ.

[77] Tyndale, *The obedie[n]ce of a Christen man*, fols 87ʳ–97ᵛ.

clerics in *The obedie[n]ce*, Johan suggests that Roman prelates are little more than mumbling players.

King Johan's suggestion that 'Latyne mummers' have caused 'Godes holy worde' to decay, highlights the reformers' commitment to the vernacularization of the Bible in contradistinction to the Catholic obfuscation of scriptural truth through the retention of its Latin liturgy and elaborate rituals. The 'play' metaphor is therefore particularly apt for, as Dillon has argued, 'both theatre and the Catholic church are seen as manifestations of Babel, proliferating words and forms promiscuously, in opposition to the kind of singleness of meaning the Reformers yearned for.'[78] A similar opposition is apparent a few hundred lines later in a lengthy scene in which the Vices debate how best to accompany each other into the playing space:

> Sures, marke well this gere   for now yt begynnyth to worke:
> False Dyssymulacyon   doth bryng in Privat Welth;
> And Usurpyd Powre,   which is more ferce than a Turcke,
> Cummeth in by hym   to decayve all spyrytuall helth;
> Than I by them bothe,   as clere experyence telth.
> We four by owre craftes   Kyng Johan wyll so subdwe
> That for three hundred yers   all Englond shall yt rewe. (*KJ* 770–76)

The scene was presumably devised to provide a visual account of the history of papal usurpation: Sedicyon orders Dissymulacyon to bring in Privat Welth, who in turn is ordered to bring in Usurpid Powre, before all three bring in Sedicyon. Walker's account of the scene is helpful: 'Polemic and dramatic purposes combine in a splendid iconographic moment as the three clerics Private Wealth, Dissimulation and Usurped Power (the first two in regular habits) carry Sedition upon their shoulders', spectacularly representing the papal suppression of monarchical authority.[79] It is, in other words, a scene in which Bale exploits the potential of the dramatic form to great polemical effect. Sedicyon's remark that 'for three hundred yers all Englond shall yt rewe', clearly echoes the argument made by Simon Fish, that ever since the fall of King John England 'wrongfully (alas for shame) hath stod tributary (not vnto any kind temporall prince, but vnto a cruell deuelisshe bloudsupper dronken in the bloude of the sayntes and marters of christ)'.[80] But the remark that Johan is to be subdued by

---

[78] Dillon, *Language and Stage in Medieval and Renaissance England*, p. 91.

[79] Walker, *Plays of Persuasion*, p. 188.

[80] Fish, *A supplicacyon for the beggers*, fol. 3ᵛ.

the Vices' 'craftes' is Bale's intervention and clearly aligns this process of monarchical submission with theatrical deception. This association is heightened by
Privat Welth's own interpretation of their proposed entrance:

> I trow thow shalt se me   now play the praty man.
> Of me, Privat Welth,   cam fyrst Usurpyd Powre:
> Ye may perseyve yt   in pagent here this howre. (*KJ* 784–86)

Identifying himself as a crafty or cunning man, Privat Welth describes the
entrance prescribed by Sedicyon as a pageant.[81] However, the potency of this
condemnatory attack on the theatricality of Catholicism is severely undermined by further, yet more insistent glosses on the action:

> SEDICYON: Nay, Usurpid Powre,   thow must go backe ageyne,
> For I must also   put the to a lytyll payne.
> USURPID POWRE: Why, fellaue Sedycyon,   what wyll thow have me do?
> SEDICYON: To bare me on thi backe   and bryng me in also
> That yt may be sayde   that first Dyssymulacyon
> Browght in Privat Welth   to every Cristen nacyon,
> And that Privat Welth   browght in Usurpid Powre,
> And then Sedycyon   in cytye, towne and tower
> That sum man may know   the feche of all owre sorte.
> USURPID POWRE: Cum on thy wayes, than,   that thow mayst make the fort.
> DISSYMULACYON: Nay, Usurped Powre,   we shall bare hym all thre,
> Thy selfe, he, and I,   yf ye wyll be rewlyd by me. (*KJ* 789–800)

With over seventy lines of explication, Bale seems anxious to ensure his point is
effectively made. But in relying on such extensive commentary, he risks undermining the dramatic effectiveness of the scene. As such, it offers a neat illustration of some of the problems Bale faced in using drama to expose and condemn
the theatricality of Catholicism.

Although it is clear that Bale did not share the implacable opposition to
religious drama witnessed in the fifteenth-century *Tretise of Miraclis Playinge*,
his plays testify to a conflict between using drama both to parody Catholic rites
and ritual and to champion reformed theology and practice. Richie Kendall
has argued that Bale attempts to resolve this conflict by distinguishing between
his own godly stagecraft and the polluted drama of the Vices. 'All the negativity
that Bale as a nonconformist found in the dramatic arts is concentrated in the

[81] 'pretty, *adj.*, 1. a', in *The Oxford English Dictionary*, 2nd edn, <http://dictionary.oed.com/cgi/entry/50188241> [accessed 5 June 2013].

demonic play of the Vices. The sense of the play as an escape from contingency and law, of its tendency to confuse rather than clarify spiritual identity, of its establishment of a world that rivals God's universe'; all these aspects are found within the Vices' histrionic sense of show.[82] In contrast, Bale's virtuous characters prioritize word over action, directness over digression. Moreover, they possess single stable identities, in contrast to the Vices' doubleness and deceit. In fact, Bale's distinction between demonic and sanctified modes of dramatic expression suggests an attempt to develop a new kind of drama, a new mode of performance in which those characters that play straight triumph over those that play fast and loose. However, though his plays might oppose these two stagecrafts as yet another manifestation of the eternal battle between Christ and Antichrist, is his attempt to advance what we might describe as a reformed dramaturgy wholly successful? Given that all drama relies on the basic conceit of one person pretending to be another, can Bale really distinguish his own pious playing from the Catholic theatricality he seeks to condemn?

Holy Histrionics

In 1544, while in exile on the continent, Bale wrote and published *The epistle exhortatorye of an Englyshe Christiane vnto his derelye beloued contrye of Englande* ([1544?]; STC 1291), his appeal to the King and people of England to abolish all vestiges of Catholicism as retained in the conservative Act of the Six Articles (1539). Like a number of his other works written at this time, Bale's invective argues that the Henrician church is merely popery without the pope, its bishops little better than Catholic clerics, unable to distinguish pious from profane practice:

> So long as they played lyes and sange bawdye songes, blaspheminge God and corruptinge mennes consciences, neuer blamed them, but were verye well contented. But sens they persuaded the people to worshyp theyr lorde God aryght according to his holye lawes and not yours, and to acknowledge Iesus Christ for their onlye redemer and sauer without lowsye legerdemaynes, ye neuer were pleased with them, whan they they tell you as the truthe is, that your Romishe father hath played the cruell Antichrist, and you his false phesicyanes in holdinge the Christen multitude so manye hondreth years in soche dampnable darknesse of sprete withoute repentaunce, ye take it vnpacientlye seekinge theyr destruccion for it.[83]

[82] Kendall, *The Drama of Dissent*, p. 109.
[83] Bale, *The Epistle exhortatorye of an Englyshe Christiane* ([1544?]; STC 1291), fols 16[r-v].

In attacking the Henrician church, Bale identifies two types of theatrical practice: played lies and bawdy songs that corrupt men's conscience; and truth-
ful plays that teach people the correct way to worship God. Implied is a distinction between the religious dramas that were historically condoned by the
Roman Church (mystery, miracle, and morality plays) and the new dramas
and interludes produced by polemicists like Bale designed to expose the fallacy
of Catholicism. In this passage, Bale further intimates a congruity between
'bawdy' theatre and those who uphold it. With their 'lowlye legerdemaynes',
trickery, deception, and hocus-pocus, the Roman priests resemble nothing quite
so much as those players who play lies.[84] In contrast, like the plays they write,
reformed dramatists are singular in their commitment to the salvific power of
Christ. Consequently, they seek to expose the jugglery of the 'Romishe' fathers
who 'playe the cruell Antichrist'.[85]

A similar distinction between godly stagecraft and Catholic playing is
apparent in the Praefatio to *God's Promises*:

> Yow therefor, good fryndes,   I lovyngely exhorte
> To waye soche matters   as wyll be uttered here,
> Of whome ye maye loke   to have no tryfelinge sporte
> In fantasyes fayned,   nor soche lyke gaudysh gere;
> But the thynges that shall   your inwarde stomake stere
> To rejoyce in God   for your justyfycacyon,
> And alone in Christ   to hope for your salvacyon.[86]

Here Bale, as Baleus Prolocutor, informs his audience that the play they are
about to see performed will not rely on a Catholic dramaturgy formed of trifling sports and idle rubbish, but will advance a pious stagecraft that will teach
the central tenets of the reformed faith.[87] In other words, the speech evolves a

---

[84] 'legerdemain, 2', in *The Oxford English Dictionary*, 2nd edn, <http://dictionary.oed.com/
cgi/entry/50131493> [accessed 5 June 2013].

[85] 'legerdemain, 1', in *The Oxford English Dictionary*, 2nd edn, <http://dictionary.oed.com/
cgi/entry/50131493> [accessed 5 June 2013]: '[s]leight of hand; the performance of tricks
which by nimble action deceive the eye; jugglery; conjuring tricks'.

[86] *God's Promises*, in Bale, *The Complete Plays*, ed. by Happé, II (1986), 1–34, (p. 2,
ll. 15–21). The play was first printed as Bale, *A tragedye or enterlude manyfestyng the chefe promyses of God*.

[87] The final couplet invokes the doctrines of *sola fide* (justification by faith alone) — 'All
oure iustifyinge then cometh of fayth, and fayth and the sprite come of God and not of vs' —
which is often recognized as the material cause of the Lutheran Reformation, and *sola gratia*

distinction between the sensual frippery of Catholic stagecraft and the pious singularity of reformed playing. Concluding this chapter, I am interested in exploring the extent to which Bale is able to sustain successfully this distinction in his own drama. Bearing in mind the polemical necessity of his dramatization of Catholic theatricality in *Three Laws* and *King Johan*, how does Bale separate the theatricality of his Catholic Vices from his own godly stagecraft?

Richie Kendall has proposed that Bale resolves his 'stage fright', his reservations about the propriety of dramatic representation, through a 'rigidly divided approach to the characterization of his Vices and Virtues'.[88] There are, he argues, two plays being performed in *Three Laws*: a tragedy, composed and directed by Infidelitas, depicting the overthrow of the divine order; and a comedy, 'compyled' by Bale, but ordained by God. The audience is always aware that Infidelitas's play-within-a-play is subsidiary to the larger comedic plot because the prologue and opening scene serve to outline the dramatic shape and offer reassurance that Infidelitas's tragedy will be arrested. Consequently, the play allows Bale to work through and resolve 'his own ambivalent attitude toward the rectitude of his vocation.'[89] Kendall's assessment is compelling, but his suggestion that Bale's anxiety about the propriety of drama is resolved by his innovative distinction between Catholic playing and pious stagecraft demands further investigation. To what extent does the Virtues' sanctified drama successfully surround and contain the Vices' polluted play? Their dramatic domain might frame the play, but is it sufficiently robust to avoid contamination by the Vices' series of plays-within-the-play? By placing the Vices' demonic interludes within the Virtues' sanctified drama, Bale ironically and perhaps unwittingly reveals their phenomenological similarities.

(salvation through grace) — 'By the lawe then we se clerely that we muste nedes haue Christe to iustifie vs with his grace.' Although the earliest complete edition of Tyndale's translation of the New Testament does not contain any prologues, the doctrine of *sola fide* is emphasized in his version of Paul's Letter to the Romans: 'We suppose therefore that a man is iustified by fayth without the dedes of lawe'; 'Because therfore thatt we are iustified by fayth we are at peace with god thorow oure lorde Jesus Christ: by whom we have a waye in thorow faith unto this faveour wherin we stoned and reioyse in hope of the prayse that shalbe geven of God.' See Tyndale's 'A prologue to the Epistle of Paule to the Romayns', in *The newe Testament, dylygently corrected [...] by Willyam Tindale* (1534; STC 2826), fols 202ᵛ–220ʳ (fols 205ʳ, 212ᵛ); and *The newe Testame[n]t*, trans. by Tyndale ([1526?]; STC 2824), fols 202ᵛ, 204ʳ.

[88] Kendall, *The Drama of Dissent*, p. 102.

[89] Kendall, *The Drama of Dissent*, p. 109.

Kendall has noted that 'the play opens with a cautious reworking of the familiar salutatory speech of God in the cycle plays':[90]

> I am Deus Pater,   a substaunce invysyble,
> All one with the Sonne   and Holy Ghost in essence.
> To Angell and Man   I am incomprehensyble,
> A strength infynyte,   a ryghteousnesse, a prudence,
> A mercy, a goodnesse,   a truth, a lyfe, a sapyence. (*TL* 36–40)

Echoing Baleus Prolocutor's instruction to 'marke therfor what He sayth' (*TL* 35), to foreground His words rather than his appearance, Deus Pater warns the audience against mistaking the signs of things for what they signify; no human actor can every really embody God. According to Kendall these lines are a testimony to Bale's continuing anxiety about the propriety of dramatic representation and represent his attempt to separate meaning from method, tenor from vehicle, and character from actor. 'By underscoring the purely abstract quality of his deity, Bale forces a perceptible wedge between the actor and the God he represents.'[91] But, as Pauline Blanc has gone on to note, '[t]he tensions are only partially dissipated [...] since a human actor necessarily evokes responses in human terms from the audience.'[92] For all that Deus Pater insists that He is an incomprehensible invisible substance, the dramatic necessity of a human actor cannot help but mean that He will be seen and understood as a visible and substantial presence. To put it another way, the phenomenological pressures of dramatic performance make it inevitable that God's 'substaunce invysyble' will, like the miracle at the heart of the Croxton *Play*, be made visibly present. Consequently, in this single, paradoxical line, Bale undoes all the oppositions upon which his polemical argument relies.

In fact, these oppositions — between inwardness and show, language and spectacle, and presence and representation; between, in other words, reformed and Catholic dramaturgies — are everywhere less stable than Bale might have hoped. Take, for instance, the first of the play's three ages, which begins with an encounter between Naturae lex and Infidelitas. Like Moseh lex and Christi lex in Acts III and IV, Naturae lex speaks to instruct the audience over matters of doctrine and practice. In fact, his very first lines in the play assert, 'The lawe in effect is a teacher generall — | What is to be done, and what is to be layed asyde'

[90] Kendall, *The Drama of Dissent*, p. 101.

[91] Kendall, *The Drama of Dissent*, p. 101.

[92] Blanc, 'Commentators, Mediators, Subversives', p. 200.

(*TL* 162–63). These lines and the rest of this opening speech are rendered in rhyme royal, which in Happé's estimation is recognizable as an exclusive and elevated verse form, used sparingly 'to establish the special tone required for authoritative doctrinal speeches'.[93] However, the decorous piety of Naturae lex's speech is rudely interrupted by the abrupt entry of Infidelitas:

> *Brom, brom, brom, brom, brom.*
> *Bye brom, bye, bye.*
> *Bromes for shoes and powcherynges,*
> *Botes and buskyns for new bromes.*
> *Brom, brom, brom.*
> Marry, God geve ye good even,
> And the holyman saynt Steven
>   Sende ye a good newe yeare.
> I wolde have brought ye the paxe,
> Or els an ymage of waxe,
>   If I had knowne ye heare. (*TL* 176–86)

In contrast to Naturae lex's sententious rhyme royal, Infidelitas adopts a rhyme scheme that directly recalls the tail rhyme used by the three lowest Vices in the *Castle of Perseverance* (*c.* 1400–25) and therefore marks his speech as corrupt and corrupting.[94] However the distinction between these two ways of speaking collapses when Naturae lex replies to Infidelitas, adopting the Vice's form of verse:

> Ye are dysposed to dallye,
> To leape and oversallye
>   The compasse of your wytte:
> I counsell ye yet in season,
> Sumwhat to folowe reason,
>   And gnawe upon the bytte. (*TL* 244–49)

Here Naturae lex does at least perceive what Kendall has described as the 'utter lawlessness' of Infidelitas's 'unsanctified speech'.[95] However, though he condemns Infidelitas's crackpot verse, his adoption of rhyme couée reflects the extent to which his own speech has been contaminated by Infidelitas's way of speaking. Infidelitas's wit has quite literally exceeded its limits; his demonic

---

[93] Happé, *John Bale*, p. 84. Deus Pater, for instance, always speaks in rhyme royal.

[94] The play's other Vices make similar use of end rhyme.

[95] Kendall, *The Drama of Dissent*, p. 103.

play properly overleaped its bounds. To put it another way, in adopting rhyme couée, Naturae lex's words exemplify the same dangers they warn against. So, far from containing the subversive play world of the Vices, his speech indicates the degree to which the Virtues are unable to police the borders between pious and impious stagecrafts.

Nowhere is the proximity of Bale's reformed dramaturgy to the Catholic theatricality of the Vices more apparent than in the doubling schemes for *King Johan* and *Three Laws*. In *Three Laws* a scheme is printed in the *c.* 1547 edition on sig. G1ᵛ below the note that 'Into fyve personages maye the partes of thys Comedy be devyded' (*TL*, p. 121). According to this scheme, the first actor should take the parts of 'The Prolocutor', 'Christen fayth', and 'Infydelyte'; the second should play 'The lawe of Nature', 'Couetousnesse', and 'False doctryne'; the third 'The lawe of Moses', 'Idolatrye', and 'Hypocresye'; the fourth 'The lawe of Christ' (i.e. the Word of God), 'Ambycyon', and 'Sodomye'; and the fifth 'Deus Pater' and 'Vindicta Dei' (*TL*, p. 121). Strikingly, the scheme is expunged from the second, 1562 edition.[96] Although there is no extant contemporary edition of *King Johan*, a doubling scheme is implicit in the play's stage directions. At line 154 a stage direction instructs '*Go owt Ynglond and drese for Clargy*'; at 312 a stage direction reads '*Her go owt Sedwsion and drese for Syvyll Ordere*'; at 556 the direction demands '*Here Kyng Johan and Sivile Order go owt: and Syvile Order drese hym for Sedewsyon*'; at 1061 Privat Welth is called to '*Here go owt and drese for Nobylyte*'; and a further stage direction at line 1397 demands the same change. According to at least two scholars, these directions date to Scribe A's correction of the original draft.[97] A further two instructions also in Scribe A's hand were also apparently included in the original text: '*Here go owt Clargy and drese for Ynglond, and Syvyll Order for Commynnalte*' (*KJ* 1490); and '*Here Nobelyte go owt and dresse for the Cardynall*' (*KJ* 1533). In addition, further directions pertaining to the doubling of parts can be found in the surviving but cancelled four pages of the 1538 A-text: '*Go owt Ynglond and dresse for Dyssymulacyon*' (*KJ* A24); and '*Here the cardynall go owt and [dresse] for Nobelyte*' (*KJ* A45). Taken together, these instructions point to a doubling scheme for three actors in which Actor A plays Englande, Clergye, and Dissymulacyon; Actor B plays Sedicyon, Cyvyle Order, and Commynnalte;

---

[96] I discuss the textual and presentational differences between the two editions of *Three Laws* in Atkin, 'Playing with Books in John Bale's *Three Laws*', pp. 250–61.

[97] Adams, 'Doubling in Bale's *King Johan*'; and Happé, 'Introduction', p. 22. This doubling scheme is discussed further in Adams, 'Introduction', pp. 8–12, 43–47; and Craik, *The Tudor Interlude*, pp. 32–33.

and Actor C plays Privat Welth and Nobylyte. However, as Barry Adams has noted, while Actor A could have easily managed the roles assigned to him, '[t] he assignments of Actors B and C present a different picture.'[98] Actor B could have played both Englande and Clergye with no difficulty, but he could not have played Dissymulacyon since he is required in the playing space at the same time as Englande. Similarly, Actor C could have played both Sedicyon and Commynnalte, but not Cyvyle Order, who on two occasions must share the playing space with Sedicyon. Blaming a defective copy-text for Scribe A's inconsistent and unworkable doubling scheme, Adams has proposed that by disregarding the stage directions at lines 312, 556, and A45 the following distribution of roles is most likely:

> ACTOR A: Nobylyte, Privat Welth
> ACTOR B: Englande, Clergye
> ACTOR C: Sedicyon
> ACTOR D: Cyvyle Order, Commynalte.[99]

Of the remaining seven roles unaccounted for by this scheme, five occur only in the B-text passages added by Bale and are therefore not relevant to the present discussion.[100] The remaining two, King Johan and Dissymulacyon, could be played by a fifth actor.

In addition to the doubling schemes demanded by the exigencies of professional performance, there is, in the words of Adams, 'a related but essentially different phenomenon which may be termed "disguising" — a practice whereby a character is made to adopt a false name and an assumed personality in order to deceive his adversary'.[101] Happé has likewise distinguished between 'doubling,

---

[98] Adams, 'Doubling in Bale's *King Johan*', pp. 113–14.

[99] Adams, 'Doubling in Bale's *King Johan*', pp. 117–18; Happé confirms this arrangement in Happé, 'Appendix IV', pp. 152–53.

[100] In their treatment of doubling in *King Johan*, both Adams and Happé are concerned with Bale's final version, the B-text. Adams has suggested a doubling scheme for five actors, with a sixth, presumably Bale himself, taking the role of The Interpreter. His Actors E and F take the roles of King Johan and Imperyall Majestye, and Usurpid Powre, Treason, and Veritas respectively. Happé has likewise proposed a scheme for five actors and The Interpretour, although he distributes the parts slightly differently. His Actor 1 corresponds to Adams's Actor E; his Actor 2 plays Englande, Clergye, and Usurpid Powre; his Actor 3 plays Sedicyon and Veritas; his Actor 4 corresponds to Adams's Actor 1; and his Actor 5 takes the roles of Cyvyle Order, Dissymulacyon, Commynnalte, and Treason. See Adams, 'Doubling in Bale's *King Johan*', pp. 119–20; and Happé, 'Appendix IV', pp. 152–53.

[101] Adams, 'Doubling in Bale's *King Johan*', p. 111.

in which the actor is to change to another character who is not an alias', and disguising, 'in which a change of costume carries forward an aspect of meaning, as the historical characters are seen to be manifesting the underlying and more permanent evil abstractions'.[102] In *King Johan* it is this second phenomena that occurs when Sedicyon becomes Stephen Langton or when Dissymulacyon becomes Simon of Swinsett and its polemical function must be to bolster and condemn the equation between Catholicism and theatricality. Like Tyndale's Catholic Antichrist the play's allegorical Vices 'go out of the Playe for a season' and then 'come in agayne with a new name and new raymente'. But if Sedicyon's plan to 'chaunge myn apparell | Unto a bysshoppe' (*KJ* 296–97) is designed to exemplify Catholic duplicity and disguise, it is also an excellent parallel to the doubling practices demanded by the play. Consequently, while it may have been Bale's intention to make explicit the reformed condemnation of the ritualistic aspects of Catholicism by presenting his Catholic Vices as players within the context of his plays, the practical requirements of contemporary performance results in a dramaturgy that resembles rather too closely the Catholicism his plays seek to condemn.

Walker has concluded his own discussion of 'polemic as drama' by suggesting that the problems of methodology exposed by plays like *King Johan* 'may partially explain Bale's eventual rejection of the dramatic form in later years in favour of less "idolatrous" prose'.[103] It is certainly true that after 1538, the year in which Bale claims to have compiled all of his surviving plays, there is no evidence to suggest he produced any new drama. And although the B-text of *King Johan* represents Bale's post-1558 revisions to the A-text, his adjustments say less about his ongoing commitment to drama, than his need to state the opposition between Catholic theatricality and reformed polemic in ever more explicit terms.[104] However, in both the A- and B-versions of this play and in *Three Laws* the phenomenological pressures of drama undermine Bale's innovative attempts to distinguish between Catholic playing and reformed stagecraft. For no matter how singular, stable, or 'unstagey' his virtuous characters are, no matter that they ultimately triumph over the dissolute, duplicitous, and histrionic Vices, Bale still relies on a mode of presentation — sensual, visual, incarnational — that is remarkably similar to the Catholic practices he is most keen to condemn. And by writing plays for his own semi-professional troupe, Bale's

---

[102] Happé, 'Introduction', p. 22; and Happé, *John Bale*, p. 134.

[103] Walker, *Plays of Persuasion*, p. 194.

[104] These revisions are discussed in Happé, *John Bale*, pp. 89–92.

dramatic economy replicates, almost exactly, the deceptive use of disguise by
his plays' Vices. In the final Chapter, I will explore these similarities between
the representational practices of theatre and the Catholic Church — between
dramatic and sacramental modes of presence — in a reading of the mid-Tudor
interlude *Jacke Jugeler*. But in the next chapter, I am interested in the efforts of
another playwright, Lewis Wager, to use drama for theological ends. Unlike
Bale, who pits two modes of playing side by side, Wager attempts to stage the
Magdalene's renovation in *The Life and Repentaunce of Mary Magdalene* as the
conversion from a profligate, histrionic mode of presentation to a pious, logo-
centric one. But are his attempts to develop new, reformed modes of playing
any more successful than Bale's fraught and perhaps ultimately unsuccessful
dramatic experiments?

STAGING ICONOCLASM:
LEWIS WAGER'S *LIFE AND REPENTAUNCE
OF MARY MAGDALENE* AND
CRANMER'S LAWS AGAINST IMAGES

D uring the summer of 1547, a little over six months after Edward VI's accession to the throne, the King's Printer, Richard Grafton, issued a set of Injunctions for a royal Visitation of the Church.[1] Though based on Cromwell's 1538 Injunctions, this new set promoted a programme of reform that went well beyond anything attempted during his chancellorship. Where the earlier set had taken steps against such extra-scriptural practices as pilgrimage and the veneration of images, the later set called for a blanket ban on all such practices and even encouraged parish priests to detect and report cases of noncompliance. Although the 1547 set far exceeded anything issued in the previous decade, a letter from Cranmer to his secretary, Ralph Morice, which calls for the Visitors' discretion in all areas of controversy, suggests that the Visitors were permitted licence to interpret the Injunctions along still more radical lines. The Injunctions against images were particularly open to such readings. In the 1538 set, abused images were banned, but following the old Gregorian defence of religious images, those that served as 'bokes of

---

[1] Church of England, *Iniunccions geuen by the kynges maiestie* (1547; STC 10087.5). The STC lists an additional eight imprints produced by Grafton on the same day (31 July 1547): STCs 10088, 10089, 10090, 10090.3, 10090.5, 10091, and 10093.5.

vnlerned men' were permitted to remain.[2] In the later set, images were denied this pedagogic function and tolerated only as mementos of 'the holy liues and conuersacion of theim, that thesaied Images do represent':[3]

> [T]hat suche ymages, as thei knowe in any of their Cures, to be or haue been so abused with pilgrimage or offrynges, or any thyng made thereunto, or shalbe hereafter censed vnto, thei (and none other priuate persons) shall for the aduoidyng of that most detestable offence of Idolatrie, furthwith take doune or cause to be taken doune and detroye thesame, [...] Admonishyng their parishioners, that Images serue for no other purpose, but to bee a remembraunce.[4]

With the removal of the 1538 distinction between feigned and unfeigned images and the extension of the definition of abuse to encompass all acts whether in the past, the present, or the future, the wording of the 1547 set left the door open for a radical interpretation which insisted on the wholesale removal and destruction of all images. Whether or not the Visitors universally followed this reading, little more than a month had passed before spontaneous and unauthorized acts of iconoclasm were taking place the length and breadth of the country. In Norwich, the civic and ecclesiastic authorities sat back and watched as a mob made up of 'diuers curates and other idle persons' ransacked local churches for images to destroy.[5] And in London, image and window breaking got so out of hand that the Privy Council tried to bring it to a halt by commanding the restoration of all images which should not have been removed. In the end the 'strife and contention' prompted by the Injunctions provided the necessary pretext for a total ban on images.[6] In a letter to Cranmer requesting the removal of 'all the Images remaining in any church or chappell', the Council explained:

---

[2] Church of England, *Iniunctions for the clerge*, fol. 1ʳ (no pagination).

[3] Church of England, *Iniunccions geuen by the kynges maiestie*, sig. A3ᵛ. All further references are to this imprint. Although the sixth Injunction permitted the retention of images that served a memorial function, paradoxically the twenty-eighth Injunction required the Visitors to 'take awaie, vtterly extincte, and destroye, all shrines, coueryng of shrines, all tables, candelstickes, tryndilles or rolles of waxe, pictures, paintynges, and all other monumentes of fained miracles, pilgremages, Idolatry, and supersticion: so that there remai, *no memory of the same*'. Ibid, sig. C2ᵛ, my emphasis.

[4] Church of England, *Iniunccions geuen by the kynges maiestie*, sig. A3ᵛ.

[5] Norwich, Record Office, Mayor's Court Book 1534–1539, fol. 52ʳ, cited in McClendon, 'Religious Toleration and the Reformation', p. 96.

[6] Foxe, *TAMO (1563 Edition)*, IV, 748. The ban was first introduced in London, but by February 1548 had been wheeled out across the whole country.

Considering therfore that almost in no place of this Realme is any sure quietnes but where all Images be whole taken away, and pulled downe alredy. To the intent that all contencion in euery parte of the Realme for this matter, may be clerly taken away, & that the lyuely Image of Christ should not contende for the dead Images [...] wee haue thought good to signify vnto you, that hys highnes pleasure, with the aduise and consent of vs the Lord protectore and the rest of the Counsayle is, that immediatly vpon the sight hereof with as conuenient diligence as you may, you shall not onely geue order that all the Images remainyng in any church or chappell [...] be remoued and taken awaye.[7]

To paraphrase Christopher Haigh, the council had blundered into a total ban on images, and they had got away with it.[8] This chapter explores the ways that Lewis Wager's *Life and Repentaunce of Mary Magdalene* (1566; STC 24932) engages with the 1547 Injunctions against images. Written around the same time as the royal Visitation, the play presents the sinful Magdalene as an abused image.[9] However, where the Injunctions called for the removal and destruction of misused images, the play promotes the Magdalene's conversion and renovation. Activating both the functional and phenomenological similarities between imagery and drama, the play can also be read as a spirited defence of the use of drama for religious instruction, and this chapter will also consider the play as a response to Martin Bucer's call for 'honest playing'.[10]

The Life and Repentaunce of Mary Magdalene

The Life and Repentaunce of Mary Magdalene was entered in the Stationers' Register for the year 1566/7 and was printed for the first time by John Charlewood as *A newe enterlude, neuer before this tyme imprinted, entreating of the life and repentaunce of Marie Magdalene: not only godlie, learned and fruitefull, but also well furnished with pleasaunt myrth and pastime, very delectable for those which shall heare or reade the same* (1566; STC 24932).[11] The play is offered as a kind of reformed alternative to medieval Magdalene saint plays. Consequently, while it dramatizes Mary's corruption at the hands of the Vices Infidelitie, Pride,

---

[7] Foxe, *TAMO (1563 Edition)*, IV, 748.

[8] Haigh, *English Reformations*, p. 170.

[9] The dating of the play is discussed below, p. 104.

[10] Bucer, 'De honestis ludis', ed. and trans. by Wickham. The Latin text is printed in Chambers, *The Elizabethan Stage*, IV, 188–90.

[11] A variant imprint appeared a year later in 1567 (STC 24932a).

Cupiditie, and Carnall Concupiscence (who, like their namesakes in Bale's moral plays, rely on disguise to achieve their intentions); her conversion by The Lawe, Knowledge of Sinne, and Christ; and her washing of Christ's feet at the house of Simon the Pharisee, it rejects such post-biblical miracles as the conversion of the king and queen of Marseille, concluding instead with a debate between Mary, Iustification, and Loue about the value of penitence, faith, and love of God. As the only surviving saint's play from the period and given the anonymity of many contemporary interludes, it is striking the author's name is given on the title page as 'the lerned clarke Lewis Wager'.[12] Very little is known about Wager.[13] The few records that survive reveal he was made subdeacon of the Franciscan order at Oxford in 1521; he was acting as a secular priest in 1536; he was made rector of St James, Garlickhithe, London in 1560; and he was buried in 1562. The birth of a son, William Wager, and the suppression of the Oxford Franciscans in 1538 suggest that his conversion may have happened around this time. If we assume that *Mary Magdalene* was written after his conversion but before he was made rector at Garlickhithe, then a composition date between 1538 and 1560 is most likely. In fact, the Prologue's reference to 'the kyng' (34), most likely Edward VI, suggests that the play was written after 1547 and certainly no later than 1553 when Mary I ascended the throne.[14] Though no record of performance survives, the title page's doubling instructions, which suggest that '[f]oure may easely play this Enterlude' support the Prologue's presentation of the play as a professional production (p. 1). The cast, the Prologue points out, 'haue ridden and gone many sundry waies' (25), performing 'this feate at the vniuersitie' (26) to audience members who have paid a 'halfpence or pence' (43) to see the show. Omitting the numerous post-scriptural accretions to the story of Mary Magdalene favoured by medieval dramatists, the play not only upholds the 'Authoritie of Scripture' (59), but also offers a platform for a variety of reformed beliefs, among them the doctrine of justification, and it is easy to imagine its appeal to a university audience, particularly at Cambridge, where the reformed cause had long been championed.

[12] Wager, *The Life and Repentaunce of Mary Magdalene*, p. 1. All further references are to this edition with line numbers given in parentheses within the text. See also Wager, *A newe enterlude [...] of Marie Magdalene* (1566 ; STC 24932), sig. A1ʳ.

[13] At fewer than 250 words Wager's *Oxford Dictionary of National Biography* entry might be the shortest I have encountered. See Happé, 'Wager, Lewis'.

[14] The definite article makes Paul Whitfield White's argument that Wager uses the word 'kynge' in the generalized sense of 'to be sovereign' unlikely. See White, 'Lewis Wager's *Life and Repentaunce of Mary Magdalene*', p. 511.

Though the basic plot derives in its entirety from Luke 7, the play's form and character owe much to this doctrinal emphasis, leading Michael O'Connell to conclude that 'it is the Pauline theology of Romans, and *not* the story of the repentant Magdalene, that finally controls the action' of Lewis Wager's play.[15] Certainly, the actions and words of The Lawe, Knowledge of Sinne, Repentaunce, Fayth, Iustification, and Loue are apiece with the Epistle's main subject of justification by faith. Given that the Pauline theology of Romans has on more than one occasion been described as 'part of the designated route that, led, inevitably [...] to the Reformation', it is perhaps fitting that Paul White has recently identified Books 2 and 3 of Calvin's *Institutes* as the source for a number of the play's doctrinally-heavy speeches.[16] Wager's use of Calvin offers a compelling example of the early reception of Calvinist theology in England and has pointed up a number of areas for critical inquiry. Noting the play's theological emphasis and its rejection of all post-scriptural accretions to the legend, including the famous *hortulanus* scene, Peter Happé suggests that *Mary Magdalene* offers what might be regarded as the only extant example of a Protestant adaptation of the saint play.[17] This idea has been extended by both Dalia Ben-Tsur and Patricia Badir, who both but independently read the Magdalene's conversion in the light of reformation controversy.[18] For them, Mary's progress from sinner to saint offers a neat allegory for the rejection of Catholic forms of worship, in particular the veneration of images, for reformed ones. For Badir, this process is only partially successful, since the Magdalene's body, heavily eroticized in the earlier half of the play, always recalls its pre-penitent self. Ultimately, she suggests, it is Wager's anxiety about the ability of drama to fully reform images and the ways in which they are used that explains the Prologue's defence against future criticism. My own reading of the play develops these arguments but differs in a number of ways. First, while Wager's commitment to gospel narrative reflects his own religious convictions, the play's presentation of the sinful Magdalene is clearly indebted to medieval versions of her story. Wager employs his knowledge of the practices associated with the medieval cult of the Magdalene to polemical purposes in order to illustrate his heroine's sinfulness.

---

[15] O'Connell, *The Idolatrous Eye: Iconoclasm and Theater*, p. 100, and more generally pp. 99–103.

[16] Cottret, *Calvin: A Biography*, p. 146; White, 'Lewis Wager's *Life and Repentaunce of Mary Magdalene*'.

[17] Happé, 'The Protestant Adaptation of the Saint Play', pp. 226–28.

[18] Badir, '"To Allure Vnto Their Loue"'; and Ben-Tsur, 'Early Ramifications of Theatrical Iconoclasm'. Badir covers similar ground in her more recent book Badir, *The Maudlin Impression*.

In short, the pre-penitent Magdalene is offered as an embodiment of the kinds of devotional practice that led to the 1547 ban of religious imagery. Secondly, though the Magdalene's conversion might be usefully read as the reformation of an abused image, by attending to the functional and phenomenological similarities between images and drama, the conversion sequence can be read as an attempt to reform drama and to develop a reformed dramaturgy. Here Wager is more like Bale than initially meets the eye, for not only do both dramatists share a conviction that drama might be successfully used to advance the reformed cause, they also seek to show in their plays the triumph of a new pious mode of playing over the drama of Catholic vice. Aligning Wager's stagecraft with the mode of playing advocated by Bucer in his great work *De regno Christi* (c. 1550) – often read as a kind of blueprint for the on-going English Reformation – Wager's play can be seen to contribute to a semi-official programme of religious propaganda. Finally, although the Prologue speaks specifically to the kinds of criticism that might be levelled against the play, its arguments can also be read as part of a more general defence of drama. The play might in the end reject the mode of playing associated with the pre-penitent Magdalene, but her ongoing presence ensures that she will always recall her earlier, sinful self. To put it another way, Wager, like Bale, is forced to admit that if bodily presence is a functional and phenomenological necessity, it is one that comes dangerously close to undermining the concept of a reformed stagecraft based not on images but on words, specifically the Word. Consequently, in concluding this chapter, I suggest that Prologue's defence of drama is proleptic of the kinds of criticism levelled at drama by the anti-theatrical writers of the later sixteenth century.

Abused Images

The medieval Magdalene was a composite of at least three biblical characters: the woman identified as Mary Magdalene from whom Jesus expels seven devils in Luke 8. 2–3, who is described in Mark 15. 40, Matthew 27. 55, and John 19. 25 as present at the crucifixion, and in Mark 16. 9 and John 20. 11–18 as the first to witness Christ's resurrection; Mary of Bethany, sister of Lazarus and Martha, who sits at Christ's feet in Luke 10. 38–42, and anoints Him with perfume in John 11. 1–2; and the unnamed female sinner in Luke 7. 36–50, who bathes Christ's feet at the home of Simon the Pharisee.[19] This understanding of

[19] The allusion to Magdalene's possession by devils in Mark 16. 9 is now known to be a later addition. In Luke 24, Mary Magdalene, Joanna, and Mary the mother of James go to Christ's tomb with the purpose of anointing His body. The Disciples do not believe them when they tell of Christ's resurrection. In Matthew 28, the Magdalene and the 'other Mary' come to visit

the Magdalene as a conflation of several separate biblical characters dates back at least to Gregory I the Great and perhaps even earlier.[20] Certainly, it was his exegetical authority that promoted and preserved the traditional identification of the Magdalene with Mary of Bethany and the unnamed sinner throughout the Middle Ages.[21] Though the nature of the nameless sinner's faults remain unnamed in the biblical account, by the thirteenth century the pre-penitent Magdalene was almost always described as a prostitute, making this composite figure a kind of patron saint for all sinners, but particularly those whose faults were sexual.[22] Few patristic or medieval texts deal to any great extent with her life before her conversion, but when they do, they commonly describe her as coming from a noble background, blaming her faults not on a sinful nature but on the corrupting influence of money and youth.[23]

the tomb just after it has been sealed and guarded under Pilate's orders. Afterwards, they return to the Disciples and meet Christ on the road. The episode recounted in Luke 7. 36–50 is told in different and less elaborate versions in Matthew 26. 6–13 and Mark 14. 3–9. However, in both of these versions Simon is identified as a leper. Although the Magdalene is not mentioned by name in any versions of the encounter, she is usually associated with this woman because of John 11. 2, which identifies Mary, 'whose brother Lazarus was sick', as the one who anointed Christ with perfume and wiped His feet with her hair. The biblical accounts from which the medieval Magdalene was constructed are further discussed in Haskins, *Mary Magdalen: Myth and Metaphor*; and Garth, *Saint Mary Magdalene in Mediaeval Literature*.

[20] See the following passages from his *Homiliae in Ezechielem* and *Homiliae in Evangelia*, in *PL*, LXXVI (1857), cols 854c, 1189b–1196d, 1238b–1244b. Gregory's role in the creation of the composite Magdalene is discussed in Garth, *Saint Mary Magdalene in Mediaeval Literature*, p. 19; Saxer, *Le Culte de Marie Madeleine en occident*, pp. 2–6; Haskins, *Mary Magdalen: Myth and Metaphor*, pp. 95–97; and Jansen, *The Making of the Magdalen*, pp. 32–35.

[21] As Clifford Davidson has noted, this tradition was eventually challenged in 1518 when Jacques Lefèvre d'Etaples published the first of two treatises that endeavoured to prove that Mary Magdalene, Lazarus's sister, and the unnamed sinner of Luke were three distinct persons. Wager, however, appears to betray 'no consciousness of the long and bitter sixteenth-century controversy over the question' and 'accepts without question the time-honoured identification' of the Magdalene with the woman who anoints Christ and cleans his feet. Davidson, 'The Middle English Saint Play and its Iconography', p. 73. See also Carpenter, 'Introduction', p. xxiv. The treatises published by d'Etaples, *De Maria Magdalena*; and d'Etaples, *De tribus et unica Magdalena*.

[22] The identification of Mary Magdalene with the sin of prostitution is, in part, a function of her association with the woman taken in adultery in John 8. 3–11. For further discussion of the sexualization of the Magdalene's sin see Hansel, *Die Maria-Magdalena-Legende*, p. 25; Karras, 'Holy Harlots', p. 18; and Jansen, 'Mary Magdalen and the Mendicants', pp. 19–21.

[23] See, for instance, Odo of Cluny's tenth- or eleventh-century sermon in praise of the Magdalene in, *PL*, CXXXIII (1853), cols 713d–721c, incorrectly cited in Karras, 'Holy Harlots', p. 19, as *PL*, CXXXII (1853), col. 714; and Jacobus de Voragine's life of Saint Mary Magdalene

Almost all of these elements are present in Wager's presentation of the Magdalene. Mary's exorcism is performed at lines 1385–96; her relationship to Lazarus and Martha is implied at line 257; and her use of ointment, tears, and her hair to anoint Jesus is described at lines 1793–1816. Her sin is identified as sexual by virtually every character in the play, including the Magdalene herself: 'the parts of my body in tymes past, | I haue made seruants to all kynd of iniquitie' (1789–90). And in the corruption sequence there are frequent allusions to Mary's background and status, 'you haue in your possession | The whole castel of Magdalene' (269–70), and the temptations of riches and youth, 'Remember that you are yong and full of dalliance | Lusty, couragious, fayre, beautifull and wise' (236–37). However, though Wager is detailed in his dramatization of the pre-ascension narrative, he pointedly rejects all aspects of the post-ascension legend that was so integral to medieval versions of the Magdalene's life.

The post-ascension portion of the Magdalene legend developed in a variety of ways, but the dominant version in the West after the twelfth century sees her travel by a rudderless boat to Marseille where she converts the ruler of the region and his consort, before retiring to the wilderness to spend the final thirty years of her life as a contemplative hermit.[24] It is this version of the legend that is narrated in Jacobus de Voragine's hugely influential *Legenda*

---

in Jacobus de Voragine, *Legenda Aura vulgo historia lombardia dicta*, ed. by Graesse, pp. 407–17. For the fifteenth-century English translation, probably by Caxton, see Jacobus de Voraigne, *Legenda aurea*, trans. by Caxton (1483; STC 24873), fols 216ʳ–219ᵛ. The *Legenda aurea* solves the problem of the namelessness of the sinner in Luke 7. 26–50 by claiming that the Magdalene forfeited her name and background when she sinned. See Jacobus de Voragine, *Legenda Aura vulgo historia lombardia dicta*, ed. by Graesse, p. 408; and Jacobus de Voraigne, *Legenda aurea*, trans. by Caxton, fol. 216ᵛ. Another tradition, noted but repudiated by the *Legenda aurea*, claims her sin stemmed from being jilted at the altar by Saint John the Evangelist. See, for example, Myrc, *A Critical Edition of John Mirk's Festial*, ed. by Powell, i, 184. The popular medieval tradition of John the Evangelist as the bridegroom at the wedding at Cana is discussed in Garth, *Saint Mary Magdalene in Mediaeval Literature*, p. 30. The popularity of the same tradition in the Eastern Church is discussed in Haskins, *Mary Magdalen: Myth and Metaphor*, pp. 106–07.

[24] As Victor Saxer and a number of subsequent historians have noted, the legend of the Magdalene in Provence derives from four separate traditions each of which developed separately: the ninth-century *Vita eremitica*, which conflated her with the desert hermit and reformed prostitute Mary of Egypt; the tenth-century *Vita apostolica* which dealt with the Magdalene's apostolic work in Gaul; an eleventh-century story which explained how her body had been rediscovered in Provence and brought to the abbey of Vézelay in Burgundy; and the twelfth-century proto-romance which told the story of Mary's conversion of the prince of Marseille. For the authoritative history of these four traditions and their amalgamation, see Saxer, *Le Culte de Marie Madeleine en occident*.

aurea (*c.* 1267), which almost certainly formed the basis for popular dramatic versions of the Magdalene's life.[25] Ending his play with the episode at the house of Simon the Pharisee, Wager rejects all of the post-ascension aspects of the Magdalene legend; a decision which effectively amounts to the simultaneous rejection of medieval dramatic treatments of her narrative. However, he also, perhaps somewhat surprisingly, ignores the traditional *hortulanus* scene as told in John 20. 11–18. Happé has attributed this omission to the strength of the play's 'doctrinal element'.[26] It is certainly possible that Wager's commitment to the reformed teaching of justification by faith through grace may have impacted upon his choice of material, but another reason for excluding the *hortulanus* episode is that the image of the sadly apparelled Magdalene in the play's final scene provides a striking and iconographically significant contrast with the image of the Magdalene as a sumptuously dressed sinner. From her first entrance '*triflyng with her garmentes*' (142 sd), attention is drawn to the Magdalene's appearance and dress. In her opening speech Mary describes her clothing as the work of 'The most bungarliest tailers' (144), and laments the twenty shillings she has paid them for the 'marryng' of her gear (162). Addressing the audience directly about these concerns three times in four quatrains, she constructs herself as an object to be seen and desired: 'Haue you eyer sene an ouerbody thus sytte?' (147); 'Thinke you in the waste I am so great?' (154); and 'Is this geare no better than to cast away?' (160). The erotic potential of her appearance is further emphasized by her exclamation that she is 'ashamed to come in any mans sight' (153), a remark that is surely ironized by the presence of a predominantly male audience. Mary's anxieties about the state of her attire are confirmed by Infidelitie, who suggests that her tailors have so botched 'the mydst' of her garment that 'it is past amendement' (171, 173). As it turns out, Infidelitie is not without 'taylers craft' (179), and proposes to 'helpe to set her forward' (317):

> Shortly my ofspryng and I shall her so dresse,
> That neither law nor prophets she shall regard,
> No though the sonne of God to her them expresse. (318–20)

---

[25] The *Legenda aurea* survives in over seven hundred manuscripts and 173 early printed editions. Its influence on English Magdalene plays is particularly prominent. For instance, the Digby play of *Mary Magdalen*, which is preserved in the early-sixteenth century manuscript Oxford, Bodl. Libr., MS Digby 133 at fols 95ʳ–145ʳ follows the episodic pattern of the *Legenda aurea* almost exactly, while the characterization of the Magdalene in the northern mystery cycles is also clearly indebted to the *Legenda aurea* tradition.

[26] Happé, 'The Protestant Adaptation of the Saint Play', p. 227.

This plan to 'dresse' Mary, as Badir has noted, clearly exploits both the sartorial and pedagogic meanings of the verb.[27] In fact as its meaning flits from 'to set in order', through 'to place or set in position', 'to make ready or prepare for any purpose', and 'to adorn or deck with apparel', to 'to turn or send in some given direction', dressing the Magdalene clearly echoes the way that devotees of her medieval cult would have dressed and adorned her statues and paintings with rich materials, jewellery, and incense.[28] And in suggesting that in her splendour the Magdalene will lose interest in God's law, Infidelitie establishes a dichotomy between art and iconography and spiritual truth in terms that validate the reformed equation of images with idols and image-worship with idolatry.[29]

By enlisting Infidelitie's offspring — Pride of Life, Cupiditie, and Carnall Concupiscence — to serve as Mary's dressers, the play neatly points up the kinds of vice associated with excessive care for one's appearance: vanity; greed; and lust. But it is equally telling that these characters do not appear as themselves, but in disguise. Here as in Bale's plays, sin is marked out as a kind of duplicity that lies dangerously close to the workings of drama. In the guise of their adopted personas of Nobilitie (Pride of Life), Utilitie (Cupiditie), and Pleasure (Carnall Concupiscence), the Vices inform Mary that her 'countenance is not ladylike inough yet' (614) and instruct her how to arrange her hair. Carnall Concupiscence suggests that she should style it so 'the most part may be in sight' (628); Infidelitie advocates the use of a hot needle 'That it may curle together in maner like a wispe' (633); Pride of Life advises the she should fold her hair, 'like Tomboyes' (637); and Cupiditie recommends she acquaint herself with 'some Goldsmyth' if the colour of her hair 'beginneth for to fade' (642, 640).[30] They offer similarly elaborate tips for the use of make-up (646–66); the arrangement of clothing (669–704); and the application of perfume (768–73). They

[27] Badir, '"To Allure Vnto Their Loue"', p. 9; Badir, *The Maudlin Impression*, p. 37. 'To make straight or right; to bring into proper order; to array, make ready, prepare, tend'; and '[t]o direct'. See 'dress, *v.* I., II.', in *The Oxford English Dictionary*, 2nd edn, <http://dictionary.oed.com/cgi/entry/50069820> [accessed 5 June 2013].

[28] 'dress, *v.*, I., 2. a, 3. a, 5. a, and II., 14. A', in *The Oxford English Dictionary*, 2nd edn, <http://dictionary.oed.com/cgi/entry/50069820> [accessed 5 June 2013].

[29] Nicholas Ridley preached to the King on this very subject three days after his coronation, on 23 February 1547. Although the sermon is lost, its contents are known from a letter written in response by Stephen Gardiner, Ridley's long-standing opponent. See Aston, *England's Iconoclasts*, p. 251.

[30] For a discussion of the semiotic connotations of blond hair see Haskins, *Mary Magdalen: Myth and Metaphor*, pp. 246–48.

also instruct her in the arts of conversation, 'set muche by your kynrede and noble blood: | Boast of them' (709–10); seduction, 'see that your louers be yong and gay, | And suche fellowes as be well able to pay' (762–3); and extortion, 'Oppresse you tenantes, take fines, and raise rentes' (815). Badir has shown the Vices' fashion advice conforms to contemporary ideals of feminine beauty and honours the medieval tradition of the fashion-conscious Magdalene.[31] While these observations are undoubtedly valid, the Vices' fashion tips also and per- haps more pressingly engage with contemporary discussions about the adorn- ment of statues.

In an anonymous text titled *The praierand [sic] complaynte of the ploweman vnto Christe* ([1531?]; STC 20036) that has, at different points, been attributed to both Tyndale and George Joye, the author complains, 'what heryenge ys it, to cloth mawmettes of stokes and of stones yn syluer and in golde and in other good coloures?'[32] Whether or not *The praierand [sic] complaynte* was written by Tyndale, elsewhere he certainly expresses comparable views about the adorn- ment of statues. In *An answere vnto Sir Thomas Mores dialoge made by Vvillyam Tindale* ([1531]; STC 24437), he argues that '[a]s for the riches that is bestowed on images and reliques they can not proue but that it is abhominable, as longe as the pore are dispised and vncared for and not first serued.'[33] During Edward VI's reign, Hugh Latimer makes the same point in a sermon preached at St Paul's in January 1548 in which he attacks the 'deckynge of ymages and gaye garnyshynge of stockes' when 'the pore and impotent' remain unclothed.[34] Latimer's sermon

---

[31] Badir, '"To Allure Vnto Their Loue"', pp. 9–10. Accounts of contemporary trends can be found in Willett and Cunnington, *The History of Underclothes*, pp. 27, 32–37; Willett and Cunnington, *Handbook of English Costume in the Sixteenth Century*, pp. 53–86, 149–89; Ewing, *Dress and Undress: A History of Women's Underwear*, pp. 21–34; and Ewing, *Fashion in Underwear*, pp. 20–31. For a discussion of the medieval Magdalene's expensive taste in clothing, see Haskins, *Mary Magdalen: Myth and Metaphor*, pp. 157–58.

[32] *The praierand [sic] complaynte of the ploweman*, sig. C5ʳ. Following his appearance before Wolsey in December 1527, Joye fled to Antwerp, and was certainly there when the first edition of *The Praierand [sic] complaynte* was published. However, the preface to the second, London imprint ([c. 1532]; STC 20036.5) is signed with Tyndale's initials. William Clebsch has made the case for the attribution to Tyndale. See Clebsch, *England's Earliest Protestants*, pp. 163, 336.

[33] Tyndale, *An answere vnto Sir Thomas Mores dialoge* ([1531]; STC 24437), fol. 37ʳ⁻ᵛ. For an earlier expression of this view see the tract on images and pilgrimages in BL, Addit. MS 24202, fols 26ʳ–28ᵛ (fol. 26), edited in *Selections from English Wycliffite Writings*, ed. by Hudson, pp. 83–88 (p. 83): 'men erren foul in [...] peynten [images] wiþ greet cost, and hangen myche siluer and gold and precious stones þeronne and aboute it, and suffren pore men, bouȝte wiþ Cristis precious blode, to be by hem nakyd, hungry, thursty and in strong preseon boundun.'

[34] *A notable sermo[n]* ([1548]; STC 15291), sig. C4ʳ.

at St Paul's coincided with the condemnation of the 'offering of money, caNdelles or tapers, to Reliques, or Images' in the 1547 Injunctions, and echoes the stance of Cranmer's 1548 catechism, which states: 'thou shalt not worshyppe ymages, that is to saye, thou shalt not gylte them, and set them in costlye tabernacles, and decke theim with coates or shertes, thou shalt not sense them.'[35] With gilt in her hair, decked with 'bon grace' (670), velvet collar, and 'wiers and houpes' (700), and incensed with 'ciuet, pommander, muske' (770), the Magdalene of the pre-conversion sequence in Wager's play resembles nothing so much as an abused image that is idolized, quite literally, by her 'yong and gay' customers (762). And following the anxiety of at least one pre-Reformation tract, that 'þe gayest and most rychely arrayed ymage raþeest wil þe puple offur' — that lavishly decorated icons serve to fill Church coffers — the Magdalene will be sure 'to get an hundred pound a yeare' by wearing 'pretie geare' (785, 784).[36]

Anticipating the Elizabethan identification of religious images with dolls, Mary is decked like a great puppet 'for olde fooles to play with'.[37] As Aston has argued, this disparagement of church images as toys 'was conveniently able to assume its disdain for the falsities of little popes — "popetry" — into the deluding manipulations of carved and jointed images — "puppetry"'.[38] Or, to put it in Badir's words, 'the tricks of "puppetry" slip both alliteratively and metaphorically into a lewd critique of "popery"'.[39] She has further noted that Pride of Life's instruction to Mary to let her 'eies roll' in her head (616), 'is evocative of the most notorious of old Catholic puppets, the Rood of Boxley'.[40] Whether or not Mary follows Pride of Life's direction, it is clear that that Mary's skill in 'catchyng and takyng' (787) echoes the use of the Rood, with its moving eyes and lips, by the monks of Boxley to extract money from people who thought

---

[35] Cranmer, *Cathechismus* (1548; STC 5993), sig. C5^r–C5^v, cited in Aston, *England's Iconoclasts*, p. 431.

[36] 'Images and Pilgrimages', in *Selections from English Wycliffite Writings*, ed. by Hudson, pp. 83–88 (p. 84).

[37] *The seconde tome of homelyes* (1563; STC 13663), sig. Xx4^v, cited in Aston, *England's Iconoclasts*, p. 403.

[38] Aston, *England's Iconoclasts*, p. 403.

[39] Badir, '"To Allure Vnto Their Loue"', p. 8; Badir, *The Maudlin Impression*, p. 36. See also Dillon, *Language and Stage in Medieval and Renaissance England*, p. 91.

[40] Badir, '"To Allure Vnto Their Loue"', p. 8. The Boxley Rood as puppet is further explored in Groeneveld, 'A Theatrical Miracle'. A number of critics have used the exhibition and exposure of the mechanics of the Boxley Rood of Grace to illuminate their discussion of early Tudor dramatic texts. See, for instance, Jones, 'Theatrical History in the Croxton *Play of the Sacrament*', pp. 243–44; and White, *Theatre and Reformation*, pp. 36–37.

'that the sayde image had so moved by the power of God'.[41] The parallels are yet more apparent in John Hoker's account of the Rood:

> There was lately discovered a wooden God of the Kentish folk, a hanging Christ who might have vied with Proteus himself. For he was able, most cunningly, to nod with his head, to scowl with his eyes, to wag his beard, to curve his body, to reject and receive the prayers of pilgrims. This [puppet] when the pied Monks lost their craft, was found in their Church, begirded with many an offering; enriched with gifts, linen, waxen, rural, oppidan, and foreign.[42]

At the time of Cromwell's 1538 Visitation, Cranmer had the Rood removed from the abbey at Boxley, and 'sett in the market place first at Maydstone':[43]

> [A]nd there shewed openlye to the people the craft of movinge the eyes and lipps, that all the people there might see the illusion that had bene used in the sayde image

---

[41] Wriothesley, *A Chronicle of England during the Reigns of the Tudors*, ed. by Hamilton, I (1875), 74. Badir has noted the stage direction at l. 618, which says, 'Mary poses, rolls her eyes'. However, what she has failed to observe is that this direction is a later interpolation by the play's most recent editor. See Badir, '"To Allure Vnto Their Loue"', p. 8. Further accounts of the showing and destruction of the Boxley Rood can be found in *Letters and Papers of the Reign of Henry VIII*, XIII, 1, ed. by James Gairdner (1892), p. 79, no. 231 (Jeffray Chamber to Cromwell); p. 283, no. 754 (Nicholas Partidge to Bullinger); p. 239, no. 643 (John Finch to Conrad Humpard); p. 239, no. 644 (William Peterson to Conrad Pulbert); and Wriothesley, *A Chronicle of England during the Reigns of the Tudors*, ed. by Hamilton, I (1875), 75–76.

[42] 'Repertus est nuper Cantianorum deus ligneus, pensilis Christus, qui cum ipso Protheo concertare potuisset. Nam et capite nutare, innuere oculis, barbam convertere, incurvare corpus, adeuntium aversari et recipere preces scitissime noverat. Hic cum monachi suâ causâ caderent, repertus est in eorum templo, plurimo cinctus anathemate, linteis, cereis agricis [...] exterisque ditatus muneribus.' For the English translation see 'John Hoker, Minister of Maidstone, To Bullinger', in *Gleanings of a Few Scattered Ears*, ed. by Gorham and Bird, pp. 17–19, no. 3 (p. 17). An abbreviated version of the letter is edited in *Letters and Papers of the Reign of Henry VIII*, XIII, 1, ed. by James Gairdner (1892), p. 120, no. 348 (John Hoker, of Maidstone, to Bullinger). For the Latin original see 'A letter to Bullinger from one of Maidstone, giving an account of an image, which seems to be the rood of Boxley in Kent', in Burnet, *The History of the Reformation of the Church of England*, VI, 194–95, no. 55. The letter was written some time after 24 February 1538, the date of Bishop Hilsey of Rochester's sermon at Paul's Cross. The original copy of the letter is no longer extant. Hoker's disparagement of the Boxley Rood as a shape-shifting Proteus is a rhetorical slight repeated by a number of Protestant reformers. For instance, in the mid-century anti-Catholic tract, *The displaying of the Popish masse*, Thomas Becon complains that '*Proteus* never turned himself into so many forms, shapes, and fashions, as your Masse hath vertues'. See Becon, *The displaying of the Popish masse*, pp. 309–10. Though written in the mid-sixteenth century, Becon's tract was not printed until 1637 (STC 1719).

[43] Wriothesley, *A Chronicle of England during the Reigns of the Tudors*, ed. by Hamilton, I (1875), 74.

by the monckes of the saide place of many yeares tyme out of mynde, whereby they had gotten riches in deceavinge the people.[44]

Discussing the public exhibition of the Boxley Rood, White has argued that, like 'Bale's iconoclastic treatment of Catholic ceremonies, the shock value derives from changing the physical context — in one instance taking the holy object to the marketplace, in the other reenacting it on stage — and from the exposure of the rite or image as a meaningless sham. In both cases, an object of holiness is displaced and demystified.'[45] Badir has suggested that White's argument can be directly applied to Wager's play, in which a 'once-venerated saint's statue is vigorously debased by its relocation in a morally and physically corrupt world'.[46] But it strikes me that it is the dressing of the Magdalene rather than her relocation that provides the closest parallel with the Boxley Rood of Grace. For in both the market and playing space, the craft is exposed and 'shewed openlye to the people'. And just as the people learn of the Boxley Rood's dependence on 'graces and engines' to delude the people of Maidstone, so Wager's audience learn of the way the unrepentant Magdalene uses hair dye, make-up, corsetry, and perfume to seduce her patrons.[47]

After its initial disparaging exhibition at Maidstone, the Boxley Rood of Grace was brought to Paul's Cross, where it was used to illustrate a sermon given by John Hilsey, bishop of Rochester. As Aston has commented, 'Hilsey made full use of the set piece placed before the congregation by demonstrating the cords and devices as he denounced the manipulation of the "engines used in old tyme" in this image.'[48] In Wriothesley's words: '[a]fter the sermon was done, the bishop tooke the said image of the roode into the pulpit and brooke the vice of the same, and after that gave it to the people againe, and then the rude people and boys brake the said image in peeces, so that they left not one

---

[44] Wriothesley, *A Chronicle of England during the Reigns of the Tudors*, ed. by Hamilton, I (1875), 74.

[45] White, *Theatre and Reformation*, p. 37.

[46] Badir, '"To Allure Vnto Their Loue"', p. 8.

[47] Wriothesley, *A Chronicle of England during the Reigns of the Tudors*, ed. by Hamilton, I (1875), 75. An editorial note suggests that 'graces' is 'probably a clerical error for vices'. See editorial note c on the same page. Later in his chronicle, Wriothesley gives an account of a sermon in which the preached 'shewed a picture of the resurrection of our Lord, made with vices, which putt out his legges of sepulchree and blessed with his hand, and turned his heade' (II, 1877). The language recalls Infidelitie's advice that to Mary: 'Your nether garments must go by gymmes and ioynts | Aboue your buttocks thei must be tied on with points' (696–97).

[48] Aston, *Faith and Fire*, p. 267.

peece whole.'[49] The self-conscious theatricality of the occasion is underlined in
Hoker's ecstatic account to Heinrich Bullinger:

> After a few days, a Sermon was preached in London, at the Metropolitan Cathedral,
> by the Bishop of Rochester [Dr John Hilsey]. The Kentish Bel stands opposite to
> Daniel, erected on the upper part of the pulpit, so that he may be conveniently seen
> by all. Here again, he opens himself; here again, the Player acts his part skilfully.
> They wonder, they are indignant, they stare with bewilderment, they are ashamed
> to find they have been so deluded by a puppet. Then when the Preacher began
> to wax warm, and the Word of God to work secretly in the hearts of his hearers,
> the wooden trunk was hurled neck-over-heels among the most crowded of the
> audience. And now was heard a tremendous clamour of all sorts of people; — he is
> snatched, torn, broken in pieces bit by bit, split into a thousand fragments, and at
> last thrown into the fire; and there was an end of him![50]

Hoker's account draws an explicit link between the word of God and iconoclasm. The association is similarly implied in Wriothesley's *Chronicle*. In
his entry for November 1547 he explains that '[a]n idol made of vices and
shewed at Paules crosse' was broken into pieces immediately following a sermon by William Barlow, bishop of Bath and Wells.[51] Although Wager's *Mary
Magdalene* likewise pits idolatrous craft against the purity of God's word, it
stops short of the overt iconoclasm witnessed in these accounts, advocating
reformation over destruction. In this the play is perhaps less radical than the
twenty-eighth Injunction of the 1547 Visitation that called for the destruction
of all 'monumentes of fained miracles, pilgremages, Idolatry, and supersticion'.[52]
Nonetheless, in transforming Mary from sinner to penitent, ornate to sad figure,
Wager dramatizes the conversion of an idolatrous image outlawed by the sixth

[49] Wriothesley, *A Chronicle of England during the Reigns of the Tudors*, ed. by Hamilton, I, 76.

[50] 'Hinc post dies aliquot habita est Londini concio, prædicabat è sacrâ cathedrâ episcopus
Roffensis; stat ex adverso Danieli Bel Cantianus, summo erectus pulpito. Hic denuò sese aperit,
hic denuò coram fabulam scitè agit. Mirantur, indignantur, stupent. Pudet ab idolo tam turpiter
fuisse delusos. Cumque jam incalesceret concionator, et verbum Dei occultè operaretur in cor-
dibus auditorum, præciptio devolvunt istum lignum truncum in confertissimos auditores. Hic
varius auditur diversorum clamor, rapitur, laceratur, frustillatim, comminuitur, sciditurque in
mille confratus partes, tandem in IGNEM mittitur. Et hic tulit exitum illum.' For the English
see 'John Hoker', in *Gleanings of a Few Scattered Ears*, ed. by Gorham and Bird, pp. 18–19. For
the Latin original see 'A letter to Bullinger', in Burnet, *The History of the Reformation of the
Church of England*, VI, 194–95.

[51] Wriothesley, *A Chronicle of England during the Reigns of the Tudors*, ed. by Hamilton, II
(1877), 1.

[52] Church of England, *Iniunccions geuen by the kynges maiestie*, sig. C2ᵛ.

of the 1547 Injunctions, to an image that remembers the biblical Magdalene's holy life and conversation and therefore permitted by it.[53]

The conversion sequence occupies some 430 lines from the entrance of The Lawe at line 1108 to Mary's exit with Fayth and Repentaunce at line 1540. In contrast to the spectacular bawdry of the pre-conversion sequence, the conversion sequence is pointedly wordy, as first The Lawe and Knowledge of Sinne, then Christ Jesus, and finally Fayth and Repentaunce, preach on the reformed doctrine of justification in terms that recall official teaching on the subject.[54] More specifically, The Lawe and Knowledge of Sinne teach God's mercy and grace, Christ teaches His role in the satisfaction of God's justice, and Fayth and Repentaunce teach God's gift of faith. These lessons are restated in the final scene between the Magdalene, Iustification, and Loue. In this scene Mary retains the sad apparel seen for the first time in the earlier scene at the house of Simon the Pharisee. The modesty of her dress is matched by the modesty of her speech, and her words are constrained by biblical account:

> [...] Many sinnes are fogiuen hir sayd he,
> Because she hath loued much, meanyng me,
> I pray you, most holy Iustification,
> Of this sentence to make a declaration. (2053–56)

Mary here repeats the words uttered by Christ Jesus in the play at line 1923, and by Jesus in the Bible in Luke 7. 47.[55] In response, Iustification makes a declaration, a sermon on the Edwardian doctrine of justification by grace through faith, concluding that 'by faith in Christ you haue Iustification/Frely of his grace, and beyond mans operation' (2083–84). White has identified Calvin as the source for Wager's treatment of this doctrine, but it is perhaps more plausible that Wager was working from a knowledge of Cranmer's *Certain sermons* (1547), which the thirty-second of the 1547 Injunctions required 'all Persones, Vicars, and Curates' to 'reade in their Churches, euery Sondaye'.[56] Taking its

---

[53] See Church of England, *Iniunccions geuen by the kynges maiestie*, sig. A3ᵛ.

[54] See, for instance, 'An homely of the Saluacion of mankynd, by onely Christe our sauiour from synne and death euerlastyng', in *Certain sermons* (1547; STC 13638.5), sigs ᵊᵛᵊᵛᵊᵛ3ʳ–ᵊᵛᵊᵛᵊᵛᵊᵛᵊᵛ3ʳ; and 'The seconde sermon of our Redemption', in Cranmer, *Cathechismus*, sigs N1ʳ–R3ᵛ.

[55] The wording follows the Great Bible exactly: 'many synnes are forgeuen her, for she loued moche.' See *The byble in Englyshe*, v: *The newe Testament in englyshe*, sig. Dd2ʳ.

[56] Church of England, *Iniunccions geuen by the kynges maiestie*, sig. C4ʳ. See White, 'Lewis Wager's *Life and Repentaunce of Mary Magdalene*', pp. 511–12; and White, *Theatre and*

cue from scripture — here Paul's letter to the Romans - - the second homily on 'the Saluacion of mankynd, by onely Christ our sauior from synne and death euerlastyng' repeatedly states '[n]o man is iustified, by the workes of the lawe, but frely by faithe in Iesus Christe' and describes how 'we receiue it of hym frely, by his mercie, without our desertes, through true and liuely faithe'.[57] His sermon concluded, Iustification is eager to bring the play to its close:

> Of this matter we might tary very long,
> But then we should do your audience wrong,
> Which gently hath heard vs here a long space,
> Wherefore we will make an end nowe by Gods grace,
> Praying God that all we example may take
> Of Mary, our synfull lyues to forsake:
> And no more to looke backe, but to go forward still
> Folowyng Christ as she did and his holy will. (2109–16)

Iustification offers the Magdalene as an exemplum through which the audience will be encouraged to forsake their sinful lives. Asking that the audience 'no more to looke backe' (2115), he commands the viewer to exchange the decadent, sensual image of the profligate Magdalene for the modest image of the sadly apparelled, repentant Mary in terms that recall directly the 1547 Injunction 'that Images serue for no other purpose, but to be a remembraunce, whereby men may be admonished, of the holy lives and conuersacion of theim, that thesaied Images doo represent'.[58] What is more, Iustification's commitment to the letter of scripture echoes the move made by a number of parishes to paint New Testament verses over their churches' newly whitewashed walls. To put it another way, attention to the spectacle of the abused image is reconfigured as attention to the Word of God.

Reformation, pp. 184–85. At least six imprints of *Certain sermons* were printed on the same day, 31 July 1547: STCs 13638.5; 13638.7; 13639; 13639.5; 13640; and 13640.5. It is worth noting that the doctrine of justification by faith is central to Reformation thought in all its diverse forms, including Lutheranism, Calvinism, and Zwinglism. As Caroline M. Stacey has noted the 1547 Book of Homilies can be grouped into two units of six of which the first concerns doctrine and the second, its application to the Christian life. See Stacey, 'Justification by Faith'. Only homilies three, four, and five are universally attributed to Cranmer. Other undisputed attributions include homily two to John Harpsfield, chaplain to Edmund Bonner, conservative bishop of London, six to Bonner himself, and eleven to Thomas Becon, Cranmer's chaplain.

[57] *Certain sermons*, sigs ꝺ3ᵛ, ꝺ1ʳ.

[58] Church of England, *Iniunccions geuen by the kynges maiestie*, sig. A3ᵛ.

Huston Diehl has argued that 'the breaking of familiar and well-loved images necessitate[d] the making of new ones', and that these 'ways of seeing' were more 'skeptical, more self-reflexive, and more attentive to what lies beyond visual representations'.[59] In concluding this chapter, I want to suggest that the reformation of the Magdalene enacts the replacement of image by word, inculcating a 'new Protestant mode of seeing' in which the playing space is textualized.[60] Taking a similar line, Badir has argued that the success of this conceit is undermined by 'the eroticism [... of ...] the highly charged act of touching Christ' in the scene at the house of Simon the Pharisee.[61] But it is not the eroticism of this encounter that threatens Wager's godly stagecraft, but his necessary reliance on the real presence of actors' bodies. Strikingly, this threat is acknowledged by The Prologue and various other characters; the result is a play that works in a disruptive way, arousing what Diehl has described as 'a wariness and uneasiness about the very act of gazing' at it.[62]

Honest Playing

In a part of his great work *De regno Christi* titled 'De honestis ludis', Martin Bucer, Regius Professor of Divinity at Cambridge, writes a defence of drama. Rejecting the wit, charm, and grace of the language of Aristophanes, Terence, and Plautus, and the dignity, subtlety, and polished style of Sophocles, Euripides, and Seneca, Bucer argues that 'religious men [...] schooled in the knowledge of Christ's Kingdom' will be needed to compose plays drawn from a variety of biblical episodes:[63]

> For these stories are thickly packed with godlike and heroic people, with emotion, with character, with actions and with unforeseen events moreover which happen contrary to expectation and which Aristotle calls 'reversals of fortune'.[64]

[59] Diehl, *Staging Reform, Reforming the Stage*, p. 46.

[60] Diehl, *Staging Reform, Reforming the Stage*, p. 63.

[61] Badir, '"To Allure Vnto Their Loue"', p. 17; Badir, *The Maudlin Impression*, p. 43.

[62] Diehl, *Staging Reform, Reforming the Stage*, p. 63.

[63] '[P]iis [...] ad regnum Christi doctis atque sapientibus virus.' Bucer, 'De honestis ludis', ed. and trans. by Wickham, p. 329. For the Latin original see Chambers, *The Elizabethan Stage*, p. 188. Though never translated in its entirety, selections were printed as Bucer, *A treatise* (STC 3965). The STC suggests a publication date of 1557, presumably on the basis that earliest known edition of the Latin original was printed in Basel in the same year. If *A tretise* was published in England it is unlikely to have been printed before the accession of Elizabeth I in 1558.

[64] 'Omnino enim refertae sunt hae historiae diuinis et heroicis personis, affectionibus, moribus, actionibus, euentibus quoque inexpectatis, atque in contrarium quam expectarentur

In addition to defining the subjects suitable for dramatization, Bucer identifies two modes of playing: one 'frivolous and theatrical'; the other 'not without value in increasing piety'.[65] Of these two styles, plays 'in which knowledge of the eternal life is manifestly clear (even if some literary niceties are lacking)' are clearly preferable to those 'in which both spirit and character are defiled by impious and disgusting interchanges of buffoonery, even if some pleasure is given by refinements of wit and language'.[66] Moreover, that these ideas were treated with something like official approbation is testified by John Cheke's presentation of *De regno Christi* to Edward VI in October 1551.

Composed by a 'lerned clarke' and rehearsing 'a fruictfull story, | Written in the .vii. of Luke' (59–60) in which the fortunes of the heroine are dramatically reversed, Wager's *Mary Magdalene* conforms to Bucer's definition of 'useful subject-matter'.[67] However, in spite of the elimination of many of the medieval additions to her story, the Magdalene as a biblical figure emerges only in the post-conversion sequence of Wager's play with the dramatization of the encounter at the house of Simon the Pharisee.[68] As a result, her reformation is imagined as a return to the Word of God and, therefore, to a subject matter capable of providing 'wholesome entertainment'.[69] What is more, the style of the post-conversion sequence is clearly different to the style of the pre-conversion sequence. In the first half of the play, the action is dominated by lewd innuendo:

> INFIDELITIE: Mistresse Mary can you not play on the virginals?
> MARY: Yes swete heart that I can, and also on the regals,
> There is no instrument but that handle I can,

---

candentibus, quae Aristoteles vocat περιπετείας.' Bucer, 'De honestis ludis', ed. and trans. by Wickham, p. 329. For the Latin original see Chambers, *The Elizabethan Stage*, p. 189.

[65] '[L]eue aut histrionicum', 'ad augendam pietatem non inutilis.' Bucer, 'De honestis ludis', ed. and trans. by Wickham, pp. 330, 329. For the Latin originl see Chambers, *The Elizabethan Stage*, pp. 189, 188.

[66] '[Q]uibus si minus ars poetica, scientia tamen vitae aeternae praeclare exhibetur', 'quibus vt ingenii linguaeque cultus aliquid iuuatur, ita animus et mores impia atque foeda et scurrili mutatione conspurcantur.' Bucer, 'De honestis ludis', ed. and trans. by Wickham, pp. 330–31, 331. For the Latin original see Chambers, *The Elizabethan Stage*, p. 190.

[67] '[V]tilus [...] materia.' Bucer, 'De honestis ludis', ed. and trans. by Wickham, p. 330. For the Latin original see Chambers, *The Elizabethan Stage*, p. 189.

[68] This observation has also been made in O'Connell, *The Idolatrous Eye: Iconoclasm and Theater*, p. 100.

[69] '[H]onesta [...] oblectatio.' Bucer, 'De honestis ludis', ed. and trans. by Wickham, p. 329. For the Latin original see Chambers, *The Elizabethan Stage*, p. 188.

>   I thynke as well as any gentlewoman.
> INFIDELITIE: If that you can play vpon the recorder,
>   I haue as fayre a one as any is in this border,
>   Truly you haue not sene a more goodlie pipe,
>   It is so bigge that your hand can it not gripe. (837–46)[70]

The Vices' theatrical bawdry, frivolous puns, and impious and disgusting exchanges of buffoonery, clearly suggest a mode of playing condemned in 'De honestis ludis'. However, after the Magdalene's conversion, Wager adopts a dramatic style that is 'religious and serious'.[71] Following Bucer's instruction that 'in every representation of sin the condemnation of the individual conscience should be perceived together with fearful respect for the judgement of God', the conversion sequence emphasizes the justice of God's judgement.[72] In The Lawe's words:

>   In me as in a glasse it doth plainly appere,
>   What God of his people doth require,
>   What the peoples duetie is, they may see here,
>   Whiche they owe vnto God in paine of hell fyre.
>
>   In me is declared the same iustice,
>   Whiche vnto God is acceptable.
>   Mans synne is here shewed, and proude enterprise,
>   Whereby he is conuicted to paines perdurable. (1121–28)

As Badir has commented, 'the stone tablets of God's Law are presented to Mary by a personified looking-glass in whom she finds "knowledge of sinne"'.[73] The allegory noted by Badir literalizes Bucer's recommendation that the 'dread of divine judgement and a horror of sin should appear' 'when the faults and sins of

---

[70] Thomas Middleton's *Chaste Maid in Cheapside* (*c.* 1613) opens with the same sexual quibble.

[71] '[S]ancta [...] et graui.' Bucer, 'De honestis ludis', ed. and trans. by Wickham, p. 330. For the Latin original see Chambers, *The Elizabethan Stage*, p. 189.

[72] '[I]n omni peccati repraesentatione sentiantur, conscientiae propriae comdenatio, et iudicio Dei horrenda trepidatio.' Bucer, 'De honestis ludis', ed. and trans. by Wickham, p. 330. For the Latin original see Chambers, *The Elizabethan Stage*, p. 189.

[73] Badir, '"To Allure Vnto Their Loue"', p. 2. White has shown the indebtedness of these lines to book three of Calvin's *Institutes*. See White, 'Lewis Wager's *Life and Repentaunce of Mary Magdalene*', pp. 509–10; White, 'Introduction', pp. xxxii–xxxiv; and White, *Theatre and Reformation*, pp. 181–82. The idea of The Lawe as a mirror is extended in Fayth's speech at lines 1497–1500: 'The word to a glasse compare we may, | For as it were therin, Faith doth od behold, | Whom as in a cloude we loke vpon always, | As hereafter more plainly it shal be told.'

men are [...] shown in action as though before our eyes'.[74] The scenes following the Magdalene's conversion are dominated by the events at the house of Simon the Pharisee, where the action as well as language closely follows Luke 7. 36–50 in the 1541 revised edition of the Great Bible:[75]

> *Let Marie creepe vnder the table, abyding there a certayne space behynd, and doe as it is specified in the Gospell.* (1828 sd)

By deferring to the authority of the Bible, which describes how Mary 'stode at his fete behynde hym wepynge, and beganne to wasshe his fete with teares, & dyd wipe them with the heeres of her heed, & kyssed his fete, and anoynted them with the oyntment', Wager directs the audience's gaze beyond the spectacle of the playing space, to the Word of God that has directed the actions performed within it.[76] What is more, just as speeches by The Lawe, Knowledge of Sinne, Fayth, and Repentaunce teach 'fearful respect for the judgement of God' in the conversion sequence, the 'good and honourable actions' of Luke 7. 36–50 are glossed with long homilies by Iustification and Loue that express as clearly as possible 'a joyful sense of divine mercy'.[77]

In *Mary Magdalene*, Wager envisages Mary's conversion in dramaturgical terms. At the moment of her transformation from profligate sinner to modest penitent, he abandons the 'impious and disgusting exchanges of buffoonery' of the pre-conversion sequence for a style that is 'religious and serious yet pleasing, at any rate to the pious'.[78] To put it another way, *Mary Magdalene* begins as 'frivolous' drama and ends as 'wholesome entertainment'.[79] Though the play

---

[74] '[T]error quidam in his diuini iudicii, et horror appareat peccati', 'cum hominum vitia et peccata [...] actione quasi oculis conspicienda exhibentur.' Bucer, 'De honestis ludis', ed. and trans. by Wickham, pp. 330, 329–30. For the Latin original see Chambers, *The Elizabethan Stage*, p. 189.

[75] Compare, for instance, the parable of the two debtors in Wager's play, at lines 1889–1932, and in *The byble in Englyshe*, v, sig. Dd3ʳ.

[76] *The byble in Englyshe*, v, sig. Dd3ʳ.

[77] '[A] iudicio Dei horrenda trepidatio', 'piae et probae [...] actiones', 'clarissime sensus divinae misericordiae.' Bucer, 'De honestis ludis', ed. and trans. by Wickham, p. 330. For the Latin original see Chambers, *The Elizabethan Stage*, p. 189.

[78] '[I]mpia atque foeda et scurrili mutatione', 'sancta [...] et graui, iucunda tamen, sanctis duntaxat.' Bucer, 'De honestis ludis', ed. and trans. by Wickham, pp. 331, 330. For the Latin original see Chambers, *The Elizabethan Stage*, pp. 190, 189.

[79] '[L]eue', 'honesta [...] oblectatio.' Bucer, 'De honestis ludis', ed. and trans. by Wickham, pp. 330, 329. For the Latin original see Chambers, *The Elizabethan Stage*, p. 189.

seems committed to dramatizing this exchange of one impious stagecraft for another that is both serious and pious, the Prologue is quick to define the entire project as virtuous:

> I maruell why they should detract our facultie:
> [...]
> Doth not our facultie learnedly extoll vertue?
>   Doth it not teache, God to be praised aboue al thing?
> What facultie doth vice more earnestly subdue?
>   Doth not it teache true obedience to the kyng?
>   What godly sentences to the mynd doth it bryng?
>   I saie, there was neuer thyng inuented
>   More worth, for mans solace to be frequented. (24–37)

He adds that the play also teaches 'godly Sapience' (47); instructs the ignorant 'what is true beleue' (53); offers 'an example of penance' (56); shows 'a loue which from Faith doth spring' (57); and affirms the 'Authoritie of Scripture' (58). Stressing the play's pedagogic value, its lessons of moral and religious worth, the Prologue defends *Mary Magdalene* against the charge of profiteering in particular:

> O (say they) muche money they doe get.
>   Truley I say, whether you geue halfpence or pence,
>   Your gayne shalbe double, before you depart hence. (42–44)

But in drawing attention to the 'halfpence or pence' paid by each member of the audience, The Prologue unwittingly likens the play to the pre-conversion Magdalene, who likewise extracts money from onlookers, thus extending the parallel between the pre-penitent Magdalene and abused images to include drama. So rather than overturning the concerns expressed by the play's detractors, The Prologue in fact substantiates some of their qualms; moreover it does so in terms that look forward directly to the anti-theatrical sentiment of the 1570s and 1580s.[80] In particular, the identification of players with 'unscrupulous merchants, engaging in economic exploitation', anticipates the condemnation by Stephen Gosson, the cleric and anti-theatrical polemicist, of theatres as 'the very markets of bawdry, where choise *with*out shame hath bene as free, as

---

[80] Whether real or imagined, the 'they' alluded to by the Prologue are the first recorded opponents to Tudor drama, predating the earliest of the anti-theatrical tracts by at least ten years. However, the condemnation of Catholicism as theatrical and of Catholic clerics as players is a charge recorded as early as 1531.

it is for your money in the royall exchaung'.[81] More generally, the implied inter-
rogation of the moral propriety of playing — the questioning of its reliance on
cross-dressing and its mixing of 'vertues with vice' (81) — foresees Gosson's
accusation that by taking on the 'signes of another', players 'falsifie, forge, and
adulterate, contrarie to the expresse rule of the worde of God'.[82]

Stephen Orgel has noted that the argument against transvestite actors warns
that male viewers 'will be seduced by the impersonation, and losing their reason
will become effeminate, which in this case means not only that they will lust
after the woman in the drama, which is bad enough, but also after the youth
beneath the woman's costume'.[83] This charge is forcefully made by Gosson, who
claims that, '[t]he diuel is not ignorant how mightely these outward spectacles
effeminate, & soften þe hearts of men, vice is learned with beholding, sense is
tickled, desire pricked, & those impressions of mind are secretly conueyed ouer
to þe gazers, which þe plaiers do counterfeit on þe stage.'[84] Characterizing plays
as 'outward spectacles' and audience members as 'gazers', Gosson stresses the
visual character of drama that is 'presented vp on the Stage'.[85] As O'Connell
has noted, 'several antitheatrical writers make the point that there is no harm
in reading plays — that the real danger comes from in the experience of seeing them performed on the stage'.[86] Certainly, this is the stance advanced by
Gosson when he argues that Gregory Nazianzus, a fourth-century theologian,
and George Buchanan, a contemporary Scots neo-Latin poet, penned their
books 'to be reade, not be played'.[87]

---

[81] White, *Theatre and Reformation*, p. 169; and Gosson, *Playes confuted in fiue actions*
([1582]; STC 12095), sig. G7ᵛ. White has convincingly proposed that these arguments against
the stage are predicated on 'Protestant teachings on divine vocation and stewardship'. He has
further suggested that some playwrights invoked such teachings to condemn social ambition
and acquisitiveness. In the 1580s and 1590s, 'within the context of theatrical commercialism,
these same notions were being applied to a new end', as the stage's opponents attacked professional players as glorified beggars who failed to contribute anything of any value to the common
welfare of the state. See White, *Theatre and Reformation*, p. 169. See also Bradbrook, *The Rise of
the Common Player*, p. 74; and Mullaney, *The Place of Stage*, p. 47.

[82] Gosson, *Playes confuted in fiue actions*, sig. E3ᵛ.

[83] Orgel, *Impersonations*, p. 29.

[84] Gosson, *Playes confuted in fiue actions*, sig. G4ʳ.

[85] Gosson, *Playes confuted in fiue actions*, sigs G4ʳ, E7ʳ.

[86] O'Connell, *The Idolatrous Eye: Iconoclasm and Theater*, p. 34.

[87] Gosson, *Playes confuted in fiue actions*, sig. E5ᵛ.

Although Wager's *Mary Magdalene* was clearly intended for performance, in its dramatization of the Magdalene's conversion, hearing and reading — word and text — are privileged over seeing and watching — image and spectacle. Referring repeatedly to the play's biblical source as the 'matter whiche we are about to *recite*' (52, my emphasis), the Prologue is keen to downplay the centrality of movement and action in the play's performance. So too is the title page to the first edition, which describes the play as an interlude 'very delectable for those which shall heare or reade the same' (p. 1). More generally, by staging her reformation as the exchange of decadent image for God's Word — bawdy playing for pious sermonizing — the play tries to redirect the audience's attention from sight to sound. Nonetheless, in the words of O'Connell, 'drama as an art requires both seeing and hearing', and in *Mary Magdalene* the attempt to textualize the action paradoxically confirms the spectacular power of stage presence.[88] Nowhere is this more apparent than in the final words of Knowledge of Sinne and Fayth. Limited in their movements, with speeches heavily indebted to Calvin's *Institutes*, both characters are envisaged as reformed exemplars of the Word. However, on exiting the playing space Fayth remarks: 'Though in person we shall no more appeare, | Yet inuisibly in your heart we we remayne' (1533–34), and Knowledge of Sinne declares:

> Though I appere not to hir carnall syght,
>   Yet by the meanes that she knoweth the lawe,
>   I shall trouble hir always both day and night,
>   And vpon hir conscience continually gnawe. (1305–08)

Claiming that their meaning will outlast their presence, Fayth and Knowledge of Sinne's words betray an anxiety that the exact opposite may in fact be true.

When the royal commissioners carried out the 1547 Visitation, they were instructed to:

> take awaie, vtterly extincte, and destroye, all shrines, coueryng of shrines, all tables, candelstickes, tryndilles or rolles of waxe, pictures, paintynges, and all other monumentes of fained miracles, pilgremages, Idolatry, and supersticion: so that there remain[n], no memory of thesame.[89]

In this chapter I have argued that Wager envisages the profligate Magdalene as a monument of 'fained miracles'. However, I have suggested that he rejects the

---

[88] O'Connell, *The Idolatrous Eye: Iconoclasm and Theater*, p. 35.

[89] Church of England, *Iniunccions geuen by the kynges maiestie*, sig. C2ᵛ.

iconoclastic subtext to the 1547 Injunctions, staging the Magdalene's conversion as the reformation of an image rather than its destruction. In the post-con-
version sequence, the sadly apparelled Magdalene, like the newly whitewashed
walls of churches around the country, provides a backdrop for the exposition
of the Word of God. Consequently, her conversion is paralleled by a change in
both subject matter, from bawdy apocrypha to scriptural truth, and dramatic
style, from impious buffoonery to serious proselytization.

The 1547 Injunction to destroy 'pictures, paintynges, and all other monumentes' recognizes that unless images are removed and destroyed people will
continue to remember them. In favouring reformation over removal, Wager
allows the memory of the pre-penitent Magdalene to pervade the post-conver-
sion sequence of his play. In fact, The Prologue's anxious defence of 'our fac-
ultie' is testimony to a wider anxiety about all stage presence. In the next and
final chapter I will explore these phenomenal pressures more fully, arguing that
the Edwardian eucharistic debate mediates in discussions about the iconicity
of drama.

Chapter 4

STAGED PRESENCE:
JACKE JUGELER AND THE EDWARDIAN
EUCHARISTIC CONTROVERSY

In 1566, students of Corpus Christi College, Oxford, mounted a production of Richard Edwards's *Palamon and Arcite*. Although the text does not survive, an extremely detailed account of the performance by Miles Windsor provides a clear indication of how the play was received. Windsor seems to perceive that the actors on stage are both themselves and representations of fictional characters. Describing Queen Elizabeth I's response to the performance, he says:

> When all the play was done, [Elizabeth I] called Mr Edwards, the maker thereof, and gave him great thanks with promise of reward. And afterwards her majesty gave unto one John Rainoldes, a scholar of Corpus Christi College who was a player in the same play, eight [g]old angels in reward. The Lady Emilia for gathering her flowers prettily in the garden and singing sweetly in the Prime of May, eight angels for a gracious reward.[1]

The passage appears to suggest that Elizabeth offers two rewards: eight angels each for John Rainolds, an actor, and Lady Emilia, a fictional character. However, the syntax is ambiguous, and it may be the case that Elizabeth offers only one reward: to John Rainolds for his portrayal of Lady Emilia. The sec-

---

[1] Oxford, Corpus Christi College, MS 257, fol. 121ʳ, quoted in King, 'Introduction', p. 80. Rainoldes would go on to become a vocal critic of commercial theatre. See pp. 147, 157.

ond sentence identifies the recipient of the angels as the sign vehicle, or actor, Rainolds; the third as the referent, or character, Emilia. Whether Windsor writes about one or two rewards, the passage suggests the absence of a standardized critical vocabulary. Should the dramatic commentator speak of actors or characters, players or roles? Windsor hedges his bet and refers to both.

As Bale and Wager discovered in their attempts to develop reformed stagecrafts, in all drama there exists a tension between the human reality of the performers and the semiotic element of the performance. An actor in a production is not merely 'like' the character he or she represents, but is in fact the same thing or at least the same *kind* of thing. Keir Elam has called this relationship 'iconic identity' and distinguishes it from the relationship between sign vehicle and referent in the other representational arts:

> The theatre is perhaps the only art form able to exploit what might be termed iconic *identity*: the sign-vehicle denoting a rich silk costume may well be a rich silk costume, rather than the illusion thereof created by pigment on canvas, an image conserved on celluloid or a description.[2]

In painting and cinema, the relationship between the sign vehicle and referent is purely iconic; the sign vehicle is an image that represents an absent referent.[3] In theatre, the relationship between sign vehicle and referent relies on both iconicity and identity; the sign vehicle, although very similar to the referent, still mediates its identity and meaning. To give Martin Carlson's example, in theatre 'a chair represents a chair and a glove, a glove, but also gestures, movements, words — the whole communicative machinery of our cultural life — appear on the stage in a form frequently indistinguishable from how they appear in daily life'.[4] In Michael O'Connell's words:

> Theatrical presence is not a mere sign but a use of corporeality to 'body forth' the fiction it portrays. Elements of stage performance – actors, their costumes and props – are not mere counters pointing semiotically to what they are not. Rather the actor playing the king is a man who portrays another man who was king.[5]

The semiotic process at work in drama is contingent on the observations of an audience. On the one hand, the audience's perception of the presence of signs

---

[2] Elam, *The Semiotics of Theatre and Drama*, pp. 22–23.

[3] I exclude Elam's third example, writing, because the sign vehicle/referent relationship is neither iconic (as it is for painting or cinema), nor one of iconic identity (as it is in drama).

[4] Carlson, *Theatre Semiotics: Signs of Life*, p. xiv.

[5] O'Connell, *The Idolatrous Eye: Iconoclasm and Theater*, p. 20.

will always mediate its understanding of the identity of whatever is presented on stage. On the other, the audience may also perceive 'that the fan held by the flirting lady in a Restoration comedy is actually a fan made in seventeenth-century England and thus recognize a true similarity in identity between the stage prop and the fictional object'.[6] '"Personation" is always in play', but there is an equal insistence on the value of the dramatic experience to move 'despite its mediated quality'.[7] In the previous two chapters, I suggested that it was the iconicity of drama that problematized the attempts made by John Bale and Lewis Wager to distinguish their own pious stagecrafts from the theatricality of their Catholic Vices. In this, the final chapter, I am interested in another play that foregrounds the relationship between presence and representation, between prop and object, and between actor and character; a play sometimes attributed to the reformed schoolmaster and playwright Nicholas Udall called *Jacke Jugeler* ([1562?]; STC 14873).[8] In dramatizing the attempt made by one character to steal the identity of another, *Jacke Jugeler* offers a dramatic illustration of the semiotic process at work in drama. This chapter begins with an exploration of the play's engagement with both the iconic and identical aspects of drama as exemplified by the characters of Jacke Jugler and Jenkin Careaway respectively. Although *Jacke Jugeler* was not printed until 1562, allusions to transubstantiation make it likely that the play was originally composed during the reign of Edward VI, when the Eucharist was the subject of a printed debate between Thomas Cranmer, archbishop of Canterbury, and the conservative Bishop of Winchester, Stephen Gardiner. In the second part of this chapter, these allusions are examined more fully. Refining the recent critical evaluation of the play as a veiled attack on transubstantiation, I argue that the play's treatment of stolen identity engages directly with contemporary debates about the correct interpretation of the words of institution: 'this is my body'.[9] The play's

---

[6] Houston, 'Transubstantiation and the Sign', p. 117.

[7] Dawson, 'Performance and Participation', in Dawson and Yachnin, *The Culture of playgoing*, pp. 11–37 (p. 26).

[8] Although Udall's name does not appear in any of the three extant editions of the play, the attribution has been convincingly argued by a number of critics. See 'Introduction', in *Three Tudor Classical Interludes*, ed. by Axton, pp. 1–33 (pp. 2–3, 21–23); Edgerton, *Nicholas Udall*, pp. 60–71; White, *Theatre and Reformation*, pp. 127–29; and Williams, 'The Date and Authorship of *Jacke Jugeler*'. For an alternative attribution see King, 'Introduction', pp. 13–15.

[9] '[H]oc est enim corpus meum.' The formula combines words from accounts of the Last Supper given in the Gospels of Mark, Matthew, and Luke, and the Pauline account in 1 Corinthians. For recent critical discussion of the play's anti-Catholicism see 'Introduction', in *Three Tudor Classical Interludes*, ed. by Axton, pp. 1–33 (pp. 19–20); Dean, '"Nothing that

title is also the name of its Vice, and the final section of this chapter examines the use, by reformed polemicists, of the words juggler and juggling to character- ize Catholic clerics and their rituals as excessively histrionic. I suggest that the established equation of transubstantiation with juggling in polemical tracts by Cranmer, Pietro Martire Vermigli (Peter Martyr), Thomas Becon, and John Bale may explain the decision to dramatize the arguments against the Catholic interpretation of the Eucharist. However, in contrast to the depiction of the Mass as drama by a number of influential early reformers, the men and women of Devon and Cornwall who rebelled against the introduction of the First Book of Common Prayer in 1549 compared Cranmer's reformed liturgy to 'a Christmas ga*m*me'.[10] More recently Julia Houston has argued that, 'Cranmer's discussion of the "special facility" of the eucharist as instructive conflates the iconographic concerns of the Mass with those of other didactic drama.'[11] Concluding this chapter, I argue that Jacke's iconic mode of self-presentation highlights similarities between drama and the reformed Lord's Supper and may suggest reasons why all drama, religious or otherwise, became the focus of dec- ades of virulent abuse.

Jacke Jugeler *and Iconic Identity*

The Roman playwright Plautus wrote approximately 130 plays, twenty-one of which survive to the present day. In the sixteenth century he was best known for his two comedies of mistaken identity, *Menaechmi* and *Amphitruo*. English adaptations of these, and other plays by Plautus, abound through the late six- teenth and early seventeenth centuries. They include Shakespeare's *Comedy of Errors* (*Menaechmi*) and *Twelfth Night* (*Amphitruo*) and Ben Jonson's *The Case is Altered* (*Aulularia* and *Captivi*). But *Jacke Jugeler*, a reworking of *Amphitruo*, is significantly earlier than any of these adaptations.[12] The play begins with

is So is So", pp. 281–83; Sedinger, "And yet woll I stiell saye that I am I'"; White, *Theatre and Reformation*, pp. 125–28; and Weimann, *Author's Pen and Actor's Voice*, pp. 117–19.

[10] L., R., *A Copye of a letter contayning certayne newes* (1549; STC 15109.3), sig. B7ʳ. The attribution is taken from the title page of the second edition, also issued in 1549 (STC 15109.7). The comparison occurs in a part of the text titled, 'The Articles of vs the Commoners of Deuonshyre and Cornewall in diuers Campes by East and Est of Excertor.' See sig. B6ʳ.

[11] Houston, 'Transubstantiation and the Sign', p. 129.

[12] Three editions of the play were printed in the sixteenth century: [Udall], *A new enterlued [...] named Jacke Jugeler* ([1562(?)]; STC 14837); [Udall], *A new enterlued [...] named Iacke Iugeler* ([1565?]; STC 14837a); and [Udall], *An enterlude [...] named Iack Iugler* ([c. 1570]; STC 14837a.5). For the dating of the play see below pp. 141–42.

The Prologue, who advertises the debt to Plautus and insists the play contains no serious matter and is designed only to make its audience 'merie and glad'.[13] The action then opens with a long speech from the roguish Vice, Jacke, a page, who reveals his plan to make Jenkin Careaway, the reprobate servant of Mayster Boungrace, believe 'That he is not him selfe, but an other man' (179). To this end he imitates Jenkin's dress and speech. Consequently, when Jenkin enters, complaining about his stern master and shrewish mistress, Dame Coye, Jacke both resembles and is able to recite all of Jenkin's movements. A farcical exchange follows, as Careaway becomes more and more frustrated at his inability to prove who he is. When Jacke finally leaves, Jenkin is in a state of total confusion about his own identity. In Douglas Bruster's words, Jenkin is left with no means of proving who he is: 'Juggler has appropriated his identity.'[14] In the scene that follows, Dame Coye enters with her maidservant, Ales Trype and Go, who tells her mistress that in his daily conversation and behaviour, Jenkin plays her 'many a lyke pranke' (661). When he enters, a few lines later, she is indifferent to his identity crisis and angrily sends him off to attend to Boungrace. At this point Jacke briefly re-enters to inform the audience that he has resumed his old identity, before leaving the playing space never to be seen again. In the next episode, Jenkin relates what has happened to him to his master, but Boungrace proves as unsympathetic a listener as his wife. Encouraged by Dame Coye who has now joined him in the playing space, Boungrace beats Jenkin for his wayward behaviour. They go off to dinner, leaving Jenkin to muse about the strange events that have befallen him. The play concludes with an Epilogue, who discourses on the subjects of truth and deception.

The opening scene of *Jacke Jugeler* teaches the audience to accept that actors are characters by presenting Jacke as an actor playing the part of Careaway. However, in doing so the audience becomes doubly aware of dramatic artifice. When Jacke reveals that he 'woll playe a jugling cast a non', he reminds the audience that the entire play is fiction presented as reality (107). Like an actor who puts on a costume before he goes on stage, Jacke's first move in his plot to impersonate Careaway is to assume his physical likeness:

> This garments, cape, and all other geare
> That now you see apon me here
> I have doon oon all like unto his (174–76)

[13] *Jacke Jugeler*, in *Three Tudor Classical Interludes*, ed. by Axton, pp. 64–93 (p. 66, l. 69). All further references are to this edition with line numbers given in parentheses within the text.

[14] Bruster, *Drama and the Market in the Age of Shakespeare*, p. 72.

The words are part of a lengthy speech of some one hundred lines made directly
to the audience. Strikingly, the entire speech comes before Careaway has made
his first entrance. The result is that the audience encounter Careaway's likeness before they encounter him. The point is strengthened by Jacke's report of
Careaway's most recent activity. The audience learns that Careaway has been
playing 'At the bukelers' (145) or fencing with shields, that he has stolen apples
'And put them in his sleve' (156), and 'Forgettyng his message' from Mayster
Boungrace to Dame Coye (162), he has been playing dice and 'lost almost all in
his porse' (165). Everything that the audience learns about Careaway is mediated
through the onstage presence of a character preparing to impersonate him. This
is true even of Careaway's language and manner of speech, which are also indicated by Jacke:

> [...] 'I must nides bee goon.
> My maister suppeth herbie, at a gentylmans place,
> And I must thither feache my dame, Maistres Boundgrace,
> But yet er I go, I care not motche
> At the bukelers to playe with the the oon faire toche.'
> To it they went, and plaied so long (141–46)

Careaway's lines are delivered to the audience by a character dressed in a disguise designed to resemble Careaway's natural attire. In this opening scene,
Jacke, a fictional character in the play *Jacke Jugeler*, foregrounds the iconic identity of his own drama by assuming the language, clothing, and immediate history of Careaway. He shows the audience that he is like, but not the same as,
his adversary. And just as the actor who plays the part of Jacke is a sign vehicle
representing the fictional character Jacke Jugler, Jacke figures himself as an actor
who represents the referent Jenkin Careaway.

   When Jacke and Careaway meet at line 330 a conflict develops over the
right to represent the referent Jenkin Careaway. Initially both characters claim
identity in relational terms. Jacke declares he is Jenkin Careaway because he is
Boungrace's servant, 'My maisters servaunt I am, for veritie' (399). Careaway
counters this claim by insisting, 'I am a servaunt of this house' (413). Both characters use a kind of syllogistic equation to prove their identity: 'I am a servant
of this house | Boungrace's servant. Jenkin Careaway is a servant of this house
| Boungrace's servant. Therefore I am Jenkin Careaway.' In this construction it
is not who one is, but what one is that confers identity. When this approach
fails to resolve the conflict, both characters assert identity by claiming the name
Jenkin Careaway. Careaway says 'I am Jenkin Carewaye' (440), to which Jacke
replies 'I am his Jenkin Carewaye' (467). However, with both characters insisting the name is theirs, the signifier 'Jenkin Careaway' is shown to bear an arbi-

trary relationship to the referent Jenkin Careaway. At this point Jacke baldly insists, 'I am he that thou saidest thou were' (480). Careaway's response is the simple, but emphatic, 'yet woll I steill saye that I am I' (497).

With name and occupation revealed as inadequate markers of identity, both characters attempt to construct selfhood grammatically. Jacke's assertion that 'I am he', joins the subjective pronoun 'I' to the subject complement 'he' by way of the verb 'to be'. 'He' is then qualified by the relative clause, 'that thou saidest thou were'. In this construction the verb 'to be' is deployed as a copula linking the subject 'I' to the predicate nominal 'he'. As such it does not itself express any action or condition, but rather serves to make the subject 'I' resemble the complement 'he'. Careaway's claim that 'I am I' is constructed in a very similar way. However, there are two distinctions. First the subject and predicate nominal are the same. This means that there is no need for a relative clause; the complement does not need to be defined because it is identical to the subjective pronoun. Secondly, the verb 'to be' in Careaway's statement of being is substantive as well as copulative. The 'am' joins the essential subject 'I' to the existential predicate 'I'. As Judith Anderson has noted in her discussion of the verb 'to be' in the words of institution, 'the translation from copulative to substantive *is* [...] reveals a historical instance in which the metaphorical potential within the verb *to be* is realized.'[15] In these terms, the grammar of Careaway's declaration reveals that he *is* Jenkin Careaway, whereas the grammatical construction of Jacke's assertion suggests that he is metaphorically Jenkin Careaway. Jacke's self-definition as a figure of Jenkin Careaway is iconic; he represents something that he is not. His statement, 'I am he', draws attention to dramatic artifice; Jacke is Jenkin Careaway in the same way an actor is a character. By contrast, Careaway's statement 'I am I' is one of likeness; he does not represent so much as present himself. His statement, although occasioned by the impersonation of a character by an actor, suggests that the character has displaced the person of the actor, that dramatic fiction has become reality.[16]

After Jacke's abrupt departure at 773, Careaway remains confused about how to distinguish himself from the person who looks, speaks, and acts like him. Attempting to explain himself to his master and mistress, he says:

[15] Anderson, 'Language and History in the Reformation', p. 27. She adds that there is an 'ambiguity inherent in the history of this verb [to be], not only in its relation to the nominal sentence but also in its subsequent relation to itself — two concepts of being, essential and existential, nominal and truly verbal, copulative and substantive, within it'. See p. 24.

[16] See Dawson, 'Performance and Participation', in Dawson and Yachnin, *The Culture of Playgoing*, pp. 11–37 (p. 29).

But I marvayll greatlye, by our lorde Jhesus,
How *he I* escapid, *I me* beat me thus.
And is not *he I* an unkind knave
That woll no more pytie on myselfe have?
Here may you see evydentlye iwis
That in *hym me* no drope of honestie is. (917–22)

The passage roughly corresponds with *Amphitruo* II. 2. 601–08. In Plautus's play Amphitruo's servant Sosia accounts for his wounds saying, 'Egomet memet, qui nunc sum domi.'[17] He identifies himself as 'memet', or 'me myself', the object of his speech, and his second self, Mercury, as 'egomet', or 'I myself', the subject. In *Jacke Jugeler*, Careaway's eccentric use of personal pronouns between lines 918 and 922 ensures that sense is contingent on the conventional position, rather than the appropriate inflection of words; it is the arrangement of subject before object that confirms Careaway has been beaten by Jacke.[18] However, while his meaning is unambiguous, Careaway's speech does highlight the representational doubleness occasioned by Jacke's impersonation of him.

'I me', 'he I', and 'hym me' are grammatical hybrids: 'I me' of case, 'he I' of person. 'He I' consists of two subjective pronouns and 'hym me' two objective pronouns, but both conflate the first with the third person. They correctly identify Jacke first as subject, then as object of the speech, but fail to differentiate between the speaker (the first person, Careaway) and the person spoken about (the third person, Jacke). Conversely, 'I me' is consistent in terms of person, but conflates subject with object, suggesting that perpetrator (the subject) and victim (the object) are identical. Careaway's speech is the result of the iconic identity between himself and the disguised Jacke. His confusion of person and case highlight the spectatorial perception of the fictional truth that Jacke is like, but not the same as, Careaway, and the theatrical truth that Jacke and Careaway are like, but not the same as, the actors that portray them.

Jacke Jugeler dramatizes the impersonation of one character, Jenkin Careaway, by another, Jacke Jugler. By attempting 'to make Jenkine bylive [...] | That he is not him selfe, but an other man', Jacke foregrounds the play's iconic identity. By assuming the language and costume of another character, Jacke

---

[17] *Amphitrvo*, in Plautus, *Comoediae*, ed. by Leo, I, 1–48 (p. 27, II. 2. 608). The quotation can be translated as follows, 'I myself, who am now at home, [beat] me myself.'

[18] It is perhaps worth noting that Latin, in contrast with English, is a fully inflected language. In English only pronouns still change their form (i.e. case) to show their grammatical function.

draws attention to the theatrical convention that an actor 'is' the character he represents. As Paul Dean has said of Shakespeare's adaption of *Amphitruo* as *Twelfth Night*, by dramatizing questions of mistaken identity, the play 'brings together the idea of an actor embodying a role and the relationship between the two elements in a metaphor'.[19] The same point is equally true of *Jacke Jugeler*, but the earlier play also encourages the audience to believe in the veracity of the actor's role, to believe that metaphorical reality is, in fact, literal reality. Given the play's mid-century date of composition, how does this representational doubleness engage with the contemporary theological debate about the correct interpretation of the sacrament of the Eucharist? To what extent does the *Jacke Jugeler*'s treatment of stage presence mediate in a more controversial discussion about the nature of Christ's presence in the Eucharist?

The Edwardian Eucharistic Controversy

Despite conventional disclaimers in the Prologue that *Jacke Jugeler* is simply a 'trifling matter' in which 'nothing but trifles may be had', critics have long acknowledged that the 'further meaning' alluded to by the Epilogue is the Eucharist (70, 68, 999). Dean has asserted that the play 'makes unambiguous allusions to transubstantiation'.[20] Paul Whitfield White has argued that 'the terms "juggler" and "juggling", had strong anti-Catholic overtones in Reformation England, and suggest compellingly that the play was intended to be polemical from the start.'[21] And Robert Weimann has noted, 'the Protestant equation, as practised by Cranmer and others, of "transubstantiation" with "juggling", and the use of "juggling" as interchangeable with "gaming", "playing", and "conjuring" is seized upon by the Vice, Jack Juggler.'[22] More recently, Tracey Sedinger has suggested that the play promotes disbelief in the real presence by exposing the logical flaws in the Catholic argument that a body can be in two places at once.[23] And noting reformed attacks on transubstantiation are often indebted to Aristotelian physics, William N. West has proposed that the play is a kind of experiment in the physics of performance.[24]

---

[19] Dean, '"Nothing that is So is So"', p. 289.

[20] Dean, '"Nothing that is So is So"', p. 281.

[21] White, *Theatre and Reformation*, p. 126.

[22] Weimann, *Author's Pen and Actor's Voice*, p. 117.

[23] Sedinger, '"And yet woll I stiell saye that I am I"'.

[24] West, 'What's the Matter in Shakespeare?'.

As all these critics note, the case for *Jacke Jugeler*'s anti-Catholicism rests largely on the association between juggling and Catholicism.[25] The eponymous Vice takes his name from the long established heterodox tradition of comparing Catholic priests with jugglers. The name first appears in the fourteenth-century alliterative poem *Piers Plowman*:

> Iakke the iogelour and Ionet of the stues
> And Danyel the dys-playere and Denote the baude
> And frere the faytour.[26]

In the poem, the name has not yet assumed its anticlerical associations, but Iakke is placed in the company with those wasters and cheats for whom Piers specifically refuses to provide food.[27] Though many manuscript copies of *Piers Plowman* were made in the fifteenth century, it was the Edwardian Reformation that seized the poem as a polemic against Rome. As Marie Axton has noted, 'three editions were issued in 1550 and soon broods of pamphlets were hatched bearing Piers' name.'[28] For instance, in the same year that *Piers* appeared in print, William Copland, the printer of the first two editions of *Jacke Jugeler*, brought out *A godly dialogue & dysputacion betwene Pyers plowman, and a popysh preest, concernyng the supper of the lorde* ([c. 1550]; STC 19903). A similar conceit is adopted in Luke Shepherd's dialogue between *John Bon and Mast Person* ([1548?]; STC 3258.5), in which a simple but honest ploughman is contrasted with a crafty, duplicitous priest:

> For thoughe I haue no learning yet I know chese from chalke
> And yche can perceiue your iuggling as crafty as ye walke.[29]

[25] Chambers distinguishes between 'the jugglers in the narrower sense, the *jouers des costeaux* who tossed and caught knives and balls, and the practitioners of sleight of hand, who generally claimed to proceed by *nigremance* or sorcery'. See Chambers, *The Mediæval Stage*, I, 71. For other meanings see 'Introduction', in *Three Tudor Classical Interludes*, ed. by Axton, pp. 1–33 (pp. 18–20).

[26] Langland, *The Vision of Piers Plowman*, ed. by Schmidt, p. 98, VI, ll. 74–76.

[27] The earliest text to equate clerics with jugglers that I have been able to trace is John Wyclif's tract *Of Prelates*, in which he writes that prelates 'bicomen þe deuelis iogelours to blynde mennus gostly eiȝen'. See *Of Prelates*, in Wycliffe, *The English Works [...] hitherto Unprinted*, ed. by Matthew, pp. 52–108 (p. 99).

[28] 'Introduction', in *Three Tudor Classical Interludes*, ed. by Axton, pp. 1–33 (p. 19).

[29] Shepherd, *John Bon and Mast person* ([1548?]; STC 3258.5), fol. 4ᵛ. Though the STC notes the attribution to Luke Shepherd, it gives the author as John Bon, but this name clearly refers to the book's title.

Here, natural reason is pitted against the '*crafty and sophistical cavillation*' of the Roman church.[30] A similar distinction is made by the Epilogue of *Jacke Jugeler* who fears that 'symple innosaintes ar deluded, | And [...] | By suttle and craftye meanes shamefullie abused' (1001–03). However, where John Bon is free to assert that he knows 'chese from chalk', the Epilogue describes how innocent men and women are 'compelled | To belive and saye: the moune is made of a grene chese, | Or ells have gret harme and percace their life lese' (1004–06).[31]

The reformed derogation of the Mass-priest as juggler is made more explicit in *The ressurreccion of the masse* (1554; STC 13457), which is frequently attributed to John Bale.[32] It describes the 'preste disgysed lyke one that wolde shewe some conueyaunce or iuglyng playe' and complains:

> To the good playne people ye turne your backes
> And playe many a pratye iugling caste,
> Brandon the iuglare had neuer goodlyer knackes
> Than ye haue at your masse, bothe fyrste and laste.[33]

The accusation that the priests 'playe many a prayte iugling caste' is also found in Udall's translation of Peter Martyr's *A discourse or traictise [...] concernynge the sacrament of the Lordes supper* ([1550]; STC 24665). Here Udall denounces 'such iugling castes, as þe aduersaies wold haue here in this matier of þe sacrament'.[34] Although there are no authorial marks in any of *Jacke*

---

[30] This phrase appears on the title page of Cranmer, *An answer of Thomas archebyshop of Canterburye* (1551), sig. A1ʳ. Hereafter *A* and placed with page references in parentheses in the text.

[31] Although he 'will name no man in particular', it has been suggested that the Epilogue's account of 'playne terani' is a reference to the Marian counter-Reformation, and that the play is a 'shrewdly executed satire on Marian Catholicism' (1039, 1048). See White, *Theatre and Reformation*, p. 125. See also Gayley, 'An Historical View of the Beginnings of English Comedy', p. lxxviii; and *Anonymous Plays: 3rd Series*, ed. by Farmer, pp. 278–79. It is my sense, however, that the play belongs to the Edwardian era, and that the Epilogue and perhaps the Prologue are later additions, possibly the work of a reformed reviser working during the reign of Mary I 'for a production before an audience of Protestant sympathizers (although the carefully guarded language would have protected him from charges of heresy)'. White, *Theatre and Reformation*, p. 125.

[32] Hilarie, *The resurreccion of the masse* (1554; STC 13457). The name Hughe Hilarie is otherwise unknown, and the question mark on the title page may imply the fictitiousness of the name. In any case, the tract is commonly attributed to Bale.

[33] Hilarie, *The resurreccion of the masse*, sig. B4ʳ.

[34] Vermigli, *A discourse or traictise [...] concernynge the sacrament of the Lordes supper*, trans. by Udall, sigs D1ᵛ–D2ʳ.

Jugeler's three editions, Udall has long been thought the most likely author. It is certainly plausible that he followed his translation of Martyr's treatise with a stage play exploring similar concerns. Moreover, Jacke's assertion that 'in fayth I woll playe a jugling caste a non' strikingly recalls Udall's condemnation of the Catholic church's 'iugling castes' (107).

Axton has noted a marginal jingle in a fifteenth-century book of homilies now in Clare College, Cambridge, that not only labels the Mass-priest a juggler, but also specifically compares the Catholic doctrine of transubstantiation to a juggling act:

> A Jack Juggelar that guggyll with a cake
> Etyng up fleche blode bonse I besh[r]ew your pate.[35]

Catholic orthodoxy maintains that with the utterance of the words of institution, the bread and wine cease to be bread and wine in their essence (or substance) and become the very body and blood of Christ, remaining bread and wine only in their outward appearance (or accidents). The jingle in the Clare manuscript expresses disbelief that the eating of the eucharistic 'cake' really involves '[e]tyng up fleche blode and bonse'.

In *Jacke Jugeler* there are a number of ways in which the thematic associations of juggling are employed in an attack on transubstantiation. Indeed, the subject matter taken, by the Prologue's own admission, from 'Plautus first commedie' (64), may have been suggested by an analogy between *Amphitruo* and transubstantiation made by Archbishop Thomas Cranmer in *An answer of Thomas archebyshop of Canterburye* ([1551]; STC 5991).

> [...] cal you not this illusion of our senses, when a thing apeareth to our senses, which is not the same thing in deed? When Jupiter and Mercury (as the comedy telleth) appeared to Alcumena in the similitude of Amphytrio and Sosia, was not Alcumena deceiued thereby? [...]Why then is not in the ministration of the holy communion an illusion of our senses, if our senses take for bread and wine that whiche is not so indeede. (*A* sigs EE1ᵛ–EE2ʳ).

Alcumena is duped by Jupiter and Mercury because her senses tell her that she is in the company of her husband and his slave. Similarly, if, as according to Catholic doctrine, Christ really is present in the Eucharist, then our senses must be deceived since all we see, touch, and taste is bread and wine. To put it another way, using *Amphitruo* to illustrate his point, Cranmer argues that a

---

[35] Cambridge, Clare College Libr., MS 13, fol. 36ᵛ, cited in 'Introduction', in *Three Tudor Classical Interludes*, ed. by Axton, pp. 1–33 (p. 19).

theology predicated on a difference or separation between appearance and reality, between accidents and substance must necessarily rely on deceit and consequently must be false. But his comparison of *Amphitruo* to transubstantiation is appropriate for more reasons than their shared programme of deception by illusion. In *Amphitruo* the appearance of Jupiter and Mercury in the guise of Amphitruo and Sosia leads to the fictive possibility of two Amphitruos and two Sosias: the real Amphitruo and Jupiter dressed as Amphitruo; and the real Sosia and Mercury dressed as Sosia. In his reply to Cranmer's *A defence*, which was printed in Rouen under the title *An explicatio[n] and assertion of the true catholique fayth* (1551; STC 11592), Stephen Gardiner, conservative bishop of Winchester, affirms Christ's presence in both heaven *and* the sacrament:

> The churche acknowledgeth, beleueth, and teacheth truely, that Christ sytteth on the right hande of his father in glory, from whence he shall come to iudge the world, & also teacheth Christes very body & bloud, & Christ himselfe God & man, to be present in the Sacrament, not by shiftyng of place, but by the determination of his will.[36]

Cranmer attacks this very point of Catholic doctrine in *A defence of the true and catholike doctrine of the sacrament of the body and bloud of our sauiour Christ*. He says:

> And a thousand thynges mo, of lyke foolishnesse doo the Papistes affirme by their Transubstantiation, contrary to all nature and reason. As that two bodies bee in one place, and one body in many places at one tyme, [...] with many suche lyke thynges, agaynst all order and principles of nature and reason.[37]

Cranmer expresses disbelief in two ideas implicit to the Catholic doctrine of transubstantiation: that numerous bodies can be in one place; and that one body can be in many places. Similar criticism is found in a number of other Protestant writings, and it seems likely the argument derives from Calvin; certainly the point is made explicit in his *Institutes*, which states that it defies both Scripture and reason to conceive of 'a twoo bodyed Christ, that the same he maye lurke hidden vnder bred, which sitteth visible in heauen'.[38] In his tract, *The display-*

---

[36] Gardiner, *An explicatio[n] and assertion of the true catholique fayth*, sig. D4ʳ. Hereafter *E* and placed with page references in parentheses in the text.

[37] Cranmer, *A defence of the true and catholike doctrine of the sacrament*, sig. F1ᵛ. Hereafter *D* and placed with page references in parentheses in the text.

[38] Calvin, *The institution of christian religion* (1561; STC 4415), trans. by Norton, IV. 17. 28, fol. 131ʳ. The final folio of this edition of *The institution* is signed T. N., for Thomas

ing of the popish masse (STC 1719), written around the middle of the sixteenth century but not printed until 1637, Becon complains that, 'it is directly against the veritie and truth of Christs naturall body, to bee at more places at once than in one, as hee must be in an hundred thousand places at once, if your doctrine bee true.'[39] And the Black Rubric inserted by order of the Privy Council into the 1552 Book of Common Prayer prohibited adoration of the consecrated bread and wine because 'they remayne styll in theyr very naturall substaunces, and therefore maye not be adored, for that were Idolatrie to be abhorred of all fayth-ful Christians. And as concerninge the naturall body and bloud of our sauiour Christ, they are in heauen and not here: for it is agaynste the trueth of Christes true natural body, to be in moe places then in one at one tyme.'[40]

The tone of incredulity that marks all these examples is found in equal pro-portion in *Jacke Jugeler*. When Careaway attempts to account for his 'other I', Boungrace exclaims with exasperated disbelief (753):

> Why thou naughtye vyllayne! darest thou affirme to me
> That which was never syne nor hereafter shalbe?
> Than on man may have too bodies and two faces?
> And that one man at on time may be in two placys? (784–87)

A number of critics have read Boungrace's words as an attack on transubstantia-tion. As White comments, 'an audience familiar with the theological dispute

---

Norton the translator. Norton's text is a translation of the Calvin's final Latin edition of 1559. In the Latin original, the relevant passage reads: 'satis ostendit se Christum bicorporem non fingere, ut occultus sub pane lateat qui in caelo visibilis sedet.' See Calvin, *Institutio Christianae religionis* (1559), IV. 17. 28, unpaginated. The text of the 1559 edition expanded and revised the preceding four editions which were published in 1536, 1539, 1543, and 1550. Although there is no explicit reference to God's two bodies in the earliest editions, in all five editions Calvin condemns the subtle evasion of those who argue that 'this body which is set forth in the Sacrament is glorious and immortal; therefore, there is nothing absurd if under the Sacrament it is contained in several places, in no place, or in no form'. See Calvin, *Institutes of the Christian Religion*, ed. by McNeill, IV. 29, p. 105. This passage appears in the Norton's translation of the 1559 edition at IV. 17. 17, fol. 125[r] as follows: 'this body whiche is geuen in the Sacrament is glorious and immortall: and that therfore it is no absurditie, if it bee conteined in many places, if in no place, if with no forme, vnder the sacrament.'

[39] Becon, *The displaying of the Popish masse*, pp. 192–93.

[40] Church of England, *The booke of common prayer*, sig. M.8[r]. The Black Rubric, or the Declaration on Kneeling as it was officially called, was inserted into the 1552 Book of Common Prayer at the last minute (see, for instance, STC 16288). In the earliest printings, it was either omitted, as in STC 16280.5, or inserted as a separate leaf, as in STC 16279. However, in the imprint I quote from, the entire Black Rubric is incorporated into the body of the text.

could hardly miss the additional significance of Mayster Boungrace's outburst.'[41] Certainly Boungrace's remarks seem to support the reformed contention that the *body* of Christ ascended to heaven at the resurrection and will not return to this world until the Second Coming, and consequently it defies 'verity and truth' 'that one man at on time may be in two placys'. However, to my knowledge, no critic has identified the immediate source of Boungrace's speech, nor has it been acknowledged how his speech can help in the dating of the play.

Boungrace dismisses Careaway's claim, that some 'other I is now your page | And I am no longer in your bondage', for two reasons (744–45): first, because it is impossible for one man to have two bodies; and secondly, because it is impossible for one man to be in more than one place at one time. Disbelief in the idea that one man can be in two places is common to all mid-Tudor attacks on the doctrine of transubstantiation. However, the notion that 'twoo bodyes cannot bee togyther in one place by the rules of nature' is found only in Cranmer's work (*A* sig. 2ᵛ). Cranmer's *A defence* was originally printed in London in 1550 by Reginald Wolfe. François Philippe's French translation, *Defence de la vraye et catholique doctrine du sacrement du corps & sang de nostre sauueur Christ* (STC 6003.5), was published in London two years later by Thomas Gualtier. In 1553 Wolfe brought out an edition of John Cheke's Latin translation under the title, *Defensio verae et catholicae doctrinae de sacramento corporis & sanguinis Christi seruatoris nostri* (STC 6004). The Swiss printer, Egidius van der Erve produced an edition of the same Latin translation in 1557 in Geneva. *An Answer* ran to two editions: Wolfe's 1551 edition; and John Day's edition of 1580 (STC 5992). It is unsurprising that these staunchly reformed texts were not printed in England for the duration of Mary I's reign. Moreover, the 1557 edition of *A defence* reflects the well-documented fact that a significant number of England's reformers spent the Marian era in self imposed exile on the Continent. Although it is likely that copies of these two works by Cranmer would have been available during Mary I's reign, the Geneva imprint of *A defence* reflects their controversial status at this time. Consequently, the publication of *A defence* in 1550 provides a definite terminus a quo for the composition of *Jacke Jugeler* and the ascension of Queen Mary in 1553 provides a plausible terminus ad quem.

An Edwardian date of composition is supported by clues about the play's original auspices embedded in the text. The title page to the first edition announces that it is 'a new enterlued for chyldren to playe', and this is confirmed by allusions to 'litle boyes handelings', 'a boye', and 'all other boyes' within the

---

[41] White, *Theatre and Reformation*, p. 127. See also Dean, '"Nothing that is So is So"', pp. 282–83; and Weimann, *Author's Pen and Actor's Voice*, p. 117.

play proper (sig. A1ʳ, 76, 105, 124).⁴² References to London —'within London wall', and 'Not all in London can shewe suche other twoo' — suggest that the play was originally intended for a London performance (117, 225). The most likely players for a play of this nature would be the Children of St Paul's, the Children of the Chapel, the boys of Eton College, where Udall, the play's most likely author, was headmaster during the 1530s, or the boys of Westminster, where he held the same post from 1554 to his death in 1556. The overt references to the well-rehearsed arguments against the Catholic theory that one man may 'be in more places at once than in one' make the play unsuitable for an original grammar school production during the Marian reign and consequently situate *Jacke Jugeler* at the end of the Edwardian era, probably to the either 1551 or 1552, making it a direct comment on, rather than a belated response to, the late-Edwardian eucharistic controversy.

Arguing that it defies sense for someone to be in two places at once, the reformers claim that their arguments against the Catholic Mass are ordained by nature and reason. Consequently, they frequently adopt the persona of the simple country labourer when expressing their views. This is clearly the case in the popular dramatic dialogues *John Bon and Mast Person* and *Pyers Plowman and a popysh preest* ([*c.* 1550]; STC 19903), in which an honest rustic debates against a crafty representative of the Catholic Church. In Cranmer's *Answer*, the interpolation of whole sections of his earlier work, *A Defence*, and the entire argument of Gardiner's *An Explicatio[n]* advances a similar effect. The treatise reads like a gregarious conversation or play script with each argument assigned to either 'Caunterbury' or 'Winchester' in much the same way that the speeches in *Jacke Jugeler* are allocated to either 'Jacke' or 'Careaway':⁴³

> For is it not plainly written of all the Papists, both lawyers and schole authors, that the body of Christ in the sacrament is made of breade, and his bloude of wyne. And they say not that his body is made present of bread & wyne, but is made of bread and wyne. (*A* sig. I3ᵛ)

Like John Bon in his dialogue with Mast Person and Pyers Plowman in his with a 'popysh preest', Cranmer assumes the position of the 'poore semple innocent', casting Gardiner as the sophistic 'schole author' (1012): 'you saye, that Christ

---

⁴² The assertion is repeated on the title pages of the two later editions.

⁴³ Shepherd, *John Bon and Mast person*, fol. 2ʳ. In *An Answer*, it is in fact Cranmer who accuses Gardiner of making '(as it were) a playe in a dialogue, between a rude man and a learned scholer'. However, Cranmer is quick to point out that, 'the matter is so learnedly handled, that the simple rude man sheweth himself to haue mire knowledge, then both you and your learned scholar.' Cranmer, *An answer of Thomas archebyshop of Canterburye* (1551), sig. DD6ᵛ.

gaue that he had consecrated, and that he made of breade, here you graunt that Christes body (whiche he gaue to his disciples at his last supper) was made of bread' (*A* sig. CC5ʳ).

The accusation that 'the body of Christ in the sacrament is made of breade' follows from Cranmer's disavowal of the idea that the accidents, or the outward appearance of bread and wine, can exist without bearing any visible relationship to the substance, or the body and the blood of Christ. It is 'agaynst all order and principles of nature and reason' to believe that accidents and substance can have separate and distinct identities (*D* sig. F1ᵛ). Consequently, when the conservatives claim that 'the body of Christ is really in the sacrament vnder the fourme of bread', Cranmer and his followers insist that form and substance being the same, Christ must be made of bread (*A* sig. G3ᵛ). However, Catholic doctrine maintains that though the bread continues to look and taste like bread, its substance is transformed into the body of Christ. In contrast, most reformers held that the words of institution do not inculcate any substantial transformation. 'The anxiety about the possibility of material transformation becomes effaced and ameliorated when attackers resort to the more comforting accusation that such ritual is simply a performative act without material efficacy.'[44] Instead, they argued that consecration turned the bread and wine into efficacious figures for the body and blood of Christ. In Cranmer's words, 'the bread and wyne bee called *examples* of Christes fleshe and bloud' (*D* sig. P4ʳ, my emphasis).

Anderson has noted that, 'perhaps the crucial difference is that for the conservatives, the translation is objective and real, whereas for the reformers, transubstantiation occurs only in language.'[45] In Catholic doctrine, 'the bread and wine do not "represent" the body and blood: they *are* the body and blood.'[46] In Cranmer's version of the Lord's Supper, 'a miracle of coming into presence does not occur, so the sacraments remain signs after consecration.'[47] Catholic interpretation makes the bread identical to the body of Christ, whereas the reformed interpretation maintained that the bread represented the body of Christ. The difference, as Theodore Beza flatly notes, is between transubstantiation and a trope.[48] In *Jacke Jugeler*, Jacke transforms himself into Jenkin

---

[44] Brunning, 'Jonson's Romish Foxe', p. 19.

[45] Anderson, 'Language and History in the Reformation', p. 29.

[46] Dean, '"Nothing that is So is So"', p. 284.

[47] Houston, 'Transubstantiation and the Sign', p. 129.

[48] Theodore Beza quoted in Pelikan, *The Christian Tradition*, IV: *Reformation of Church and Dogma (1300–1700)* (1984), p. 201. Stephen Greenblatt has suggested that, 'the eucha-

Careaway. Weimann has noted that, 'for a sixteenth-century performer, "to transubstantiate" could — in addition to either its theological meaning or its pejorative connotation of "juggling" — also have the secular meaning recorded in the *O[xford] E[nglish] D[ictionary]*, of "to transform, transmute"'.[49] Just as the bread transubstantiates into the body of Christ, Jacke transubstantiates into the body of Jenkin Careaway. Consequently, Jacke embodies an attack on the Catholic doctrine of transubstantiation. He dupes Careaway into believing in the existence of an 'other I', just as the reformers insist that the Papists dupe their congregants into believing that Christ 'is truely present, & therefore in substaunce present' (*E* sig. D4ʳ). However, Jacke's transformation, unlike Catholic transubstantiation, is one of accidents, not substance. Like an actor dressing up as a character and performing a role, he takes on the appearance of Jenkin Careaway, whilst remaining substantially Jacke Jugler. To the audience, who know that Jacke has assumed the likeness of Jenkin Careaway from the play's opening — 'This garments, cape, and all other geare | That now you see apon me here | I have doon oon all like unto his' (174–76) — Jacke is a figure for Boungrace's page in much the same way that the Reformers' sacramental bread is a figure for Christ's flesh.

As I noted in the previous section, the confrontation between Jack and Careaway between lines 331 and 601 is littered with an abundance of 'I am' sayings. When Careaway says 'I am I' his words directly recall God's self naming in Exodus 3. 14 (497).[50] God's statement of self-definition, 'I am that I am', indicates a state of existence independent of anything or anybody else.[51] As

---

ristic formula for the bread and wine [...] is a figure of speech, specifically, a metonym in which "the sign borrows the name of the truth that it figures"'. See Greenblatt, 'The Mousetrap', p. 146, quoting from Cottret, 'Pour une sémiotique de la Réforme', p. 268. However, Sarah Beckwith is right to acknowledge that 'the English Church's reformed communion still retains a version of presence and is utterly opposed to bare memorialism'. See Beckwith, 'Stephen Greenblatt's *Hamlet* and the Forms of Oblivion', p. 254. For Cranmer the bread and wine are not simple tropes, but efficacious signs: 'also they be called his *very* fleshe and blode, to signifie vnto vs, that as they feade vs carnally, so do they admonishe vs that Christe with this fleshe and bloud doth feade vs spiritually, and moste truely vnto euerlastyng life' (*D* sig. P4ʳ, my emphasis). In Cranmer's writings the linguistic figures of the bread and wine have an internal effect: 'figuratiuely [Christ] is in the breade and wyne, and spiritually he is in them that worthyly eate and drinke the bread and wyne, but really, carnally, and corporally he is onely in heauen' (*D* sig. T3ʳ).

[49] Weimann, *Author's Pen and Actor's Voice*, p. 117.

[50] Henry Janowitz catalogues some Shakespearian examples. See Janowitz, 'Exodus 3. 14 as the Source'.

[51] 'I am that I am' is the traditional rendering of the Hebrew *ehyeh asher ehyeh*. Ancient

Dean has recently noted, 'God can say "I am what I am" because his essence and his existence are one; there is no analogy, no tenor or vehicle, in the absoluteness of his being.'[52] Careaway's statement belies the truth that he is a fictional character represented by an actor playing a part. His statement is an attempt to communicate the idea that, like God in Exodus, his essence and existence are one. Conversely, when Jacke says 'I am Jenkyne Careawaye' his words evoke the 'I am' sayings of Jesus in St John's Gospel, some of which are cited by Cranmer against his adversary, Gardiner. Jesus's 'I am' sayings are metaphorical: 'he is the vine, but not *a* vine; the lamb, but not a lamb; the living bread which came down from Heaven, but not bread itself':[53]

> And Christ hym selfe often tymes spake in similitudes, parables, and figures, as whan he said: The field is the worlde, the enemy is the dyuell, the sede is the worde of God [...]. These with an infinite numbre of like sentences, Christe spake in Parables, Metaphores, tropes and figures. But chiefly whan he spake of the sacramentes, he vsed figuratiue speches. (*D* sig S.iii^v–S.iv)

Cranmer insists that the words of institution are figurative speech. He writes 'whe*n* Christ said, This is my body, it was bread he called his body' (*A* sig. N1^r). In Cranmer's opinion the verb 'to be' is a simple copulative joining the sign vehicle, the bread, to the referent, Christ's body, in much the same way that 'is', in Jacke's statements of self naming, join the sign vehicle, Jacke, to the referent, 'Jenkin Careaway'. Consequently, if *Jacke Jugeler* was written as an allegorical attack on duplicitous Roman priests and their baffling, incomprehensible rituals, its eponymous Vice represents himself in language that approaches rather too closely Cranmer's interpretation of the Eucharist.

In the late Edwardian era the terms 'juggler' and 'juggling' were used by reforming theologians and popular pamphleteers alike to deride the Mass-priest as 'one who plays tricks by sleight of hand', and transubstantiation as 'cheating, deceptive'.[54] But in addition to conveying describing 'one who deceives by trick-

---

Hebrew does not have past, present, or future tenses. Instead, it has imperfective and perfective aspects as indicators of time, with no actual determined time. *Ehyeh* is in the imperfective aspect and can be understood as God saying that he is 'in the process of being'; in other words, his work is not yet complete and may never be complete.

[52] Dean, '"Nothing that is So is So"', p. 286.

[53] Dean, '"Nothing that is So is So"', p. 286.

[54] 'juggler, 2.', in *The Oxford English Dictionary*, 2nd edn, <http://dictionary.oed.com/cgi/entry/50124577> [accessed 5 June 2013]; and 'juggling, *ppl. a.*', in *The Oxford English Dictionary*, 2nd edn, <http://dictionary.oed.com/cgi/entry/50124581> [5 June 2013].

ery; a trickster; one who plays fast and loose', the word 'juggler' also describes 'a *performer* of legerdemain'.[55] To put it another way, the terms 'juggler' and 'juggling' belong to a dramatic critical lexis which was frequently deployed by writers to deride Catholic practice and ritual as theatrical. In the final part of this chapter I want to explore the use of the term 'juggling' by reformed polemicists to characterize Catholicism as excessively histrionic. I will argue that these associations between juggling and drama may elucidate the decision to dramatize the arguments against transubstantiation. But I will also suggest that if *Jacke Jugeler* was designed as an attack on the Mass as drama, its own semiotic process uncomfortably replicates the semiotic process of the Lord's Supper.

Drama as Metaphor

The identification of 'juggling' with 'the art of tossing and catching a number of objects continuously' is a recent development from the sense 'one who works marvels' as the specific skill gained recognition as a form of entertainment distinct from conjuring.[56] In the sixteenth century the word 'juggling', in addition to its pejorative employ by reformers, was used interchangeably with 'gaming', 'playing', and 'conjuring', and the term 'juggler' often used to describe the Vice of interlude drama. Axton notes that the identification of 'juggler' with a Vice is made explicit by John Higgins in 1585:

> mimus: a vice in a plaie, a jester, a juggler or a merrie conceited fellow.[57]

The conception of juggling as a mode of dramatic display is commonly used by reformers to bolster the equation between Catholicism and theatricality and to deride the Mass as a piece of drama. For instance, in his dedicatory epistle to the earl of Essex which prefaced his translation of Peter Martyr's eucharistic tract, Udall denounces 'the iugleyng sleyghtes of Romysh Babylon' claim-

---

[55] 'juggler, 2.', in *The Oxford English Dictionary*, 2nd edn, <http://dictionary.oed.com/cgi/entry/50124577> [accessed 5 June 2013].

[56] 'juggling, *vbl. n.*', *Oxford English Dictionary Additional Series* (1997) <http://dictionary.oed.com/cgi/entry/5012480> [accessed 5 June 2013]; and 'juggler, 2', *The Oxford English Dictionary*, 2nd edn, <http://dictionary.oed.com/cgi/entry/50124577> [2 January 2012]. Juggling in our sense of the word as tossing and catching balls or pins does not appear until 1836 when a handbill of attractions at Vauxhall Gardens advertises 'Double Juggling'.

[57] 'Introduction', in *Three Tudor Classical Interludes*, ed. by Axton, pp. 1–33 (p. 18), citing Junius, *The nomenclator, or remembrancer*, trans. by Higgins (1585; STC 14860), fol. 15ʳ.

ing that Catholic ritual is deceptive and thus performative.[58] Similarly John
Jewel objects to the 'scenic apparatus' of Catholic worship, while John Rainolds
worries that the priests 'have transformed the celebrating of the Sacrament of
the *Lords supper* into a *Masse-game*, and all other parts of *Ecclesiaticall service*
into *theatricall sights* so, in steede of *preaching the word*, they caused it to be
played'.[59] Becon likewise complains that the Catholic clergy, dressed in 'gay,
gawdie, gallant, gorgious gameplayers garments', come to their altars 'as a game-
player unto his stage'.[60] And Cranmer compares the Catholic liturgy to a play
script supplied to the player-priest who 'ha[s] forgotten his part' (*A* sig. I3ᵛ).

Casting Jacke as the archetypal Vice, the play makes explicit the connection
between juggling, dramatic display, and reformed attacks on transubstantiation.[61] Like the stage Vices discussed in the previous two chapters, Jacke is likened to an actor who pretends to be someone else in order to delude innocent
people. And, like Bale's Vices, 'he may be dressed in the likeness of a Catholic
priest at his first entrance before changing into Careaway's servant attire, if
the woodcut on the title page of the play's first edition is any indication.[62]
Usurping the looks, habits, and identity of Careaway, Jacke turns the play into
a gleeful display of counterfeiting, masquerading, role playing, and disguise,
which evokes both conventional reformed sleights on the doctrine of transubstantiation and modern theories about drama as a representational practice. As
Weimann has noted, 'to think of "transubstantiation" as transforming one's self
into a role and, vice versa, a role into one's own, presenting self, was to moralize
more than two meanings in one word, and it was contrariously to foreground
the craft and craftsmanship of playing *qua* juggling.'[63] To put it another way,
Jacke embodies both an attack on the doctrine of transubstantiation and a powerful illustration of the semiotics of drama.

[58] Vermigli, *A discourse or traictise [...] concernynge the sacrament of the Lordes supper*, trans.
by Udall, sig. *2ᵛ.

[59] 'John Jewel to Peter Martyr', in *The Zurich Letters* ed. and trans. by Robinson, I (1842),
23–25 (p. 23), quoted in Barish, *The Antitheatrical Prejudice*, p. 162. Rainolds, *Th'ouerthrow of
stage-playes* (1599; STC 20616), p. 161, cited in Barish, *The Antitheatrical Prejudice*, pp. 162–63.
Rainolds's comments are striking in light of his acting experience. See above, pp. 127–28.

[60] Becon, *The displaying of the Popish masse*, pp. 77, 70.

[61] For a list of typical Vice traits see 'Introduction', in *Three Tudor Classical Interludes*, ed. by
Axton, pp. 1–33 (pp. 18–19).

[62] White, *Theatre and Reformation*, p. 127.

[63] White, *Theatre and Reformation*, p. 117.

However, although well-attested sixteenth-century opinion construed the Roman service as theatrical, there is contemporary evidence to suggest that some Catholics criticized the dramatic qualities of the reformed Lord's Supper. In addition to the accusation that 'the new service [...] is but like a Christmas game', Gardiner labels Cranmer a 'scoffer' and suggests his doctrine is equivalent to an act of dramatic buffoonery 'to supply when his felowe had forgotten his parte' (*E* sig. E5ʳ). However, these attacks are fairly generic and fail to isolate *how* Communion approaches drama. As I have already argued, the late Edwardian reformed interpretation of the sacrament of the Eucharist in general, and the words of institution in particular, places emphasis on figurative, as opposed to real, presence. In Cranmer's words, 'Christe, knowing vs to be in this world (as it were) but babes and weakelynges in faith, hath ordeined sensible signes and tokens, wherby to allure and drawe vs to more strengthe and more constaunt faith in hym' (*D* sig. C2ᵛ–C3ʳ). Houston categorizes this interpretation of the sacrament of the Eucharist as theatrical, suggesting that Cranmer's treatment of 'the sacraments wholly as signs [...] stresses the iconic properties of the wine and bread themselves', thus turning 'the "miracle" of the Lord's Supper into a dramatic presentation'.[64] Claiming iconicity for the bread and wine, Houston asserts that Cranmer's interpretation of the eucharistic rite suggests a link between sign vehicle (bread or wine) and referent (body or blood) that is similar to the relationship between an actor and the role that he performs. Strikingly, a number of reformed commentators seem to have been aware of the parallel between their version of eucharistic presence and dramatic self-presentation and are at pains to separate their own interpretation of the sacrament, a figure, from a merely fictive one, 'a bare signe or a figure' such as 'a vile persone gorgiouslye apparailled maye represent a kyng or prince in a playe'.[65] The figures of the bread and wine, stresses Udall in his translation of Martyr, are 'not like to thynges signifyed in a comedie or tragedie. For in suche enterludes, any of the players beyng disguised in his players apparell maye represente the persone of Hector or Priamus [...] but whan he hathe plaied his parte he is the same man that he was before.'[66]

In *Jacke Jugeler* the impersonation of Jenkin Careaway by Jacke Jugler foregrounds the iconic element of drama and reminds the audience that the representation of Jenkin Careaway by Jacke is performed by an actor who represents

---

[64] Houston, 'Transubstantiation and the Sign', p. 113.

[65] Ridley, *A brief declaracion of the Lordes supper* ([1555]; STC 21046), sig. A7ʳ.

[66] Vermigli, *A discourse or traictise [...] concernynge the sacrament of the Lordes supper*, trans. by Udall, sig. D1ᵛ.

Jacke. This aligns the play with the iconic features of Cranmer's interpretation
of the eucharistic sacrament. In contrast, plays which foreground the identical
aspect of drama and which encourage the audience to believe in 'the value and
meaning of theatrical experience itself' have much in common with Cranmer's
understanding of transubstantiation as deceptive.[67] But if *Jacke Jugeler* was
intended as an allegorical attack on transubstantiation it must be admitted that
on some levels it fails. Certainly, the play's assimilation of reformed associations of the words 'juggler' and 'juggling', Jacke's plot to 'playe a jugling cast',
and Boungrace's disbelief in the idea that 'one man at on time may be in two
placys', aligns the play with those English reformers who categorized priests
as conjurors and transubstantiation as both deceptive and incredible (107,
787). However, Jacke's impersonation of Jenkin Careaway and his metaphorical statements of self naming closely resemble the role of the bread and wine
in the Lord's Supper and Cranmer's interpretation of the words of institution. Consequently the play draws attention to the theatrical qualities of the
Communion service that reformers like Nicholas Ridley, Martyr, and Udall
were so keen to downplay or dissemble.

   In the 1570s and 1580s a spate of anti-theatrical pamphlets appeared with
titles such as *A tretise wherein dicing, dauncing, vaine playes or enterluds with
other idle pastimes [et]c. commonly vsed on the Sabboth day, are reproued by the
authoritie of the word of God and auntient writers* ([1577?]; STC 18670), and
*The schoole of abuse, conteining a plesaunt [sic] inuectiue against poets, pipers,
plaiers, iester, and such like caterpillers of a co[m]monwelth* (1579; STC 12097)
Most of these works featured drama as one of a range of unsavoury activities that
included dancing, gaming, dicing, and conjuring, all of which can be classified
as 'juggling' in the Tudor sense of the word. It is striking to observe that *Jacke
Jugeler*, a play that attempts to inveigh against the deceptive, theatrical nature of
the Catholic Mass, opens with a list of pursuits, all of which are proscribed by the
anti-theatricalists. Careaway has been 'Pricking, praunsing, and springing in his
short cote', 'At the bukelers to playe', 'snatching [...] an apple, [...] and put[ting]
them in his sleve', and playing with dice, and all while he should be fetching his
mistress for supper (138, 145, 154–56). His actions read like a litany of Stephen
Gosson's 'abuses' or John Northbrooke's 'idle pastimes' and overall seem to support the pejorative association of the Mass with theatre.[68]

---

[67] Dawson, 'Performance and Participation', in Dawson and Yachnin, *The Culture of
Playgoing*, pp. 11–37, (p. 26).
[68] Gosson, *The shoole [sic] of abuse*; Northbrooke, *Spiritus est* ([1577?]; STC 18670).

Michael O'Connell has commented that 'the religious preoccupation with what theater is, both the worry that theater is idolatry and the characterization of the "idolatry" of Catholic worship as theater, goes some way toward explaining the extraordinary vehemence of the antitheatrical rhetoric and why the writers could not be satisfied with mere reform of the conditions of playing.'[69] Certainly, the activities condemned by the anti-theatricalists can be typified as fraudulent in much the same way as reformers like Tyndale, Bale, and Cranmer classified Catholic worship as deceptive. However, as Houston has noted, 'Cranmer's emphasis on the Eucharist's iconicity and his denial of identity puts the Eucharist in the same category of religious objects used to communicate to the spectator through iconic indicators: the category of icons.'[70] Consequently, a stage tradition that similarly emphasizes iconicity and denies, or at least downplays, identity, can but highlight those features of the reformed religion that approach both theatricality and idolatry.[71]

In his opening speech, Jacke Jugler explains why he intends to impersonate Jenkin Careaway:

> This Jenkine and I been fallen at great debate
> For a mattier that fell betwine us a late
> And hitherto of him I could never revengid bee
> For his maister mentainyth him and lovethe not mee; (118–21)

Between 1551 and 1553, when *Jacke Jugeler* was being written, *the* 'great debate' was over the 'mattier' of the Eucharist: did the words 'this is my body' turn the bread into the body of Christ or did they transform the bread into an efficacious sign of Christ's sacrifice? *Jacke Jugeler* clearly engages with this topical debate, and it seems probable that the 'mattiers substancyall' alluded to by the Prologue are, in fact, the supreme substantial matter, the nature of Christ's presence in the sacrament (73). *Jacke Jugeler*'s dramatization of the eucharistic debate highlights those features of Catholic ritual that the reformers derided as theatrical. Catholic insistence on the substantial transformation of the bread to body was commonly criticized as false because the sacrament continued to look like bread. Similarly, Careaway's insistence that 'I am I' is undermined by

[69] O'Connell, *The Idolatrous Eye: Iconoclasm and Theater*, p. 15.

[70] Houston, 'Transubstantiation and the Sign', p. 129.

[71] While disguise and mistaken identity were central features of Roman Comedy, iconic drama is rare in England until the Tudor period when Roman New Comedy was frequently translated and adapted for modern performance.

Jacke's role playing, which reminds the audience of the physical presence of the actor's body (497). However, the play's specific interest in the interpretation of the words of institution cannot help but emphasize the similarities between reformed and theatrical versions of presence. Cranmer's treatment of the verb 'to be' in the words of institution is copulative: 'is' literally carries across the bread to the body. Likewise, Jacke's 'I am he' transforms Jacke into a figure for Jenkin Careaway (480). To put it another way, the Plautine subject matter of *Jack Jugeler*, in which one character impersonates another, draws attention to the iconic elements of both drama and reformed practice.

Unlike the plays discussed in the previous two chapters, the subject matter of *Jacke Jugeler* is entirely secular. What is more, in its allegorical treatment of the sacrament of the Eucharist, it is neither a straightforward attack on Catholicism, like Bale's *Three Laws* or *King Johan*, nor is it a simple illustration of reformed doctrine and practice, like Wager's *Mary Magdalene*. It does, nonetheless, offer a dramatic response to contemporary religious controversy. Put simply, the play comically dramatizes two versions of eucharistic and dramatic presence. However, by revealing the theatrical necessity of an 'imagined identity between sign and referent', the play latently suggests that the correspondence between earthly bread and Christ's body in Cranmer's interpretation of the Eucharist is as arbitrary as the relationship between actor and character in the mid-Tudor playing space.[72]

[72] Dawson, 'Props, Pleasure and Idolatry', in Dawson and Yachnin, *The Culture of Playgoing*, p. 134.

CONCLUSION

In the fourteenth and fifteenth centuries several orthodox writers and preachers contributed to the creation of what W. R. Jones has identified as 'a small but important corpus of English iconodule literature'.[1] Responding to the Lollard attack on images as 'sensible signes', a group of Oxford educated anti-Wycliffite scholars, among them the Dominican Roger Dymmok, the Carmelite Thomas Netter, the Franciscan William Woodford, and the Augustinian Walter Hilton, produced a series of texts in defence of the use of images in worship.[2] Writing as part of this organized effort against Lollardy, Reginald Pecock, bishop of Chichester and religious author, champions the faculty of sight as the most effective mode of religious instruction:[3]

the iȝe siȝt schewith and bringith into the ymaginacioun and into the mynde with-ynne in the heed of a man myche mater and longer mater sooner, and with lasse

---

[1] Jones, 'Lollards and Images', p. 37.

[2] The term 'sensible signes' is taken from a Lollard sermon that is quoted by G. R. Owst. The relevant passage reads: 'And now men shulden be more gostly and take lesse hede to siche sensible signes [...] For oure lord dwellis by grace in gode mennes soulis.' See Owst, *Literature and Pulpit in Medieval England*, p. 144. In addition to the friars and canons mentioned above, W. R. Jones has identified Robert Rypon, Robert Alyngton, and Reginald Pecock 'among the most prominent and easily identifiable of the contributors to the defense of image-worship'. See Jones, 'Lollards and Images', p. 37.

[3] V. H. H. Green has usefully asked whether *The Repressor* 'formed a reply to Wyclif's own works or to works written by his followers'. As Margaret Aston has noted, on the leading question of images, 'it seems abundantly plain that Pecock was [...] concerned with the contemporary mid-fifteenth-century state of affairs, which (in both writings and actions) had developed a great deal since Wycliffe's death.' See Green, *Bishop Reginald Pecock*, pp. 89–90; and Aston, *Lollards and Reformers*, p. 184.

labour and traueil and peine, than the heering of the eere dooth. And if this now seid is trewe of a man which can rede in bokis stories writun, than myche sooner and in schortir tyme and with lasse labour and pein in his brayne he schall come into remembraunce of a long storie bi si3t than bi the heering of othere mennys reding or bi heering of his owne reding; miche rather this is trewe of all tho persoones whiche kunnen not rede in bokis namelich sithin thei schulen not fynde men so redi for to rede a dosen leeuys of a book to hem, as their schulen fynde redy the wallis of a chirche peintid or a clooth steyned or ymagis sprad abroad in dyuerse placis of the chirche.[4]

As Margaret Aston has commented, Pecock here states, 'in his own unique way, a fact of human perception that was known in antiquity and is known with us still: that visual images are more readily assimilated and more lasting than acoustic messages: the picture's advantage over the page.'[5] To paraphrase Pecock, such is the immediacy of sight that one glance at a picture can communicate the same wisdom as twelve pages of a book. Pecock began *The Repressor of Over Much Blaming of the Clergy* sometime after his appointment as master of Whittington College, a London college of priests, in 1431. It was completed and published around 1455. Less than a hundred years later the humanist and diplomat Sir Richard Morison reproduces the same argument in defence of religious drama. He writes that, '[i]nto the common people thynges sooner enter by the eies, than by the eares: remembryng more better that they seen then that they heere.'[6] Like Pecock, Morison stresses the faculty of sight over that of hearing, arguing that reading imagery is easier and more effective in the dissemination of religious knowledge than reading books. And just as Pecock

---

[4] Pecock, *The Repressor of Over Much Blaming of the Clergy*, ed. by Babington, I, 212–23. The quotation is situated within the broader context of Pecock's vernacular theology in Campbell, *The Call to Read*. Stating that 'no Christen man now lyuyng hath [the conditions] anentis the person of Crist in his manhode, as hath a stok or a stoon graued into the likenes of Crist hanging on a cros naked and woundid [...] except whanne a quyck man is sett in a pley to be hangid nakid on a cros and to be in semyng woundid and scourgid', it is clear that Pecock places plays firmly in the same phenomenological realm as images. See Pecock, *The Repressor of Over Much Blaming of the Clergy*, ed. by Babington, I, 221. For a consideration of the defence of images in the *Repressor* as a defence of drama see Lerud, 'Quick Images: Memory and the English Corpus Christi Drama', pp. 222–24.

[5] Aston, *Lollards and Reformers*, p. 184.

[6] Richard Morison, *A Discourse touching the Reformation of the Lawes of England*, in BL, MS Cotton Faustina C. ii, fols 5ʳ–22ʳ (fol. 18ᵛ). An extract is edited in Anglo, 'An Early Tudor Programme for Plays', pp. 177–79. The passage from which I have quoted appears on p. 179. All further references are to this edition. Morison's defence of drama is also treated briefly in Chapter 2. See pp. 68–69.

categorizes images as copious aids to memory and spiritual understanding, as 'rememoratijf visible signes', so Morison notes the power of plays in the stimulation of memory.[7] In Diana Webb's words, both 'endorsed the long-held belief that images were not merely useful to the illiterate, but possessed a superior affective power over what was merely heard or read', a power to stir the emotions and excite the memory.[8]

Although Pecock and Morison defend religious imagery and drama in the same terms, they occupy opposing positions on the confessional spectrum. Though subsequently convicted of heresy and deprived of his see, Pecock was committed to the refutation of Lollardy, and *The Repressor* offers a staunch defence of orthodox doctrine and practice.[9] In contrast, Morison openly expressed Lutheran ideas and spent much of his adult life in the writing and dissemination of reformed propaganda.[10] Indeed, his 'Programme for Plays', which appears in his *A Discourse Touching the Reformation of the Lawes of England*, is written in support of the use of drama 'Against the Pope'.[11] Paul Whitfield White has argued that the Reformation 'did not impose radical changes on English attitudes towards drama, nor did it suppress its traditional function as a popular pastime and as an effective means of winning popular consent for officially sanctioned religious policy and practice'.[12] Of course, what did change between the writing of *The Repressor* and *A Discourse touching the Reformation*

[7] Pecock, *The Repressor of Over Much Blaming of the Clergy*, ed. by Babington, I, 182. As Aston has noted, Pecock's 'rememoratijf signes' is a translation of the scholastic 'signa recordativa', used regularly in discussions of imagery. See Aston, *Lollards and Reformers*, p. 183.

[8] Webb, *Pilgrimage in Medieval England*, p. 244. Webb's comments are directed at Pecock's defence of images in his *Repressor*, and also at the corresponding parts of Thomas More's '*Dialogue concerning Heresies*' (1529), written when Lutheran criticism was beginning to turn the Lollard trickle into something more like a flood'. See Webb, *Pilgrimage in Medieval England*, p. 244.

[9] Given Archbishop Thomas Arundel's prohibition of the discussion of theological questions in the vernacular it may well be that Pecock's commitment to reasoned expositions of Christianity in English ultimately laid him open to prosecution for heresy.

[10] Morison's conversion evidently occurred before December 1533. Writing from Venice to congratulate Cranmer on his advance to the archbishopric, Morison asks, 'why should I write this to you, since religion expects her restoration only from you and Latimer? You have a prince such as you could scarcely have expected from Heaven. The whole nobility is opposed to superstition, and supports religion, being well aware that ceremonies once instituted for good purpose have now degenerated into lucre.' See *Letters and Papers of the Reign of Henry VIII*, VI, ed. by James Gairdner (1882), p. 643, no. 1582 ([Moryson to Cranmer]).

[11] Morison, 'Extract from "A Discourse Touching the Reformation of the Lawes of England"', p. 176.

[12] White, *Theatre and Reformation*, p. 163.

was the relationship between State-sanctioned Christian teaching and the Roman Church. So, while both Pecock and Morison support the use of specta-cle in the war on heresy, what was officially sanctioned when Pecock wrote *The Repressor* had, by the time Morison wrote *A Discourse touching the Reformation*, become the subject of official abuse.

Developing arguments made by such critics as Greg Walker and Paul Whitfield White, in this book I have suggested that Reformation playwrights extended rather than ended the traditional union of religion and drama. However, by the late 1570s this pro-theatrical consensus had begun to break down as writers like Phillip Stubbes, Anthony Munday, and Stephen Gosson began to attack the theatre as idolatry. Significantly, their criticisms are often couched in the same language that Pecock and Morison use to defend religious spectacle. So, in the section of *A second and third blast of retrait from plaies and theatres* (1580; STC 21677), usually attributed to Munday, the reader learns:

> There cometh much euil in at the eares, but more at the eies, by these two open windowes death breaketh into the soule. Nothing entreth in more effectualie into the memorie, than that which commeth by seeing, things heard do lightlie passe awaie, but the tokens of that which wee haue seene, saith *Petrach*, sticke fast in vs whether we wil or no.[13]

Though Munday shares Morison's evaluation of the centrality of sight to spec-tacle, he rejects his arguments in favour of drama. So while Morison argues for drama's effectiveness on the grounds of its physicality, Munday believes that its sensual appeal is what makes it dangerous. For Munday and the other anti-theatrical writers, 'plays were idolatrous in the etymological sense: they were εἴδωλα, *imagines*, images, things seen'.[14] For Morison, plays 'are to be born withal, [...] specially whan they declare' the abomination of 'the bysshop of Rome, who provoked and forced us to commytt suche Idolatrie'.[15] Put simply, for Morison, drama is a weapon against idolatry; for Munday it is idolatry.

---

[13] Salvian, *A second and third blast* (1580; STC 21677), pp. 95–96. The rest of the title page reads, '*the one wherof was sounded by a reuerend byshop dead long since; the other by a worshipful and zealous gentleman now aliue: the one showing the filthiness of plaies in times past; the other the abhomination of theatres in the time present: both expresly prouing that that common-weale is nigh vnto the cursse of God, wherein either plaiers be made of, or theaters maintained. Set forth by Anglo-phile Eutheo.*' The 'second blast' is a translation of Book 6 of *De gubernatione Dei* by Salvian (*c.* 400–*c.* 480). The 'third blast' is commonly attributed to Munday (i.e. Anglophile Eutheo). The 'first blast' was Gosson, *The shoole [sic] of abuse.*

[14] O'Connell, *The Idolatrous Eye: Iconoclasm and Theater*, p. 19.

[15] Morison, 'Extract from "A Discourse Touching the Reformation of the Lawes of

It is more than a coincidence that Morison's equation of Catholicism with idolatry is adopted by the anti-theatricalists to equate drama with idolatry for, as Michael O'Connell has commented, 'behind the attack on theater as idolatry lies a religious preoccupation, a preoccupation that surfaces in an obverse way when Reformed writers attack what they see as the theatricality of Catholic worship.'[16] As I have already argued, this negative identification of Catholicism with theatricality can be traced to William Tyndale. But the charge was still being upheld at the end of the sixteenth century, when John Rainolds, former actor, Oxford cleric, and fiery opponent of the stage, writes:

> For, whereas the profane and wicked toyes of *Passion-playes*, playes setting foorth *Christs passion*, procured by *Popish priests*, who, being *corrupted from the simplicitie* that is Christ, as they have transformed the celebrating of the Sacrament into a *Masse-game*, and all other *Ecclesiasticall service* into *theatrical sights*; so instead of *preaching the word*, they cause it to be played.[17]

Here Rainolds's attack on 'playes setting foorth *Christs* passion' slips almost imperceptibly into a condemnation of '*Popish priests*' and their ceremonies as theatrical. By contrasting the '*theatrical sights*' of Catholic worship with '*the simplicite* that is Christ', Rainolds implicitly suggests that theatricality is tantamount to duplicity. This identification of theatricality with deceit is clearly indebted to Tyndale's assertion that, 'Christ is no hypocrite or digised player that playeth a parte in a play and representeth a persone or state whiche he is not. But is alwaye that his name signifieth.'[18] Christ is what he is; the signifier 'Christ' and the referent Christ are one. The actor on the other hand is what he is not; he resembles, but is distinct from, the part he plays. All but one of the plays studied in this book feature Vice characters who adopt false names and assumed identities in order to deceive their adversaries. In *King Johan*, several scenes after his early appearance as the Vice, Sedicyon appears in the guise of the monk Good Perfection in order to extract Nobylyte's confession. In *Three Laws*, Infidelitas deceives Naturae lex dressed as a pedlar and dupes Moseh lex disguised as a Franciscan friar. In *The Life and Repentaunce of Mary Magdalene*, Infidelitie, Pride, Cupiditie, and Carnall Concupiscence are given new names

England'", p. 178.

[16] O'Connell, *The Idolatrous Eye: Iconoclasm and Theater*, p. 14.

[17] Rainolds, *Th'ouerthrow of stage-playes*, p. 161. This quotation is discussed above. See Chapter 4, p. 147.

[18] Tyndale, *The exposition of the fyste epistle of seynt Jhon* (1531; STC 24443), sig. E1r.

to hide their true identities from the Magdalene. And in *Jacke Jugeler*, the entire play turns about Jacke's decision to impersonate Jenkin Careaway and make him believe '[t]hat he is not him selfe, but an other man'.[19] By going 'out of the Playe for a season' and re-entering with a 'new name and new raymente', these characters draw attention to impersonation as a phenomenal requirement of all drama.[20] For, by assuming a disguise — an alternative persona — the Vice destabilizes the relationship between sign and referent and reminds the audience that the actor is not the character that he represents, but that he 'playeth a part in a play and representeth a person of state which his is not'.[21] The plays that have been the subject of this study stand at an important juncture in theatrical history, illustrating for the first time the correspondence between the Vice and actors that is a feature of all anti-theatrical rhetoric. And it is in this rhetoric that the indictment of Catholicism as drama is eventually turned against itself by suggesting that all drama is in fact popery.

---

[19] *Jacke Jugeler*, in *Three Tudor Classical Interludes*, ed. by Axton, pp. 64–93 (p. 69, l. 179)

[20] Tyndale, *That fayth the mother of all good works iustifieth us*, sig. A4ʳ.

[21] Tyndale, *That fayth the mother of all good works iustifieth us*, sig. E1ʳ.

Bibliography

Manuscripts and Archival Resources

Cambridge, Clare College Library, MS 13
Cambridge, Corpus Christi College, MS 152
Cambridge, Cambridge University Library, MS Additional 6969
Cambridge, Cambridge University Library, MS Ff. 6. 2
Chippenham, Wiltshire and Swindon History Centre, D1/2/14
Dublin, Trinity College, MS F. 4. 20
Kew, The National Archives (formerly Public Record Office), SP 1/111
Lichfield, Record Office, MS B/C/13
Lincoln, Archive Office, Episcopal Register XX
London, British Library, Additional MS 24202
London, British Library, Additional MS 33383
London, British Library, MS Cotton Cleopatra E. iv
London, British Library, MS Cotton Faustina C. ii
London, British Library, MS Cotton Vespasian D. xviii
London, British Library, MS Harley 353
London, British Library, MS Harley 3838
London, Lambeth Palace Library, MS 464
Longleat, The Marquis of Bath, MS 14
Manchester, Chetham's Library, MS 6690
Norwich, Record Office, Mayor's Court Book 1534–1539
Oxford, Bodleian Library, MS Bodley 53
Oxford, Bodleian Library, MS Bodley 131
Oxford, Bodleian Library, MS Bodley 649
Oxford, Bodleian Library, MS Digby 133
Oxford, Bodleian Library, MS Hatton 31
Oxford, Bodleian Library, MS Selden Supra 41
Oxford, Corpus Christi College, MS 257
Oxford, Wadham College, MS 5
San Marino, CA, Huntington Library, MS HM 3

Early Printed Books

Bale, John, *The actes of Englysh votaryes* ([Antwerpen: Steven Mierdman], 1546; STC 1270)

——, *The actes of Englysh votaryes* (London: Thomas Raynalde, 1548; STC 1271)

——, *A comedy concernynge thre laws* ([Wesel: Derick van der Straten, c. 1547]; STC 1287)

——, *The Epistle exhortatorye of an Englyshe Christiane* ([Antwerpen: Catherine van Ruremond, 1544?]; STC 1291)

——, *The first two partes of the actes of the Englysh votaryes*, 2 parts (London: [Steven Mierdman] for John Bale, [1551]; STC 1273.5)

——, *Illustrium Maioris Britanniae scriptorium, summariu[m]* ([Wesel: Derick van der Straten for] John Overton, 1548; STC 1295)

——, *A mysterye of inyquiyte contayned within the heretycall genealogye of P. Pantolabus* ([Antwerpen: Antonius Goinus], 1545; STC 1303)

——, *A newe comedy or enterlude, concernyng thre laws* (London: Thomas Colwell, 1562; STC 1288)

——, *Scriptorum illustriu[m] maioris Brytannie quam nunc Angliam & Scotiam uocant catalogus*, 2 vols (Basel: Johannes Oporinus, [1557])

——, *A tragedye or enterlude manyfestyng the chefe promyses of God vnto man* ([Wesel: Derick van der Straten, 1547?]; STC 1305)

——, *The vocacyon of Joha[n] Bale to the bishoprick of Ossorie in Irela[n]de* ([Wesel?: Joos Lambrecht? for Hugh Singleton], 1553; STC 1307)

——, *Yet a course at the romyshe fox* ([Antwerpen: Antonius Goinus], 1543; STC 1309)

Barnes, Robert, *A supplicacion vnto the most gracyous prynce H. the .viij.* (London: John Byddell, 1534; STC 1471)

Becon, Thomas, *The displaying of the popish masse* (London: Anne Griffin, 1637; STC 1719)

Bromyard, John, *Doctissimi viri fratis Joha[n]nis de Bromyard, ordinis predicatorum: in Summam predicantium: op[us] vtiq[ue] co[m]me[n]datissimu[m]* ([Nuremberg]: Antonius Koberger, 1485)

Bucer, Martin, *A treatise, how by the worde of God, christian mens almose ought to be distributed* ([n.p.: n. pub., 1557?]; STC 3965)

✗ *The byble in Englyshe* [i.e. *The Great Bible*], 5 pts ([Paris: Francis Regnault; London]: Richard Grafton and Edward Whitchurch, 1539; STC 2068)

Calvin, John, *An excellent treatise of the immortalytie of the soule*, trans. by Thomas Stocker (London: John Daye, 1581; STC 4409)

——, *Institutio Christianae religionis* (Geneva: Robert Estienne, 1559)

——, *The institution of christian religion*, trans. by Thomas Norton (London: Reginald Wolfe and Richard Harison, 1561; STC 4415)

Certain sermons, or homilies (London: Richard Grafton, 1547; STC 13638.5)

Certain sermons, or Homilies (London: Richard Grafton, 1547; STC 13638.7)

Certain sermons or homilies (London: Richard Grafton, 1547; STC 13639)

Certain sermons, or homelies (London: Richard Grafton, 1547; STC 13639.5)

Certayne sermons, or homelies (London: Richard Grafton, 1547; STC 13640)

Certayne sermons, or homelies (London: Richard Grafton, 1547; STC 13640.5)

Church of England, *Articles deuised by the kynges highnes maiestie* (London: Thomas Berthelet, [1536]; STC 10033)

——, *The boke of common prayer* (London: Edward Whitchurch, 1552; STC 16279)

——, *The boke of common prayer* (London: Edward Whitchurch, 1552; STC 16280.5)

——, *The booke of common prayer* (London: Edward Whitchurch, [1552?]; STC 16288)

——, *Iniunccions geuen by the kynges maiestie* (London: Richard Grafton, [1547]; STC 10087.5)

——, *Iniunctions geuen by the moste excellente prince, Edward the .IV.* (London: Richard Grafton, 1547; STC 10088)

——, *Iniunccions geuen by the most [...] Edward the sixte* (London: Richard Grafton, 1547; STC 10089)

——, *Iniunccions geuen by the most [...] Edward the sixte* (London: Richard Grafton, 1547; STC 10090)

——, *Iniunccions geuen by the most [...] Edward the sixte* (London: Richard Grafton, 1547; STC 10090.3)

——, *Iniunccions geuen by the most [...] Edward the sixte* (London: Richard Grafton, 1547; STC 10090.5)

——, *Iniunccions geuen by the most [...] Edward the sixte* (London: Richard Grafton, 1547; STC 10091)

——, *Iniunccions geuen, by the most [...] Edward the sixt* (London: Richard Grafton, 1547; STC 10093.5)

——, *Iniunctions for the clerge* ([London: Thomas Berthelet, 1538]; STC 10086)

——, *Iniunctions gyuen [by the auc]toritie of the kynges highness to the clergie* ([n.p.]: Thomas Berthelet, [1536]; STC 10084.7)

Cranmer, Thomas, *An answer of Thomas archebyshop of Canterburye* (London: Reginald Wolfe, 1551; STC 5991)

——, *An aunswere by the reuerend father in God Thomas Archbyshop of Canterbury* (London: John Day, 1580; STC 5992)

——, *Cathechismus* (London: Nicholas Hill, 1548; STC 5993)

——, *Defence de la vraye et catholique doctrine du sacrement du corps & sang de nostre sauueur Christ*, trans. by François Phillipe (London: [Thomas Gaultier?] for Pierre Angelin, 1552; STC 6003.5)

——, *A defence of the true and catholike doctrine of the sacrament of the body and bloud of Christ* (London: Reginald Wolfe, 1550; STC 6000)

——, *Defensio verae et catholicae doctrinae de sacramento corporis & sanguinis Christi seruatoris nostri*, trans. by John Cheke (London: [Reginald Wolfe], 1553; STC 6004)

England, *Anno tricesimo primo Henrici octaui* (London: Thomas Berthelet, 1539; STC 9397)

d'Etaples, Jaques Lefèvre, *De Maria Magdalena et triduo Christi disceptatio* (Paris: Henri Estienne, 1518)

——, *De tribus et unica Magdalena disceptatio secunda* (Paris: Henri Estienne, 1519)

Fish, Simon, *A supplicacyon for the beggers* ([Antwerpen?: Johannes Grapheus?, 1529?]; STC 10883)

Gardiner, Stephen, *De vera obedientia* ([Wesel?: Joos Lambrecht for Hugh Singleton], 1553; STC 11587)

——, *An explicatio[n] and assertion of the true catholique fayth* ([Rouen: Robert Caly, 1551]; STC 11592)

A godly dialogue & dysputacion betwene Pyers plowman, and a popysh preest, concernyng the supper of the lorde ([London: William Copland, *c.* 1550]; STC 19903)

Gosson, Stephen, *Playes confuted in fiue actions* (London: [n. pub. for] Thomas Gosson, [1582]; STC 12095)

——, *The shoole [sic] of abuse* (London: [Thomas Dawson for] Thomas Woodcock, 1579; STC 12097)

Hilarie, Hugh, *The resurreccion of the masse* ([Wesel?: Joos Lambrecht? for Hugh Singleton], 1554; STC 13457)

The institution of a Christen man [i.e. *The Bishops' Book*] (London: Thomas Berthelet, 1537; STC 5164)

Jacobus de Voraigne, *Thus endeth the legend named in latyn legenda aurea*, trans. by William Caxton (London: William Caxton, 1483; STC 24873)

Junius, Adrian, *The nomenclator, or remembrancer*, trans. by John Higgins (London: Ralph Newberie and Henry Denham, 1585; STC 14860)

Le Jeu et Mystere de la Sainte Hostie par personages (Paris: Jean Bonfors, [*c.*1547–66])

L., R., *A copye of a letter contayning certayne newes* ([n.p.: John Day and William Seres], 1549; STC 15109.3)

——, *A copye of a letter contayning certayne newes* ([London: John Day and William Seres], 1549; STC 15109.7)

Latimer, Hugh, *A notable sermo[n] [on the plough] of maister Hughe Latemer* (London, John Daye and William Seres, [1548]; STC 15291)

Le mistere de la saincte hostie (Paris: Veuve Trepperl, [*c.* 1512–19])

Le mistere de la saincte hostie nouuellement imprime (Paris: [Jean Trepperel II or Alain Lotrian], [*c.* 1530–37])

A new enterlude drawen oute of the holy scripture of godly queene Hester (London: William Pickering and Thomas Hacket, 1561; STC 13251)

The newe Testame[n]t as it was written and caused to be writte[n] by them which herde yt, trans. by William Tyndale ([Worms: Peter Schöffer?, 1526?]; STC 2824)

The newe Testament, dylygently corrected and compared with the Greke by Willyam Tindale, ed. and trans. by William Tyndale (Antwerpen: Marten Emperowr, 1534; STC 2826)

Northbrooke, John, *Spiritus est [...] A treatise wherein dicing, dauncing, vaine playes or enterluds, are reproued* (London: Henry Bynneman for George Bishop, [1577?]; STC 18670)

[*The ploughman's tale. In verse.*] (London: Thomas Godfrey, [*c.* 1535]; STC 5099.5)

The praierand [sic] complaynte of the ploweman vnto Christe ([Antwerpen: Marten de Keyser, 1531?]; STC 20036)

The prayer and complaynt of the ploweman vnto Christ ([London: Thomas Godfrey, *c.* 1532]; STC 20036.5)

Prynne, William, *Histrio-mastix The players scourge* (London: Edward Alldc and others, 1633; STC 20464)

Rainolds, John, *Th'ouerthrow of stage-playes* [Middleburg: Richard Schilders], 1599; STC 20616)

La Rappresentazione d'un miracolo del Corpo di Cristo ([Firenze: Bartolomeo de'Libri, c. 1498])

Ridley, Nicholas, *A brief declaracion of the Lordes supper* ([Emden: Egidius van der Erve, 1555]; STC 21046)

Salvian, *A second and third blast of retrait from plaies and theaters* (London: Henry Denham, 1580; STC 21677)

The seconde tome of homelyes (London: Richard Jugge and John Cawood, 1563; STC 13663)

Shepherd, Luke, *John Bon and Mast person* (London: John Daye and William Seres, [1548?]; STC 3258.5)

Skelton, John, *Here after foloweth a lytell boke, whiche hath to name, why come ye nat to courte* (London: [Robert Copland] for Richard Kele, [1545?]; STC 22615)

Stubbes, Phillip, *The anatomie of abuses* (London: [John Kingston for] Richard Jones, 1583; STC 23376)

Tyndale, William, *An answere vnto Sir Thomas Mores dialoge* ([Antwerpen: Simon Cock, 1531]; STC 24437)

——, *The exposition of the fyrste epistle of seynt Jhon with a prologge before it* ([Antwerpen: Marten de Keyser], 1531; STC 24443)

——, *An exposicion vppon the. v. vi. vii. chapters of Mathew* ([Antwerpen: Johannes Grapheus?, 1533?]; STC 24440)

——, *The obedie[n]ce of a Christen man and how Christe[n] rulers ought to governe* ([Antwerpen: Joannes Hoochstraten], 1528; STC 24446)

——, *[The parable of the wicked mammon] That fayth the mother of all good works iustifieth vs* ([Antwerpen: Joannes Hoochstraten, 1528]; STC 24454)

——, *The practyse of prelates* ([Antwerpen: Joannes Hoochstraten], 1530; STC 24465)

——, *The practyse of prelates* (London: Anthony Scoloker and William Seres, 1548; STC 24466)

——, *The practyse of prelates* (London: Anthony Scoloker and William Seres, [1549?]; STC 24467)

[Udall, Nicholas], *A new enterlued for children to playe named Jacke Jugeler* (London: William Copland, [1562?]; STC 14837)

——, *A new enterlued for children to playe, named Iacke Iugeler* (London: William Copland, [1565?]; STC 14837a)

——, *An enterlude for children to play named Iack Iugler* (London: John Allde, [c. 1570]; STC 14837a.5)

Vermigli, Pietro Martire, *A discourse or traictise of Petur Martyr Vermill a Flore[n]tine wherin he declared his iudgemente concernynge the sacrament of the Lordes supper*, trans. by Nicholas Udall (London: Robert Stoughton [really Edward Whitchurch] for Nicholas Udall [1550]; STC 24665)

Wager, Lewis, *A newe enterlude, neuer before this tyme imprinted, of the life and repentaunce of Marie Magdalene* (London: John Charlewood, 1566; STC 24932)

——, *A new enterlude, neuer before the tyme imprinted, of the life and repentaunce of Marie Magdalene* (London: John Charlewood, 1567; STC 24932a)

Wyclif, John [sic], *Uvicklieffes wicket* ([London: John Day?, 1548?], STC 25591)

——, *Uvicklieffes wicket* ([London: John Day?, 1548?], STC 25591a)

——, *wycklyffes wycket* ([London: John Day?], 1546; STC 25590)

——, *Wyclyffes wicket* ([London: John Day?], 1546; STC 25590.5)

Other Primary Sources

A Short-Title Catalogue of Books Printed in England, Scotland & Ireland and of English Books Printed Abroad, 1475–1640, ed. by A. W. Pollard and others, 2nd edn, 3 vols (London: Bibliographical Society, 1976–91)

Adam of Eynsham, *The Life of Saint Hugh of Lincoln*, ed. and trans. by Decima L. Douie and David Hugh Farmer, 2nd edn, 2 vols (Oxford: Clarendon Press, 1985)

Anonymous Plays: 3rd Series, ed. by John S. Farmer (London: Early English Drama Society, 1906)

Aquinas, Thomas, *Summa theologica: Latin Text and English Translation*, ed. and trans. by Thomas Gilby and others, 61 vols (London: Blackfriars, [1964–81])

Aristotle, *Aristotle's Ars poetica*, ed. by R. Kassel (Oxford: Oxford University Press, 1966)

Augustine, *The City of God*, ed. and trans. by Henry Bettenson (Harmondsworth: Penguin, 1984)

——, *Confessions*, ed. and trans. by Henry Chadwick (Oxford: Oxford University Press, 1992)

——, *Confessions*, ed. by James J. O'Donnell, 3 vols (Oxford: Clarendon Press, 1991)

——, *S. Aurelii Augustini [. . .] De civitate Dei contra paganos libri XXII*, ed. by J. E. C. Welldon, 2 vols (London: Society for the Promotion of Christian Knowledge, 1924)

Averroes, *Averroes' Middle Commentary on Aristotle's Poetics*, ed. by Charles E. Butterworth (Princeton: Princeton University Press, 1986)

——, *De arte poetica, cum Averrois expositione*, trans. by Hermannus Alemannus and ed. by Laurentius Minio-Paluello, Corpus philosophorum medii aevi: Aristoteles Latinus, 33, 2nd edn (Brussels: De Brouwer, 1968)

Bale, John, *The Complete Plays of John Bale*, ed. by Peter Happé, Tudor Interludes, 4–5, 2 vols (Cambridge: Brewer, 1985–86)

The Blood Libel Legend: A Casebook in Anti-Semitic Folklore, ed. by Alan Dundes (Madison: University of Wisconsin Press, 1991)

Brinton, Thomas, *The Sermons of Thomas Brinton, Bishop of Rochester (1373–1389)*, ed. by Sister Mary Aquinas Devlin, Camden 3rd series, 85–86, 2 vols (London: Offices of the Royal Historical Society, 1954)

Bucer, Martin, 'De honestis ludis', ed. and trans. as 'Appendix C' of Glynne Wickham, *Early English Stages, 1300 to 1600*, 4 vols in 5 parts (London: Routledge & Kegan Paul, 1959–81; repr. 2002), II: *1576 to 1660*, part 1, pp. 329–31

Calvin, John, *Institutes of the Christian Religion*, ed. by John T. McNeill and trans. by Ford Lewis Battle and others, Library of Christian Classics, 20–21, 2 vols (London: S. C. M., 1961)

Chaucer, Geoffrey, *The Riverside Chaucer*, ed. by Larry D. Benson, 3rd edn (Oxford: Oxford University Press, 1988)

The Coventry Leet Book, or, Mayor's Register, Containing the Records of the City Leet or View of Flankpledge, A. D. 1420–1555, with Divers other Matters, ed. by Mary Dormer Harris, Early English Text Society, o.s., 134, 135, 138, and 146, 4 vols (London: Kegan Paul, Trench, Trübner, 1907–13)

Cranmer, Thomas, *The Works of Thomas Cranmer, Archbishop of Canterbury, Martyr, 1556*, ed. by John Edmund Cox, Parker Society, 12, 24, 2 vols ([n.p.]: Parker Society, 1844–46)

The Croxton Play of the Sacrament, in *Medieval Drama*, ed. by David Bevington (Boston: Houghton Mifflin, 1975), pp. 754–88

The Croxton Play of the Sacrament, in *Medieval Drama: An Anthology*, ed. by Greg Walker (Oxford: Blackwell, 2000), pp. 213–33

The Croxton Play of the Sacrament, in *Non-Cycle Plays and Fragments*, ed. by Norman Davis, Early English Text Society, s.s., 1 (London: Oxford University Press, 1970), pp. 58–89

Cyprian, *De lapsis*, in *De lapsis; and De Ecclesiae Catholicae unitate*, ed. and trans. by Maurice Bévenot (Oxford: Clarendon Press, 1971), pp. 2–55

Dives and Pauper, ed. by Priscilla Heath Barnum, Early English Text Society, o.s., 275, 280, 323, 3 vols (Oxford: Oxford University Press, 1976)

Dymmok, Roger, *Liber contra XII errores et hereses Lollardorum*, ed. by Harry S. Cronin (London: Kegan Paul, Trench, Trübner, 1922)

Ely Episcopal Records: A Calendar and Concise View of the Episcopal Records Preserved in the Muniment Room of the Palace of Ely, ed. by Alfred Gibbons (Lincoln: Williamson, 1891)

Foxe, John, *The Unabridged Acts and Monuments Online or TAMO (1563 Edition)*, 5 vols (Sheffield: HRI Online Publications, 2011) <http//www.johnfoxe.org> [accessed 18 April 2013]

——, *The Unabridged Acts and Monuments Online or TAMO (1570 Edition)*, 12 vols (Sheffield: HRI Online Publications, 2011) <http//www.johnfoxe.org> [accessed 18 April 2013]

——, *The Unabridged Acts and Monuments Online or TAMO (1576 Edition)*, 12 vols (Sheffield: HRI Online Publications, 2011) <http//www.johnfoxe.org> [accessed 18 April 2013]

——, *The Unabridged Acts and Monuments Online or TAMO (1583 Edition)*, 12 vols (Sheffield: HRI Online Publications, 2011) <http//www.johnfoxe.org> [accessed 18 April 2013]

Gleanings of a Few Scattered Ears, During the Period of the Reformation in England and of the Times Immediately Succeeding, A.D. 1533 to A.D. 1588, etc., ed. by George M. Gorham and Charles S. Bird (London: Bell and Daldy, 1857)

Great Britain Record Commission, *State Papers Published under the Authority of His Majesty's Commission: Henry the Eighth*, 11 vols ([London]: Murray, 1830[–1852])

The History of the Creeds, ed. by Philip Schaff, 2nd edn, 3 vols (London: Hodder and Stoughton, 1877–78)

Jacobus de Voragine, *A Critical Edition of the Legend of Mary Magdalena from Caxton's Golden Legende of 1483*, ed. by David A. Mycoff, Salzburg Studies in English Literature, 92, Elizabethan & Renaissance Studies, 11 (Salzburg: Institut für Anglistik und Amerikanistik, Universität Salzburg, 1985)

——, *Jacobi a Voragine Legenda Aura vulgo historia lombardia dicta*, ed. by Johann Georg Theodor Graesse (Dresden and Leipzig: [n. pub.], 1846)

Julleville, L. Petit de, *Histoire du théâtre en France: les mystères*, 2 vols (Paris: Hachette, 1880; repr. Geneva: Slatkine, 1968)

Kent Heresy Proceedings, 1511–12, ed. by Norman Tanner, Kent Records, 26 (Maidstone: Kent Archaeological Society, 1997)

Langland, William, *The Vision of Piers Plowman*, ed. by A. V. C. Schmidt (London: Dent, 1978)

Letters and Papers, Foreign and Domestic, of the Reign of Henry VIII: Preserved in the Public Record Office, the British Museum, and Elsewhere, 21 vols (London: Longman, Green, Longman, Roberts & Green, 1862–1932)

Lincoln Diocese Documents: 1450–1544, ed. by Andrew Clark, Early English Text Society, o.s., 149 (London: Oxford University Press, 1914)

Lollards of Coventry, ed. and trans. by Shannon McSheffrey and Norman Tanner, Camden 5th ser., 23 (Cambridge: Cambridge University Press, 2003)

Love, Nicholas, *The Mirror of the Blessed Life of Jesus Christ: A Full Critical Edition Based on Cambridge University Library Additional MSS 6578 and 6686 with Introduction, Notes and Glossary*, ed. by Michael G. Sargent (Exeter: University of Exeter Press, 2005)

The Macro Plays, ed. by Mark Eccles, Early English Text Society, o.s., 262 (London: Oxford University Press, 1969)

The Minor Poems of the Vernon Manuscript, ed. by Carl Horstmann and Frederick J. Furnivall, Early English Text Society, o.s., 98 and 117, 2 vols (London: Kegan Paul, Trench, Trübner, 1892–1901)

Le Mistere de la Saincte Hostie, ed. by Camille Salatko Petryszcze <http://www.sites.univ-rennes2.fr/celam/cetm/Edition%20Hostie/ostie.html#Le_mistere_de_la_saincte_hostie> [accessed 26 June 2013]

Le mistere de la saincte hostie nouuellement imprime A Paris (Paris: [Jean Trepperel ii or Alain Lotrian, *c.* 1530–37]; repr. Aix: Augustin Pontier, 1817)

Morison, Richard, 'Extract from "A Discourse Touching the Reformation of the Lawes of England"', in Sydney Anglo, 'An Early Tudor Programme for Plays and Other Demonstrations against the Pope', *Journal of the Warburg and Courtauld Institutes*, 20 (1957), 177–79.

Myrc, John, *A Critical Edition of John Mirk's Festial, Edited from British Library MS Cotton Claudius A. ii*, ed. by Susan Powell, Early English Text Society, o.s., 334–35, 2 vols (Oxford: Oxford University Press, 2010)

——, *Instructions for Parish Priests*, ed. by Edward Peacock, Early English Text Society, o.s., 31, rev. edn (London: Kegan Paul, Trench, Trübner, 1902)

The N-Town Play: Cotton MS Vespasian D. 8, ed. by Stephen Spector, Early English Text Society, s.s., 11–12, 2 vols (Oxford: Oxford University Press, 1991)

Norwich Consistory Court Depositions, 1499–1512 and 1518–1530, ed. by Edward D. Stone and Basil Cozens-Hardy, Norfolk Record Society, 10 ([London: Fackenham and Reading, Wyman & Sons], 1938)

Original Letters Relative to the English Reformation: Written during the Reigns of King Henry VIII, King Edward VI, and Queen Mary, Chiefly from the Archives of Zurich, ed. and trans. by Hastings Robinson, Publications of the Parker Society, 37, 38, 2 vols (Cambridge: Cambridge University Press, 1846–47)

Patrologia cursus completus: series latina, ed. by Jacques-Paul Migne, 221 vols in 222 (Paris: Migne, 1844[–64])

Pecock, Reginald, *The Repressor of Over Much Blaming of the Clergy*, ed. by Churchill Babington, 2 vols (London: Longman, Green, Longman, and Roberts, 1860)

Plautus, *Plauti comoediae*, ed. by Friedrich Leo, 2 vols (Berlin: Weidmann, 1895–96)

Records of Plays and Players in Norfolk and Suffolk, 1330–1642, ed. by David Galloway and John Wasson, Malone Society Collections, 11 (Oxford: Malone Society, 1980–81)

A Select Library of Nicene and Post-Nicene Fathers of the Christian Church: Second Series, ed. by Philip Schaff and Peter Wace, 14 vols (Oxford: James Parker; New York: Christian Literature, 1890–1900)

Selections from English Wycliffite Writings, ed. by Anne Hudson, Medieval Academy Reprints for Teaching, 38, rev. edn (Toronto: University of Toronto Press, 1997)

Thomas, William, *The Pilgrim*, ed. by James A. Froude (London: Parker, Son, and Bourne, 1861)

——, *The Works of William Thomas*, ed. by Abraham D'Aubant (London: Almon, 1774)

Three Tudor Classical Interludes, ed. by Marie Axton, Tudor Interludes (Woodbridge: Brewer, 1982)

The Towneley Plays, ed. by George England, Early English Text Society, e.s., 71 (London: Kegan Paul, Trench, Trübner, 1897; repr. London: Milford, 1952)

A Tretise of Miraclis Pleyinge, ed. by Clifford Davidson, rev. edn (Kalamazoo: Medieval Institute Publications, 1993)

Wager, Lewis, *The Life and Repentaunce of Mary Magdalene*, in *Reformation Biblical Drama in England: An Old-Spelling Critical Edition*, ed. by Paul Whitfield White (New York: Garland, 1992), pp. 1–66

Wilkins, David, *Concilia Magnae Britanniae et Hiberniae, a synodo Verolamiensi, A. D. 446 ad Londinensem, A. D. 1717*, 4 vols (London: [n. pub.], 1737)

William of Shoreham, *The Poems of William of Shoreham*, ed. by Matthias Konrath, Early English Text Society, e.s., 86 (London: Kegan Paul, Trench, Trübner, 1902)

Wriothesley, Charles, *A Chronicle of England during the Reigns of the Tudors, from A.D. 1485 to 1559*, ed. by William Douglas Hamilton, Works of the Camden Society, n.s., 11, 20, 2 vols (London: Camden Society, 1875–77)

Wycliffe, John, *The English Works of Wyclif hitherto Unprinted*, ed. by F. D. Matthew, Early English Text Society, o.s., 74 (London: Trübner, 1880)

——, *Select English Works of John Wyclif*, ed. by Thomas Arnold, 3 vols (Oxford: Clarendon Press, 1869–71)

The Zurich Letters: Comprising the Correspondence of Several English Bishops and others, ed. and trans. by Hastings Robinson, 2 vols (Cambridge: Cambridge University Press, 1842–1845)

Secondary Works

Acker, Lievan van, 'Introduction', in *Agobardi Lugdunensis: opera omnia*, ed. by Lievan van Acker, Corpus Christianorum Continuatio mediaevalis, 52 (Turnhout: Brepols, 1981), pp. i–lxvii

Adair, John, *The Pilgrims' Way: Shrines and Saints in Britain and Ireland* (London: Thames and Hudson, 1978)

Adams, Barry B., 'Doubling in Bale's *King Johan*', *Studies in Philology*, 62 (1965), 111–20

——, 'Introduction', in *John Bale's King Johan*, ed. by Barry B. Adams (San Marino: Huntington Library, 1969), pp. 1–69

Adler, Michael, *Jews of Medieval England* ([n.p.]: Goldston for the Jewish Historical Society, 1939)

Aers, David, 'New Historicism and the Eucharist', *Journal of Medieval and Early Modern Studies*, 33 (2003), 241–59

——, *Sanctifying Signs: Making Christian Tradition in Late Medieval England* (Notre Dame: University of Notre Dame Press, 2004)

Almasy, Rudolph P., '"I am That I Preach": Tyndale as Mediator in *The Parable of the Wicked Mammon*', *Renaissance and Reformation/Renaissance et Réforme*, 26 (2002), 5–22

Alvarez Recio, Leticia, *Fighting the Antichrist: A Cultural History of Anti-Catholicism in Tudor History* (Eastbourne: Sussex Academic Press, 2011)

Anderson, George K., *The Legend of the Wandering Jew* (Hanover: Brown University Press, 1965)

Anderson, Judith H., 'Language and History in the Reformation: Cranmer, Gardiner and the Words of Institution', *Renaissance Quarterly*, 54 (2001), 20–51

Anderson, Marvin, 'Rhetoric and Reality: Peter Martyr and the English Reformation', *Sixteenth-Century Journal*, 19 (1988), 451–69

Anglo, Sydney, 'An Early Tudor Programme for Plays and Other Demonstrations against the Pope', *Journal of the Warburg and Courtauld Institutes*, 20 (1957), 176–79

——, *Spectacle, Pageantry, and Early Tudor Policy* (Oxford: Clarendon Press, 1969)

Arbesmann, Rudolph, 'The Concept of "Christus Medicus" in St. Augustine', *Traditio*, 10 (1954), 1–28

Asher, Lyell, 'The Dangerous Fruit of Augustine's *Confessions*', *Journal of the American Academy of Religion*, 66 (1998), 227–55

Aston, Margaret, *England's Iconoclasts, 1: Laws against Images* (Oxford: Clarendon Press, 1988)

——, *Faith and Fire: Popular and Unpopular Religion, 1350–1600* (London: Hambledon, 1993)

——, 'Iconoclasm in England: Official and Clandestine', in *Iconoclasm vs. Art and Drama*, ed. by Clifford Davidson and Ann Eljenholm Nichols, Early Drama, Art, and Music Monograph Series, 11 (Kalamazoo: Medieval Institute Publications, 1989), pp. 47–91

——, *Lollards and Reformers: Images and Literacy in Late Medieval Religion* (London: Hambledon Press, 1984)

Atkin, Tamara, 'Playbooks and Printed Drama: A Reassessment of the Date and Layout of the Manuscript of the Croxton *Play of the Sacrament*', *Review of English Studies*, 60 (2009), 194–205

——, 'Playing with Books in John Bale's *Three Laws*', *Yearbook of English Studies*, 43 (2013), 243–61.

Badir, Patricia, *The Maudlin Impression: English Literary Images of Mary Magdalene, 1550–1700* (Notre Dame: University of Notre Dame Press, 2009)

——, 'Medieval Poetics and Protestant Magdalenes', in *Reading the Medieval in Early Modern England*, ed. by Gordon McMullan and David Matthews (Cambridge: Cambridge University Press, 2007), pp. 205–19

——, '"To Allure Vnto Their Loue": Iconoclasm and Striptease in Lewis Wager's *The Life and Repentaunce of Marie Magdalene*', *Theatre Journal*, 51 (1999), 1–20

Baker, Donald C., 'The Angel in English Renaissance Literature', *Studies in the Renaissance*, 6 (1959), 85–93

——, 'The Date of *Mankind*', *Philological Quarterly*, 42 (1963), 90–91

Bale, Anthony Paul, *The Jew in the Medieval Book: English Antisemitisms, 1350–1500* (Cambridge: Cambridge University Press, 2006)

Barish, Jonas, *The Antitheatrical Prejudice* (Berkeley: University of California Press, 1981)

——, 'Exhibitionism and the Antitheatrical Prejudice', *English Literary History*, 36 (1969), 1–29

Barnes, T. D., 'Christians and the Theater', in *Roman Theater and Society: E. Togo Salmon Papers I*, ed. by William J. Slater (Ann Arbor: University of Michigan Press, 1996), pp. 161–80

Barns, Florence E., 'The Background and Sources of the Croxton *Play of the Sacrament*' (unpublished doctoral thesis, University of Chicago, 1926)

Bauckham, Richard, *Tudor Apocalypse: Sixteenth-Century Apocalypticism, Millenarianism and the English Reformation, from John Bale to John Foxe and Thomas Brightman*, Courtenay Library of Reformation Classics, 8 (Oxford: The Sutton Courtenay Press, 1978)

Beadle, Richard, '"Devoute Ymaginacion" and the Dramatic Sense in Love's *Mirror* and the N-Town Plays', in *Nicolas Love at Waseda: Proceedings of the International Conference, 20–22 July 1995*, ed. by Shoichi Oguro, Richard Beadle, and Michael G. Sargent (Cambridge: Brewer, 1997), pp. 1–18

——, 'Plays and Playing at Thetford and Nearby, 1498–1540', *Theatre Notebook*, 32 (1978), 4–11

Beckwith, Sarah, 'Ritual, Church, and Theatre: Medieval Dramas of the Sacred Body', in *Culture and History, 1350–1600: Essays on Communities, Identities and Writing*, ed. by David Aers (London: Harvester Wheatsheaf, 1992), pp. 65–89

——, 'Stephen Greenblatt's *Hamlet* and the Forms of Oblivion', *Journal of Medieval and Early Modern Studies*, 33 (2003), 261–80

Bennet, J., 'The Meaning of the Digby *Mary Magdalen*', *Studies in Philology*, 101 (2004), 38–47

Bennett, H. S., *English Books and Readers, 1558–1603* (Cambridge: Cambridge University Press, 1965)

Ben-Tsur, Dalia, 'Early Ramifications of Theatrical Iconoclasm: The Conversion of Catholic Biblical Plays into Protestant Drama', *Partial Answers*, 3 (2005), 43–56

Bevington, David, *From Mankind to Marlowe: Growth of Structure in the Popular Drama of Tudor England* (Cambridge, MA: Harvard University Press, 1968)

——, *Tudor Drama and Politics: A Critical Approach to Topical Meaning* (Cambridge, MA: Harvard University Press, 1968)

Bilhauer, Bettina, *Medieval Blood* (Cardiff: University of Wales Press, 2006)

Blackburn, Ruth H., *Biblical Drama under the Tudors*, Studies in English Literature, 65 (Den Haag: Mouton, 1971)

Blanc, Pauline, 'Commentators, Mediators, Subversives Within and Without John Bale's Nonconformist Play World', *Theta*, 7 (2007), 197–208

——, 'Corrosive Images of the Roman Catholic Church in John Bale's Protestant Propagandistic Works', in *Pouvouirs de l'image aux XVe, XVIe et XVIIe siècles: Pour un nouvel éclairage sur la pratique des Lettres àla Renaissance*, ed. by M. Couton and others (Clermont-Ferrand: Presses Universitaires Blaise Pascal, 2009), pp. 189–99

Blatt, Thora Balslev, *The Plays of John Bale* (København: Gad, 1968)

Boas, Frederick, *University Drama in the Tudor Age* (Oxford: Oxford University Press, 1914)

Bose, Mishtooni, 'Reginald Pecock's Vernacular Voice', in *Lollards and their Influence in Late Medieval England*, ed. by Fiona Somerset, Jill C. Havens, and Derrick G. Pitard (Woodbridge: Boydell, 2003), pp. 237–50

Bradbrook, M. C., *The Rise of the Common Player: A Study of Actor and Society in Shakespeare's England* (London: Chatto & Windus, 1962)

Bradshaw, Christopher J., 'John Bale and the Use of English Bible Imagery', *Reformation*, 2 (1997), 173–89

Brigden, Susan, *London and the Reformation* (Oxford: Clarendon Press, 1989)

——, 'Youth and the English Reformation', *Past and Present*, 95 (1982), 37–67

Briscoe, Marianne, 'Some Clerical Notions of Dramatic Decorum in Late Medieval England', *Comparative Drama*, 19 (1985), 1–13

Brooks, Peter Newman, *Thomas Cranmer's Doctrine of the Eucharist: An Essay in Historical Detail* (Basingstoke: Macmillan, 1965)

Brown, E. H. Phelps, and Sheila V. Hopkins, 'Seven Centuries of Building Wages', in *Essays in Economic History*, ed. by E. M. Carus-Wilson, 3 vols (London: Edward Arnold, 1954–62), II (1962), 168–78

Brown, Peter Robert Lamont, *The Cult of the Saints: Its Rise and Function in Latin Christianity*, Haskell Lectures on History of Religions, n.s., 2 (Chicago: University of Chicago Press, [1981])

Brunning, Alison, 'Jonson's Romish Foxe: Anti-Catholic Discourse in *Volpone*', *Early Modern Literary Studies*, 6 (2000), 1–32

Bruster, Douglas, *Drama and the Market in the Age of Shakespeare*, Cambridge Studies in Renaissance Literature and Culture, 1 (Cambridge: Cambridge University Press, 1992)

Bryant, James C., *Tudor Drama and Religious Controversy* (Macon: Mercer University Press, 1984)

Burnet, Gilbert, *The History of the Reformation of the Church of England*, rev. by Nicholas Pocock, 7 vols (Oxford: Clarendon Press, 1865)

Butterworth, Philip, *Magic on the Early English Stage* (Cambridge: Cambridge University Press, 2005)

——, *Theatre of Fire: Special Effects in Early English and Scottish Theatre* (London: Society for Theatre Research, 1998)

Cabansis, Allen, *Amalarius of Metz* (Amsterdam: North-Holland Publishing, 1954)

Campbell, Ethan, "'Be Ware of the Key": Anticlerical Critique in the "Play of the Sacrament"', *Fifteenth Century Studies*, 36 (2011), 1–24

Campbell, Kirsty, *The Call to Read: Reginald Pecock's Books and Textual Communities* (Notre Dame: University of Notre Dame, 2010)

Caputo, Nicoletta, 'A "Deformed" Christianity: Ethical Transubstantiation in English Reformation Plays', in *The Poetics of Transubstantiation: From Theology to Metaphor*, ed. by Douglas Burnham and Enrico Giaccherini, Studies in European Cultural Transition, 27 (Aldershot: Ashgate, 2005), pp. 63–74

Carlson, Martin, *Theatre Semiotics: Signs of Life* (Bloomington: Indiana University Press, 1990)

Carpenter, Frederic Ives, 'Introduction', in Lewis Wager, *The Life and Repentaunce of Marie Magdalene, a Morality Play*, ed. by F. I. Carpenter (Chicago: University of Chicago Press, 1902), pp. i–xxxv

Catto, Jeremy, 'John Wycliff and the Cult of the Eucharist', in *The Bible in the Medieval World: Essays in Memory of Beryl Smalley*, ed. by Katherine Walsh and Diana Wood, Studies in Church History, Subsidia 4 (Oxford: Oxford University Press, 1985), pp. 269–86

Cavanagh, Dermot, 'The Paradox of Sedition in John Bale's *King Johan*', *English Literary Renaissance*, 31 (2001), 171–91

——, 'Reforming Sovereignty: John Bale and Tragic Drama', in *Interludes and Early Modern Society: Studies in Gender, Power and Theatricality*, ed. by Peter Happé and Wim Hüskin, Ludus, 9 (Amsterdam: Rodopi, 2007), pp. 191–210

Cevone, Thea, 'The King's Phantom: Staging Majesty in Bale's *Kynge Johan*', in *Defining Medievalism(s)*, ed. by Karl Fugelso (Cambridge: Brewer, 2009), pp. 185–202

Chambers, E. K., *The Elizabethan Stage*, 4 vols (Oxford: Clarendon Press, 1923)

——, *The Mediæval Stage*, 2 vols (Oxford: Clarendon Press, 1903)

Chazan, Robert, *Medieval Jewry in Northern France: A Political and Social History*, The Johns Hopkins University Studies in Historical and Political Science, 91st ser., 2 (Baltimore: Johns Hopkins University Press, 1973)

Cigman, Gloria, *The Jew as an Absent-Presence in Late Medieval England*, Sacks Lecture, 17 (Yarnton: Oxford Centre for Postgraduate Hebrew Studies, 1991)

Ciobanu, Estella Antoaneta, '"City of God?" City Merchants, Bloody Trade and the Eucharist in the Croxton *Play of the Sacrament*', in *Images of the City*, ed. by Agnieszka Rasmus and Magdalena Cieślak (Newcastle upon Tyne: Cambridge Scholars, 2009), pp. 50–70

Clark, Peter, *English Provincial Society from the Reformation to the Revolution: Religion, Politics and Society in Kent, 1500–1640* (Hassocks: Harvester Press, 1977)

Clark, Robert L. A., and Claire Sponsler, 'Othered Bodies: Racial Crossdressing in the *Mistere de la Sainte Hostie* and the Croxton *Play of the Sacrament*', *Journal of Medieval and Early Modern Studies*, 29 (1999), 61–87

Clebsch, William A., *England's Earliest Protestants, 1520–1535* (New Haven: Yale University Press, 1964)

Clopper, Lawrence M., *Drama, Play, and Game: English Festive Culture in the Medieval and Early Modern Period* (Chicago: University of Chicago Press, 2001)

Coleman, David, *Drama and the Sacraments in Sixteenth-Century England: Indelible Characters* (Basingstoke: Palgrave Macmillan, 2007)

Coletti, Theresa, *Mary Magdalene and the Drama of the Saints: Theater, Gender, and Religion in Late Medieval England* (Philadelphia: University of Pennsylvania Press, 2004)

Collinson, Patrick, *The Birthpangs of Protestant England* (Basingstoke: Macmillan, 1988)

Cottret, Bernard, *Calvin: A Biography* (Grand Rapids: Eerdmans, 2000)

——, 'Pour une sémiotique de la Réforme: le *Consensus Tigurinus* (1549) et la *Brève Résoluyion* (1555) de Calvin', *Annales Économies, Sociétés, Civilisations*, 39 (1984), 265–85

Cox, John D., *The Devil and the Sacred in English Drama* (Cambridge: Cambridge University Press, 2000)

——, 'Devils and Vices in English Non-Cycle Plays: Sacrament and Social Body', *Comparative Drama*, 30 (1996), 188–220

——, 'Stage Devils in English Reformation Plays', *Comparative Drama*, 32 (1998), 85–116

Craig, H., *English Religious Drama of the Middle Ages* (Oxford: Oxford University Press, 1955)

Craik, T. W., *The Tudor Interlude: Stage, Costume, and Acting* (Leicester: University Press, 1958)

Cremeans, Charles D., *The Reception of Calvinistic Thought in England*, Illinois Studies in the Social Sciences, 31 (Urbana: University of Illinois Press, 1949)

Crewe, Jonathan V., 'The Theater of the Idols: Theatrical and Anti-Theatrical Discourse', in *Staging the Renaissance: Reinterpretations of Elizabethan and Jacobean Drama*, ed. by David Scott Kastan and Peter Stallybrass (New York: Routledge, 1991), pp. 49–56

Crockett, Bryan, *The Play of Paradox: Stage and Sermon in Renaissance England* (Philadelphia: University of Pennsylvania Press, 1995)

Crockett, Peter, 'Staging *Antichrist* and the Performance of Miracles', in *Spectacle and Public Performance in the Late Middle Ages and the Renaissance*, ed. by Robert Stillman, Studies in Medieval and Reformation Traditions, 113 (Leiden: Brill, 2006), pp. 31–50

Cutts, Cecilia, 'The Croxton *Play*: An Anti-Lollard Piece', *Modern Languages Quarterly*, 5 (1944), 45–60

——, 'The English Background of the *Play of the Sacrament*' (unpublished doctoral thesis, University of Washington, 1938)

Damon, John, 'Enacting Liturgy: *Estote fortes* in the Croxton *Play of the Sacrament*', in *Romance and Rhetoric: Essays in Honour of Dhira B. Mahoney*, ed. by Georgiana Donanvin and Anita Obermeier (Turnhout: Brepols, 2010), pp. 171–92

Daston, Lorraine, 'Marvelous Facts and Miraculous Evidence in Early Modern Europe', *Critical Inquiry*, 18 (1991), 93–124

Davidson, Clifford, 'The Anti-Visual Prejudice', in *Iconoclasm vs. Art and Drama*, ed. by Clifford Davidson and Ann Eljenholm Nichols, Early Drama, Art, and Music Monograph Series, 11 (Kalamazoo: Medieval Institute Publications, 1989), pp. 33–46

——, '"The Devil's Guts": Allegations of Superstition and Fraud in Religious Drama and Art during the Reformation', in *Iconoclasm vs. Art and Drama*, ed. by Clifford Davidson and Ann Eljenholm Nichols, Early Drama, Art, and Music Monograph Series, 11 (Kalamazoo: Medieval Institute Publications, 1989), pp. 112–21

——, 'Introduction', in *A Tretise of Miraclis Pleyinge*, ed. by Clifford Davidson, rev. edn (Kalamazoo: Medieval Institute Publications, 1993), pp. 1–52

——, 'The Middle English Saint Play and its Iconography', in *The Saint Play in Medieval Europe*, ed. by Clifford Davidson (Kalamazoo: Medieval Institute Publications, 1986), pp. 31–122

——, *Religion, History and Violence: Cultural Contexts for Medieval and Renaissance Drama*, Collected Studies, 744 (Aldershot: Ashgate, 2002)

——, 'Sacred Blood and the Late Medieval Stage', *Comparative Drama*, 31 (1997), 436–59

Davies, Catharine, *A Religion of the Word: The Defence of the Reformation in the Reign of Edward VI* (Manchester: Manchester University Press, 2002)

Davies, Horton, *Worship and Theology in England*, 5 vols (Princeton: Princeton University Press, 1961–75), I: *From Cranmer to Hooker, 1534–1603*

Davis, Nicholas, 'Another View of the *Tretise of Miraclis Pleyinge*', *Medieval English Theatre*, 4 (1982), 48–55

Davis, Norman, 'Introduction to *The Croxton Play of the Sacrament*', in *Non-Cycle Plays and Fragments*, ed. by Norman Davis, Early English Text Society, s.s., 1 (London: Oxford University Press, 1970), pp. lxx–lxxxv

Dawson, Anthony B., and Paul Yachnin, *The Culture of Playgoing: A Collaborative Debate* (Cambridge: Cambridge University Press, 2001)

Dean, Paul, '"Nothing that is So is So": *Twelfth Night* and Transubstantiation', *Literature and Theology*, 17 (2003), 281–97

Debax, Jean-Paul, and Yves Peyré, 'Spectacle in Early Theatre: England and France', *Medieval English Theatre*, 16 (1994), 1–16

Denery, Dallas G., II, 'From Sacred Mystery to Divine Deception: Robert Holkot, John Wyclif, and the Transformation of Fourteenth-Century Eucharistic Discourse', *Journal of Religious History*, 29 (2005), 129–44

Dessen, Alan C., *Elizabethan Drama and the Viewer's Eye* (Chapel Hill: University of North Carolina Press, 1977)

Dickens, A. G., *The English Reformation* (London: Batsford, 1964)

——, *Lollards and Protestants in the Diocese of York, 1509–1558*, History Series, 10 (London: Hambledon, 1982)

——, *Reformation Studies*, History Series, 9 (London: Hambledon, 1982)

Diehl, Huston, 'Observing the Lord's Supper and the Lord's Chamberlain's Men: The Visual Rhetoric of Ritual and Play in Early Modern England', *Renaissance Drama*, n.s., 22 (1991), 147–74

——, *Staging Reform, Reforming the Stage: Protestantism and Popular Theater in Early Modern Europe* (Ithaca: Cornell University Press, 1997)

Dillon, Janette, *Language and Stage in Medieval and Renaissance England* (Cambridge: Cambridge University Press, 1998)

——, *Performance and Spectacle in Hall's Chronicle* (London: Society for Theatre Research, 2002)

——, 'Theatre and Controversy, 1603–1642', in *The Cambridge History of British Theatre*, ed. by Peter Thomson, 3 vols (Cambridge: Cambridge University Press, 2004), I: *Origins to 1660*, ed. by Jane Milling and Peter Thomson, pp. 364–382

——, 'What Sacrament? Excess, Taboo and Truth in the Croxton *Play of the Sacrament*', *European Medieval Drama*, 4 (2000), 169–79

Dorsten, Jan van, 'Literary Patronage in Elizabethan England: The Early Phase', in *Patronage in the Renaissance*, ed. by Guy Fitch Lytle and Stephen Orgel (Princeton: Princeton University Press, 1981), pp. 191–206

Dox, Donnalee, '*De tragoediis* and the Redemption of Classical Theatre', *Viator*, 33 (2002), 43–53

——, 'The Eyes of the Body and the Veil of Faith', *Theatre Journal*, 56 (2004), 29–45

——, *The Idea of the Theater in Latin Christian Thought* (Ann Arbor: University of Michigan Press, 2004)

——, 'Medieval Drama as Documentation: "Real Presence" in the Croxton *Conversion of Ser Jonathas the Jewe by the Myracle of the Blessid Sacrament*', *Theatre Survey*, 38 (1997), 97–115

——, 'Roman Theatre and Roman Rite: Twelfth-Century Transformations in Allegory, Ritual, and the Idea of Theatre', in *The Appearances of Medieval Rituals: The Play of Construction and Modification*, ed. by Nils Holger Peterson and others (Turnhout: Brepols, 2004), pp. 33–48

——, 'Theatrical Space, Mutable Space, and the Space of Imagination: Three Readings of the Croxton *Play of the Sacrament*', in *Medieval Practices of Space*, ed. by Barbara A. Hanawalt and Michal Kobialka, Medieval Cultures, 23 (Minneapolis: University of Minnesota Press, 2000), pp. 167–98

Doyle, A. I., 'Reflections on Some Manuscripts of Nicholas Love's *Myrrour of the Blessed Lyf of Jesu Christ*', *Leeds Studies in English*, n.s., 14 (1983), 82–93

Duffy, Eammon, *The Stripping of the Altars: Traditional Religion in England, 1400–1580* (New Haven: Yale University Press, 1992)

Eccles, Mark, *Brief Lives: Tudor and Stuart Authors* (Chapel Hill: University of North Carolina Press, 1982)

Edgerton, William L., *Nicholas Udall*, Twayne's English Authors Series, 30 (New York: Twayne, 1965)

Elam, Keir, *The Semiotics of Theatre and Drama* (London: Methuen, 1980)

Elk, Martine van, 'Urban Misidentification in *The Comedy of Errors* and the Cony-Catching Pamphlets', *Studies in English Literature 1500–1900*, 43 (2003), 323–46

Elton, G. R., *Policy and Police: The Enforcement of the Reformation in the Age of Thomas Cromwell* (Cambridge: Cambridge University Press, 1972)

Elukin, Jonathan M., 'From Jew to Christian? Conversion and Immutability in Medieval Europe', in *Varieties of Religious Conversion in the Middle Ages*, ed. by James Muldoon (Gainesville: University Press of Florida, 1997), pp. 171–90

Emmerson, Richard K., 'Renaissance "Eliding the Medieval": "New Historicism" and Sixteenth-Century Drama', in *The Performance of Middle English Culture: Essays on Chaucer and the Drama in Honor of Martin Stevens*, ed. by James J. Paxson, Lawrence M. Clopper, and Sylvia Tomasch (Cambridge: Brewer, 1998), pp. 25–41

Enders, Jody, 'Dramatic Memories and Tortured Spaces in the *Mistere de la Sainte Hostie*', in *Medieval Practices of Space*, ed. by Barbara A. Hanawalt and Michal Kobialka, Medieval Cultures, 23 (Minneapolis: University of Minnesota Press, 2000), pp. 199–222

——, 'Theater Makes History: Ritual Murder by Proxy in the *Mistere de la Sainte Hostie*', *Speculum*, 79 (2004), 991–1016

Ewing, Elizabeth, *Dress and Undress: A History of Women's Underwear* (London: Batsford, 1978)

——, *Fashion in Underwear* (London: Batsford, 1971)

Fairfield, Leslie P., *John Bale: Mythmaker for the English Reformation* (West Lafayette: Purdue University Press, 1976)

Fendt, Gene, 'The (Moral) Problem of Reading *Confessions*: Augustine's Double Argument against Drama', *Proceedings of the American Catholic Philosophical Association*, 72 (1998), 171–84

Fichte, Joerg O., 'The Appearance of the Commonwealth and the People in Tudor Drama', in *Drama and Cultural Change: Turning Around Shakespeare*, ed. by Matthias Bauer and Angelika Zirker (Trier: Wissenschaftlicher Verlag Trier, 2009), pp. 5–22

——, 'New Wine in Old Bottles: The Protestant Adaptation of the Morality Play', *Anglia*, 110 (1992), 65–84

Finucane, Ronald C., *Miracles and Pilgrimages: Popular Beliefs in Medieval England*, rev. edn (Basingstoke: Macmillan, 1995)

Fitzpatrick, P. J., *In Breaking of Bread: The Eucharist and Ritual* (Cambridge: Cambridge University Press, 1993)

Fletcher, Alan, and Diarmaid MacCulloch, *Tudor Rebellions*, 5th rev. edn (London: Pearson Longman, 2008)

Forest-Hill, Lynn, 'Maidens and Matrons: The Theatricality of Gender in the Tudor Interludes', in *Interludes and Early Modern Society: Studies in Gender, Power and Theatricality*, ed. by Peter Happé and Wim Hüskin, Ludus, 9 (Amsterdam: Rodopi, 2007), pp. 43–70

——, *Transgressive Language in Medieval English Drama: Signs of Challenge and Change* (Aldershot: Ashgate, 2000)

Fuller, Thomas, *The History of the Worthies of England*, ed. by P. Austin Nuttall, 3 vols (London: Tegg, 1840; repr. New York: AMS, 1965)

Garth, Helen Meredith, *Saint Mary Magdalene in Mediaeval Literature*, Johns Hopkins University Studies in Historical and Political Science, ser. 67, 3 (Baltimore: Johns Hopkins University Press, 1950)

Gayk, Shannon, *Image, Text, and Religious Reform in Fifteenth-Century England* (Cambridge: Cambridge University Press, 2010)

Gayley, Charles Mills, 'An Historical View of the Beginnings of English Comedy', in *Representative English Comedies: With Introductory Essays and Notes, an Historical View of Our Earlier Comedy, and other Monographs*, ed. by Charles Mills Gayley, 4 vols (New York: Macmillan, 1903–36), I: *From the Beginnings to Shakespeare* (1903; repr. 1912), pp. xiii–xcii

Ghosh, Kantik, 'Bishop Reginald Pecock and the Idea of "Lollardy"', in *Text and Controversy from Wyclif to Bale: Essays in Honour of Anne Hudson*, ed. by Helen Barr and Ann M. Hutchinson, Medieval Church Studies, 4 (Turnhout: Brepols, 2005), pp. 251–67

——, *The Wycliffite Heresy: Authority and the Interpretation of Texts*, Cambridge Studies in Medieval Literature, 45 (Cambridge: Cambridge University Press, 2002)

Gibson, Gail McMurray, *The Theater of Devotion: East Anglian Drama and Society in the Late Middle Ages* (Chicago: University of Chicago Press, 1989)

Godfrey, Bob, 'Feminine Singularity: The Representation of Young Women in Some Early Tudor Interludes', in *Interludes and Early Modern Society: Studies in Gender, Power and Theatricality*, ed. by Peter Happé and Wim Hüskin, Ludus, 9 (Amsterdam: Rodopi, 2007), pp. 141–62

——, 'The Machinery of Spectacle: The Performance Dynamic of the Play of Mary Magdalen and Related Matters', in *Papers from the Third International Conference on European Medieval Drama, Camerino, July 1998*, ed. by Sydney Higgins with the European Medieval Drama Council (= *European Medieval Drama*, 3 (1999)), 145–60

Gourley, Brian, 'Carnavalising Apocalyptic History in John Bale's *King Johan* and *Three Laws*', in *Renaissance Medievalisms*, ed. by Konrad Eisenbichler, Essays and Studies, 18 (Toronto: Centre for Reformation and Renaissance Studies, 2009), pp. 169–89

Grantley, Darryll, *English Dramatic Interludes, 1300–1580: A Reference Guide* (Cambridge: Cambridge University Press, 2004)

——, 'Producing Miracles', in *Aspects of Early English Drama*, ed. by Paula Neuss (Cambridge: Brewer, 1983), pp. 78–91

Green, V. H. H., *Bishop Reginald Pecock: A Study in Ecclesiastical History and Thought*, Thirwall Prize Essay, 1941 (Cambridge: Cambridge University Press, 1945)

Greenblatt, Stephen, 'The Mousetrap', in *Practicing New Historicism*, ed. by Catherine Gallagher and Stephen Greenblatt (Chicago: University of Chicago Press, 2000), pp. 136–63

Greg, W. W., *A Companion to Arber: Being a Calender of Documents in Edward Arber's 'Transcript of the Registers of the Company of Stationers of London, 1554–1640' with Text and Calender of Supplementary Documents* (Oxford: Clarendon Press, 1967)

——, 'Notes on Some Early Plays', *The Library*, 11 (1930), 44–60

Griffin, Benjamin, 'The Birth of the History Play: Saint, Sacrifice, and Reformation', *Studies in English Literature 1500–1900*, 39 (1999), 217–37

——, *Playing the Past: Approaches to English Historical Drama, 1385–1600* (Woodbridge: Brewer, 2001)

Groeneveld, Leanne, 'A Theatrical Miracle: The Boxley Rood of Grace as Puppet', *Early*
Theatre, 10 (2007), 11–50

Haigh, Christopher, *English Reformations: Religion, Politics, and Society under the Tudors* (Oxford: Clarendon Press, 1993)

Hale, William, *A Series of Precedents and Proceedings in Criminal Causes from 1475 to 1640, Extracted from the Act-Books of Ecclesiastical Courts in the Diocese of London* (London: [n. pub.], 1847)

Hansel, Hans, *Die Maria-Magdalena-Legende: eine Quellenuntersuchung* (Greifswald: Dallmeyer, 1937)

Happé, Peter, 'Appendix IV', in *The Complete Plays of John Bale*, ed. by Peter Happé, Tudor Interludes, 4–5, 2 vols (Cambridge: Brewer, 1985–86), I, 152–56

——, 'Dramatic Images of Kingship in Heywood and Bale', *Studies in English Literature 1500–1900*, 39 (1999), 239–53

——, 'Introduction', in *The Complete Plays of John Bale*, ed. by Peter Happé, Tudor Interludes, 4–5, 2 vols (Cambridge: Brewer, 1985–86), I, 1–28

——, *John Bale*, Twayne's English Authors Series, 520 (New York: Twayne, 1996)

——, 'John Bale's Lost Mystery Cycle', *Cahiers Elisabéthains*, 60 (2001), 1–12

——, 'Notes to *King Johan*', in *The Complete Plays of John Bale*, ed. by Peter Happé, Tudor Interludes, 4–5, 2 vols (Cambridge: Brewer, 1985–86), I, 100–41

——, 'Notes to *Three Laws*', in *The Complete Plays of John Bale*, ed. by Peter Happé, Tudor Interludes, 4–5, 2 vols (Cambridge: Brewer, 1985–86), II, 157–80

——, 'The Protestant Adaptation of the Saint Play', in *The Saint Play in Medieval Europe*, ed. by Clifford Davidson (Kalamazoo: Medieval Institute Publications, 1986), pp. 205–40

——, 'Wager, Lewis (*d*. 1562)', in *Oxford Dictionary of National Biography* (Oxford: Oxford University Press, 2004; online edn updated October 2008) <http://www.oxforddnb.com> [accessed 18 April 2013]

Hardison, O. B., Jr, *Christian Rite and Christian Drama in the Middle Ages: Essays in the Origin and Early History of Modern Drama* (Baltimore: Johns Hopkins University Press, 1965)

——, 'The Place of Averroes' Commentary on the *Poetics* in the History of Medieval Criticism', *Medieval and Renaissance Studies*, 4 (1970), 57–82

Harris, Jesse W., *John Bale: A Study of the Minor Literature of the Reformation*, Illinois Studies in Language and Literature, 24 (Urbana: The University of Illinois Press, 1940)

Harris, John Wesley, *Medieval Theatre in Context: An Introduction* (London: Routledge, 1991)

Harris, Max, *Theatre and Incarnation* (London: Macmillan, 1990)

Haskins, Susan, *Mary Magdalen: Myth and Metaphor* (London: Harper Collins, 1993)

Henshaw, Millett, 'The Attitude of the Church toward the Stage at the End of the Middle Ages', *Medievalia et humanistica*, 4 (1952), 3–17

Hermen, Peter C., *The Squitter-Wits and Muse-Haters: Sidney, Spenser, Milton, and Renaissance Antipoetic Sentiment* (Detroit: Wayne State University Press, 1996)

Higginbotham, Derrick, 'Impersonators in the Market: Merchants and the Premodern Nation in the Croxton *Play of the Sacrament*', *Exemplaria*, 19 (2007), 163–82

Hill-Vásquez, Heather, "'The Precious Body of Crist that they Tretyn in Ther Hondis": "Miraclis Pleyinge" and the Croxton *Play of the Sacrament*', *Early Theatre*, 4 (2001), 53–72

——, *Sacred Players: The Politics of Response in Middle English Religious Drama* (Washington, D.C.: Catholic University of America Press, 2007)

Holder, R. Ward, 'Calvin as Commentator on the Pauline Epistles', in *Calvin and the Bible*, ed. by Donald K. McKim (Cambridge: Cambridge University Press, 2006), pp. 224–56

Homan, Richard L., 'Devotional Themes of Violence and Humor of the *Play of the Sacrament*', *Comparative Drama*, 20 (1986), 327–40

——, 'Two Exempla: Analogues to the *Play of the Sacrament* and *Dux Moraud*', *Comparative Drama*, 18 (1984), 24–51

Hopf, Constantin, *Martin Bucer and the English Reformation* (Oxford: Blackwell, 1946)

Hornback, Robert, 'The Development of Heresy: Doctrinal Variation in English Lollard Dissent, 1381–1521' (unpublished doctoral thesis, University of Oxford, 2007)

——, 'Lost Conventions of Godly Comedy in Udall's *Thersites*', *Studies in English Literature 1500–1900*, 47 (2007), 282–303

Hornbeck, J. Patrick, II, *What is a Lollard?: Dissent and Belief in Late Medieval England*, Oxford Theological Monographs (Oxford: Oxford University Press, 2010)

Houston, Julia, 'Transubstantiation and the Sign: Cranmer's Drama of the Last Supper', *Journal of Medieval and Renaissance Studies*, 24 (1994), 113–30

Hudson, Anne, 'The Mouse in the Pyx: Popular Heresy and the Eucharist', *Trivium*, 26 (1991), 40–53

——, *The Premature Reformation: Wycliffite Texts and Lollard History* (Oxford: Clarendon Press, 1988)

Hufstader, Anselm, 'Jacques Lefèvre d'Etaples and the Magdalen', *Studies in the Renaissance*, 16 (1969), 31–60

Hughes, Jonathan, *Pastors and Visionaries: Religion and Secular Life in Late Medieval Yorkshire* (Woodbridge: Boydell, 1988)

Hunt, Alice, *The Drama of Coronation: Medieval Ceremony in Early Modern England* (Cambridge: Cambridge University Press, 2008)

Irigoin, Jean, 'La Datation par les filigranes du papier', *Codicologica*, 5 (1980), 9–36

Ivry, Alfred, 'Averroës on Aristotle', in *Uses and Abuses of the Classics: Western Interpretations of Greek Philosophy*, ed. by Jorge J. E. Garcia and Jiyuan Yu (Aldershot: Ashgate, 2004), pp. 125–36

James, Mervyn, 'Ritual, Drama and Social Body in the Late Medieval English Town', *Past and Present*, 98 (1983), 3–29

Janowitz, H. D., 'Exodus 3. 14 as the Source and Target of Shakespeare's Variations on "I Am That I Am"', *English Language Notes*, 38 (2002), 33–36

Jansen, Katherine L., *The Making of the Magdalen: Preaching and Popular Devotion in the Later Middle Ages* (Princeton: Princeton University Press, 2000)

——, 'Mary Magdalen and the Mendicants: The Preaching of Penance in the Late Middle Ages', *Journal of Medieval History*, 21 (1995), 1–25

Jones, Joseph R., 'Isidore and Theatre', in *Drama in the Middle Ages: Comparative and Cultural Essays*, ed. by Clifford Davidson and John H. Stroupe, 2nd ser. (New York: AMS, 1993), pp. 1–23

Jones, Michael, '"The Place of the Jews": Anti-Judaism and Theatricality in Medieval Culture', *Exemplaria* (2000), 327–57

——, 'Theatrical History in the Croxton *Play of the Sacrament*', *English Literary History*, 66 (1999), 223–60

Jones, W. R., 'Lollards and Images: The Defence of Religious Art in Later Medieval England', *Journal of the History of Ideas*, 34 (1973), 27–50

Jurkowski, Maureen, 'Lollardy and Social Status in East Anglia', *Speculum*, 82 (2007), 120–52

Kang, Ji-Soo, 'The Significance of the Eucharist Scenes in the Croxton *Play of the Sacrament*', *Medieval English Studies*, 9 (2001), 131–53

Karras, Ruth Mazo, 'Holy Harlots: Prostitute Saints in Medieval Legend', *Journal of the History of Sexuality*, 1 (1990), 3–32

Kastan, David Scott, '"Holy Wurdes" and "Slypper Wit": John Bale's *King Johan* and the Poetics of Propaganda', in *Rethinking the Henrician Era: Essays on Early Tudor Texts and Contexts*, ed. by Peter C. Herman (Urbana: University of Illinois Press, [1994]), pp. 267–82

Kelemen, Erick, 'Drama in Sermons: Quotation, Performativity, and Conversion in a Middle English Sermon on the Prodigal Son and in *A Tretise of Miraclis Pleyinge*', *English Literary History*, 69 (2002), 1–19

Kelly, Henry Ansgar, 'Aristotle-Averroes-Alemannus on Tragedy: The Influence of the *Poetics* on the Latin Middle Ages', *Viator*, 10 (1979), 161–209

——, *Ideas and Forms of Tragedy from Aristotle to the Middle Ages* (Cambridge: Cambridge University Press, 1993)

Kendall, Richie, *The Drama of Dissent: The Radical Poetics of Nonconformity, 1380–1590* (Chapel Hill: University of North Carolina Press, 1986)

King, John N., *English Reformation Literature: The Tudor Origins of the Protestant Tradition* (Princeton: Princeton University Press, 1982)

King, Pamela M., 'Minority Plays: Two Interludes for Edward VI', *Medieval English Theatre*, 15 (1993), 87–102

King, Ros, 'Introduction', in *The Works of Richard Edwards: Politics, Poetry and Performances in Sixteenth-Century England*, ed. by Ros King (Manchester: Manchester University Press, 2001), pp. 1–108

Kolbialka, Michal, *This Is My Body: Representational Practices in the Early Middle Ages* (Ann Arbor: University of Michigan Press, 1999)

Kolve, V. A., *The Play Called Corpus Christi* (Stanford: Stanford University Press, 1966)

Kruger, Stephen, 'The Bodies of Jews in the Middle Ages', in *The Idea of Medieval Literature: New Essays on Chaucer and Medieval Culture in Honor of Donald R. Howard*, ed. by James M. Dean and Christian Zacher (Newark: University of Delaware Press, 1992), pp. 307–23

——, 'The Spectral Jew', *New Medieval Literatures*, 2 (1998), 2–35

Lampert, Lisa, *Gender and Jewish Difference from Paul to Shakespeare* (Philadelphia: University of Pennsylvania Press, 2004)

——, 'The Once and Future Jew: Little Robert of Bury, Historical Memory and the Croxton *Play of the Sacrament*', *Jewish History*, 15 (2001), 235–55

Lancashire, Ian, *Dramatic Texts and Records of Britain: A Chronological Topography to 1558* (Cambridge: Cambridge University Press, 1984)

Lane, Belden C., 'Spirituality as the Performance of Desire: Calvin on the World as a Theatre of God's Glory', *Spiritus*, 1 (2001), 1–30

Lascombes, André, 'Revisiting the Croxton *Play of the Sacrament*', in *European Medieval Drama, 1997: Papers from the Second International Conference on 'Aspects of Medieval Drama', Camerino, 4–6 July 1997*, ed. by Sydney Higgins (Camerino: Università degli studi di Camerino, Centro linguistico di Ateneo, 1997), 261–75

Lawton, David A., 'Sacrilege and Theatricality: The Croxton *Play of the Sacrament*', *Journal of Medieval and Early Modern Studies*, 33 (2002), 281–309

Leff, Gordon, 'Ockham and Wyclif on the Eucharist', *Reading Medieval Studies*, 2 (1976), 1–13

Lerer, Seth, '"Represented Now in Yower Syght": The Culture of Spectatorship in Late Fifteenth-Century England', in *Bodies and Disciplines: Intersections of Literature and History in Fifteenth-Century England*, ed. by Barbara A. Hanawalt and David Wallace (Minneapolis: University of Minnesota Press, 1996), pp. 29–62

Lerud, Theodore K., 'Quick Images: Memory and the English Corpus Christi Drama', in *Moving Subjects: Processional Performance in the Middle Ages and the Renaissance*, ed. by Kathleen Ashley and Wim Hüsken, Ludus, 5 (Amsterdam: Rodopi, 2001), pp. 213–38

Lewis, Suzanne, *The Art of Matthew Paris*, California Studies in the History of Art, 21 (Berkeley: University of California Press, 1987)

MacCulloch, Diarmaid, *The Later Reformation in England, 1547–1603* (Basingstoke: Macmillan, 1990)

——, *Thomas Cranmer: A Life* (New Haven: Yale University Press, 1996)

——, *Tudor Church Militant: Edward VI and the Protestant Reformation* (London: Lane, 1999)

Maltman, Sister Nicholas, 'Meaning and Art in the Croxton *Play of the Sacrament*', *English Literary History*, 41 (1974), 149–64

Malvern, Marjorie, *Venus in a Sackcloth: The Magdalen's Origins and Metamorphoses* (Carbondale: Southern Illinois University Press, 1975)

Marshall, Mary H., 'Theatre in the Middle Ages: Evidence From Dictionaries and Glosses', *Symposium*, 4 (1950), 1–36, 366–89

Martin, Ian, 'The Manuscript and Editorial Traditions of William Thomas's *The Pilgrim*', *Bibliothèque d'Humanisme et Renaissance*, 59 (1997), 621–41

Martin, Thomas F., 'Paul the Patient: *Christus Medicus* and the *"Stimulis Carnis"* (II Corinthians 12. 7): A Consideration of Augustine's Medical Christology', *Augustinian Studies*, 32 (2001), 219–56

McClendon, Muriel C., 'Religious Toleration and the Reformation: Norwich Magistrates in the Sixteenth Century', in *England's Long Reformation, 1500–1800*, ed. by Nicholas Tyacke (London: University College London Press, 1998), pp. 87–115.

McCusker, Honor, *John Bale, Dramatist and Antiquary* (Bryn Mawr: [n. pub.], 1942)

McMillan, Sharon L., *Episcopal Ordination and Ecclesiastical Consensus* (Collegeville: Liturgical Press, 2005)

Menache, Sophia, 'Faith, Myth, and Politics: The Stereotype of the Jews and their Expulsion from England and France', *The Jewish Quarterly Review*, n.s., 75 (1985), 351–74

Miller, Edwin Shepard, 'The Roman Rite in Bale's *King John*', *Publications of the Modern Languages Associations*, 64 (1949), 802–22

Mills, David, '"Look at Me When I'm Speaking to You": The "Behold and See" Convention in Medieval Drama', *Medieval English Theatre*, 7 (1985), 4–12

Milner, Matthew, *The Senses and the English Reformation*, St Andrews Studies in Reformation History (Farnham: Ashgate, 2011)

Motter, Vail T. H., *The School Drama in England* ([n.p.]: Longmans, 1929; repr. Port Washington: Kennikat Press, 1968)

Muir, Lynette R., 'Further Thoughts on the Tale of the Profaned Host', *Early Drama, Art and Music Review*, 21 (1999), 88–97

Mullaney, Steven, *The Place of Stage: License, Play and Power in Renaissance England* (Ann Arbor: University of Michigan Press, 1982; repr. Chicago: University of Chicago Press, 1988)

Mundill, Robin R., *England's Jewish Solution: Experiment and Expulsion, 1262–1290* (Cambridge: Cambridge University Press, 1998)

Nelson, Alan H., ed., *Cambridge*, Records of Early English Drama, 2 vols (Toronto: University of Toronto Press, 1989)

Nichols, Ann Eljenholm, 'The Croxton *Play of the Sacrament*: A Re-Reading', *Comparative Drama*, 22 (1988), 117–37

——, 'Lollard Language in the Croxton *Play of the Sacrament*', *Notes and Queries*, 36 (1989), 23–25

——, *Seeable Signs: The Iconography of the Seven Sacraments, 1350–1544* (Woodbridge: Boydell, 1994)

Nisse, Ruth, *Defining Acts: Drama and the Politics of Interpretation in Late Medieval England* (Notre Dame: University of Notre Dame Press, 2005)

——, 'Reversing Discipline: The *Tretise of Miraclis Pleyinge*, Lollard Exegesis, and the Failure of Representation', *Yearbook of Langland Studies*, 11 (1997), 163–98

Norland, Howard B., *Drama in Early Tudor Britian, 1485–1558* (Lincoln: University of Nebraska Press, 1995)

O'Connell, Michael, 'God's Body: Incarnation, Physical Embodiment and the Fate of Biblical Theatre in the Sixteenth Century', in *Subjects on the World's Stage: Essays on British Literature of the Middle Ages and the Renaissance*, ed. by David G. Allen and Robert A. White (Newark: University of Delaware Press, 1995), pp. 62–87

——, *The Idolatrous Eye: Iconoclasm and Theater in Early-Modern England* (New York: Oxford University Press, 2000)

——, 'The Idolatrous Eye: Iconoclasm, Anti-Theatricalism, and the Image of the Elizabethan Theater', *English Literary History*, 52 (1985), 279–310

The Oxford English Dictionary, 2nd edn (Oxford: Oxford University Press, 1989), in *OED Online* <http://oed.com> [accessed 5 June 2013]

Oxford English Dictionary Additional Series (Oxford: Oxford University Press, 1997), in *OED Online* <http://dictionary.oed.com> [accessed 5 June 2013]

Olson, Glending, 'Plays as Play: A Medieval Ethical Theory of Performance and the Intellectual Context of the *Tretise of Miraclis Pleyinge*', *Viator*, 26 (1995), 195–221

Orgel, Stephen, *Impersonations: The Performance of Gender in Shakespeare's England* (Cambridge: Cambridge University Press, 1996)

Owens, Margaret E., *Stages of Dismemberment: The Fragmented Body in Late Medieval and Early Modern Drama* (Newark: University of Delaware Press, 2005)

Owst, G. R., *Literature and Pulpit in Medieval England*, 2nd edn (Oxford: Blackwell, 1961)

Pafford, John Henry Pyle, 'Introduction', in John Bale, *King Johan*, ed. by John Henry Pyle Pafford (Oxford: The Malone Society Reprints, 1931), pp. v–xxxiv

Parish, Helen L., *Monks, Miracles and Magic: Reformation Representations of the Medieval Church* (London: Routledge, 2005)

Pasachoff, Naomi E., *Playwrights, Preachers and Politicians: A Study of Four Tudor Old Testament Dramas*, Salzburg Studies in English Literature, Elizabethan & Renaissance Studies, 45 (Salzburg: Institut für Englische Sprache und Literatur, 1975)

Pelikan, Jaroslav, *The Christian Tradition: A History of the Development of Doctrine*, 5 vols (Chicago: University of Chicago Press, 1979–89)

Phelps, Wayne H., 'The Date of Lewis Wager's Death', *Notes and Queries*, 223 (1978), 420–21

Phillips, Heather, 'John Wyclif's *De eucharistia* in its Medieval Setting' (unpublished doctoral thesis, University of Toronto, 1980), pp. 241–303

Phillips, John, *The Reformation of Images: Destruction of Art in England, 1535–1660* (Berkeley: University of California Press, 1973)

Pineas, Rainer, 'The English Morality Play as a Weapon of Religious Controversy', *Studies in English Literature 1500–1900*, 2 (1962), 157–80

——, *Tudor and Early Stuart Anti-Catholic Drama*, Bibliotecheca humanistica & reformatorica, 5 (Nieuwkoop: De Graaf, 1972)

Postlewait, Thomas, 'Theatricality and Antitheatricality in Renaissance London', in *Theatricality*, ed. by Tracy C. Davis and Thomas Postlewait (Cambridge: Cambridge University Press, 2004), pp. 90–126

Reames, Sherry L., 'The Legend of Mary Magdalen, Penitent and Apostle: Introduction', in *Middle English Legends of Woman Saints*, ed. by Sherry L. Reames (Kalamazoo: Medieval Institute Publications, 2003), in *TEAMS Middle English Texts* <http://www.lib.rochester.edu/camelot/teams/11sr.htm> [accessed 5 June 2013]

Reid-Schwartz, Alexandra, 'Economies of Salvation: Commerce and the Eucharist in the *Profanation of the Host* and the Croxton *Play of the Sacrament*', *Comitatus*, 25 (1994), 1–20

Richardson, H. G., 'Review of Sister Mary Aquinas Devlin O.P., ed., The Sermons of Thomas Brinton, Bishop of Rochester (1373–1389). (Camden Third Series, Volumes lxxxv and lxxxvi.) London: Royal Historical Society, 1954. Pp. xxxviii, 518', *Speculum*, 30 (1955), 267–71

von Rosador, Kurt Tetzeli, 'The Sacralizing Sign: Religion and Magic in Bale, Greene and Early Shakespeare', *The Yearbook of English Studies*, 23 (1993), 30–45

Rosenberg, Eleanor, *Leicester: Patron of Letters* (New York: Columbia University Press, 1955)

Rubin, Miri, *Corpus Christi: The Eucharist in Late Medieval Culture* (Cambridge: Cambridge University Press, 1991)

——, *Gentile Tales: The Narrative Assault on Late Medieval Jews* (New Haven: Yale University Press, 1999)

Sargent, Michael G., 'Introduction', in Nicholas Love, *The Mirror of the Blessed Life of Jesus Christ: A Full Critical Edition Based on Cambridge University Library Additional MSS 6578 and 6686 with Introduction, Notes and Glossary*, ed. by Michael G. Sargent (Exeter: University of Exeter Press, 2005), pp. intro 1–intro 163

Saxer, Victor, *Le Culte de Marie Madeleine en occident: des origines à la fin du Moyen Âge* (Auxerre: Publications de la société des fouilles archéologiques et des monuments historiques de l'Yonne, 1959)

——, 'Santa Maria Maddalena della storia evangelica alla leggenda e all'arte', in *La Maddalena tra sacro e profano*, ed. Marilena Mosco (Milano: Mondadori, 1986), pp. 24–28

Scase, Wendy, *Reginald Pecock*, Authors of the Middle Ages: English Writers of the Middle Ages, 8 (Aldershot: Ashgate, 1996)

Schaberg, Jane, *The Resurrection of Mary Magdalene: Legends, Apocrypha, and the Christian Testament* (London: Continuum, 2002)

Scherb, Victor I., 'Blasphemy and the Grotesque in the Digby *Mary Magdalene*', *Studies in Philology*, 96 (1999), 223–60

——, 'The Earthly and Divine Physicians: Christus Medicus in the Croxton *Play of the Sacrament*', in *The Body and the Text: Comparative Essays in Literature and Medicine*, ed. by Bruce Clarke and Wendell Aycock (Lubbock: Texas Tech University Press, 1990), pp. 161–71

——, *Staging Faith: East-Anglian Drama in the Later Middle Ages* (London: Associated University Presses, 2001)

Schneider, Brian W., *The Framing Text in Early Modern English Drama: 'Whining' Prologues and 'Armed' Epilogues* (Farnham: Ashgate, 2011)

Schnusenberg, Christine Catharina, *The Relationship between the Church and the Theatre Exemplified by Selected Writings of the Church Fathers and by Liturgical Texts Until Amalarius of Metz, 775–852 A.D.* (Lanham: University Press of America, 1988)

Sedinger, Tracey, '"And yet woll I stiell saye that I am I": *Jack Juggler*, the Lord's Supper, and Disguise', *English Literary History*, 74 (2007), 239–69

Shrank, Cathy, 'John Bale and Reconfiguring the "Medieval" in Reformation England', in *Reading the Medieval in Early Modern England*, ed. by Gordon McMullan and David Matthews (Cambridge: Cambridge University Press, 2007), pp. 179–92

Shuger, Debora K., *The Renaissance Bible: Scholarship, Sacrifice, and Subjectivity*, New Historicism, 29 (Berkeley: University of California Press, 1994)

Sider, John W., '"One Man in his Time Plays Many Parts": Authorial Theatrics of Doubling in Early English Renaissance Drama', *Studies in Philology*, 91 (1994), 359–89

Siemon, James R., *Shakespearean Iconoclasm* (Berkeley: University of California Press, 1985)

Simpson, James, *Reform and Cultural Revolution, 1350–1547*, Oxford English Literary History, 2 (Oxford: Oxford University Press, 2002)

——, 'Three Laws', in *The Oxford Handbook to Tudor Drama*, ed. by Tom Betteridge and Greg Walker (Oxford: Oxford University Press, 2012), pp. 109-22

Sinanoglou, Leah, 'The Christ Child as Sacrifice: A Medieval Tradition and the Corpus Christi Plays', *Speculum*, 48 (1973), 491–509

Smith, James K. A., 'Staging the Incarnation: Revisioning Augustine's Critique of Theatre', *Literature and Theology*, 15 (2001), 123–39

Snoek, G. J. C., *Medieval Piety from Relics to the Eucharist: A Process of Mutual Interaction*, Studies in the History of Christian Thought, 63 (Leiden: Brill, 1995)

Sofer, Andrew, *The Stage Life of Props* (Ann Arbor: University of Michigan Press, 2003)

Somerset, Fiona, 'Here, There, and Everywhere? Wycliffite Conceptions of the Eucharist and Chaucer's "Other" Lollard Joke', in *Lollards and their Influence in Late Medieval England*, ed. by Fiona Somerset, Jill C. Havens, and Derrick G. Pitard (Woodbridge: Boydell, 2003), pp. 127–40

Southern, Richard, *The Staging of Plays before Shakespeare* (London: Faber, 1973)

Sowerby, Tracey, *Renaissance and Reform in Tudor England: The Careers of Sir Richard Morison, c.1513–1556*, Oxford Historical Monographs (Oxford: Oxford University Press, 2010)

Spivack, Bernard, *Shakespeare and the Allegory of Evil* (New York: Columbia University Press, 1958)

Sponsler, Claire, *Drama and Resistance: Bodies, Goods, and Theatricality in Late Medieval England*, Medieval Cultures, 10 (Minneapolis: University of Minnesota Press, 1997)

Stacey, Caroline M., 'Justification by Faith in the Two Books of Homilies (1547 and 1571)', *Anglican Theological Review*, 83 (2001), 255–79

Stacey, Robert, 'The Conversion of Jews to Christianity in Thirteenth-Century England', *Speculum*, 67 (1992), 263–83

Stanbury, Sarah, *The Visual Object of Desire in Late Medieval England* (Philadelphia: University of Pennsylvania Press, 2007)

Stevens, Martin, and Margeret Dorrell, 'The "Ordo Paginarium" Gathering of the York "A/Y Memorandum Book"', *Modern Philology*, 72 (1974), 45–59

Stewart, Alan, '"Ydolatricall Sodometrye": John Bale's Allegory', *Medieval English Theatre*, 15 (1993), 3–20

Strohm, Paul, 'The Croxton *Play of the Sacrament*: Commemoration and Repetition in Late Medieval Culture', in *Performances of the Sacred in Late Medieval and Early Modern England*, ed. by Susanne Rupp and Robias Döring (Amsterdam: Rodopi, 2005), pp. 33–44

——, *England's Empty Throne: Usurpation and the Language of Legitimation, 1399–1422* (New Haven: Yale University Press, 1998)

Targoff, Ramie, *Common Prayer: Models of Public Devotion in Early Modern England* (Chicago: University of Chicago Press, 2001)

Taylor, Andrew, 'The Reformation of History in John Bale's Biblical Dramas', in *English Historical Drama, 1500–1600: Forms Outside the Canon*, ed. by Teresa Grant and Barbara Ravelhofer (Basingstoke: Palgrave Macmillan, 2008), pp. 58–97

Thomas, Keith, *Religion and the Decline of Magic: Studies in Popular Beliefs in Sixteenth- and Seventeenth-Century England* (London: Weidenfeld and Nicolson, 1971)

Thomson, John A. F., 'John Foxe and Some Sources for Lollard History: Notes for Some Critical Appraisal', *Studies in Church History*, 2 (1965), 251–57

——, *The Later Lollards, 1414–1520* (Oxford: Oxford University Press, 1965)

Thomson, Peter, 'Sound City Jests and Country Pretty Jests: *Jack Juggler* and *Gammer Gurton's Needle*', in *Interludes and Early Modern Society: Studies in Gender, Power and Theatricality*, ed. by Peter Happé and Wim Hüskin, Ludus, 9 (Amsterdam: Rodopi, 2007), pp. 315–30

Troup, Frances B. Rose, *The Western Rebellion of 1549: An Account of the Insurrections in Devonshire and Cornwall Against Religious Innovations* (London: Smith, Elder & Co., 1913)

Truman, James C. W., 'John Foxe and the Desires of Reformation Martyrology', *English Literary History*, 70 (2003), 35–66

Tydeman, William, *English Medieval Theatre, 1400–1500* (London: Routledge & Kegan Paul, 1986)

——, *The Theatre in the Middle Ages: Western European Stage Conditions, c. 800–1576* (Cambridge: Cambridge University Press, 1978)

Van Court, Elisa Narin, 'Socially Marginal, Culturally Central: Representing Jews in Late Medieval English Literature', *Exemplaria*, 12 (2000), 293–326

Voss, Paul J., 'Printing Conventions and the Early Modern Play', *Medieval and Renaissance Drama in England*, 15 (2002), 98–115

Walker, Greg, 'The Corpus Christi in York and Croxton', in *Readings in Medieval Texts: Interpreting Old and Middle English Literature*, ed. by David F. Johnson and Elaine Treharne (Oxford: Oxford University Press, 2005), pp. 370–85

——, *Plays of Persuasion: Drama and Politics at the Court of Henry VIII* (Cambridge: Cambridge University Press, 1991)

——, *The Politics of Performance in Early Renaissance Drama* (Cambridge: Cambridge University Press, 1998)

Wallace, Dewey D. Jr, *Puritans and Predestination: Grace in English Protestant Theology, 1525–1695* (Chapel Hill: University of North Carolina Press, 1982)

Wandel, Lee Palmer, *The Eucharist in the Reformation: Incarnation and Liturgy* (Cambridge: Cambridge University Press, 2006)

Waswo, Richard, *Language and Meaning in the Renaissance* (Princeton: Princeton University Press, 1987)

Watson, Nicholas, 'Censorship and Cultural Change in Late-Medieval England: Vernacular Theology, the Oxford Translation Debate, and Arundel's Constitutions of 1409', *Speculum*, 70 (1995), 822–64

Webb, Diana, *Pilgrimage in Medieval England* (London: Hambledon, 2007)

Weimann, Robert, *Author's Pen and Actor's Voice: Playing and Writing in Shakespeare's Theatre*, ed. by Helen Higbee and William West, Cambridge Studies in Renaissance Literature and Culture, 39 (New York: Cambridge University Press, 2000)

Werrell, Ralph S., *The Theology of William Tyndale* (Cambridge: Clarke, 2006)

West, William N., 'What's the Matter in Shakespeare?: Physics, Identity, Playing', *South Central Review*, 26 (2009), 103–26

Westfall, Suzanne, 'The Boy Who Would Be King: Court Revels of King Edward VI, 1547–1553', *Comparative Drama*, 35 (2001), 271–90

——, *Patrons and Performance: Early Tudor Household Revels* (Oxford: Clarendon Press, 1990)

White, Paul Whitfield, 'The Bible as Play in Reformation England', in *The Cambridge History of British Theatre*, ed. by Jane Milling and others, 3 vols (Cambridge: Cambridge University Press, 1999), I: *Origins to 1660*, ed. by Jane Milling and Peter Thomson, pp. 87–115

——, 'Introduction', in *Reformation Biblical Drama in England: An Old-Spelling Critical Edition*, ed. by Paul Whitfield White (New York: Garland, 1992), pp. i–xlvi

——, 'Lewis Wager's *Life and Repentaunce of Mary Magdalene* and John Calvin', *Notes and Queries*, 226 (1981), 508–12

——, 'Theatre and Religious Culture', in *A New History of Early English Drama*, ed. by John D. Cox and David Scott Kastan (New York: Columbia University Press, 1997), pp. 133–52

——, *Theatre and Reformation: Protestantism, Patronage and Playing in Tudor England* (Cambridge: Cambridge University Press, 1993)

White, P. O. G., *Predestination, Policy and Polemic: Conflict and Consensus in the English Church from the Reformation to the Civil War* (Cambridge: Cambridge University Press, 1992)

Wickham, Glynne, *Early English Stages, 1300 to 1600*, 4 vols in 5 parts (London: Routledge & Kegan Paul, 1959–81; repr. 2002)

——, 'The Staging of Saint Plays in Europe', in *The Medieval Drama*, ed. by Sandro Sticca (Albany: State University of New York Press, 1972), pp. 99–120

Willett, C., and Phillis Cunnington, *Handbook of English Costume in the Sixteenth Century* (London: Faber and Faber, 1954)

——, *The History of Underclothes*, rev. by A. D. Mansfield and Valerie Mansfield (London: Faber and Faber, 1981)

Williams, William H., 'The Date and Authorship of *Jacke Jugeler*', *Modern Language Notes*, 7 (1912), 289–95

Woolf, Rosemary, *The English Mystery Plays* (London: Routledge & Kegan Paul, 1972)

Wright, Stephen K., 'What's so "English" about Medieval English Drama? An East Anglican [sic] Miracle Play and Its Continental Counterpart', in *To Make his Englissh Sweete upon his Tonge*, ed. by Marcin Krygier and Liliana Sikorska (Frankfurt: Lang, 2007), pp. 71–91

Young, Karl, *The Drama of the Medieval Church*, 2 vols (Oxford: Clarendon Press, 1933)

INDEX

LATE MEDIEVAL AND EARLY MODERN STUDIES

All volumes in this series are evaluated by an Editorial Board, strictly on academic grounds, based on reports prepared by referees who have been commissioned by virtue of their specialism in the appropriate field. The Board ensures that the screening is done independently and without conflicts of interest. The definitive texts supplied by authors are also subject to review by the Board before being approved for publication. Further, the volumes are copyedited to conform to the publisher's stylebook and to the best international academic standards in the field.

Titles in Series

Contextualizing the Renaissance: Returns to History, ed. by Albert H. Tricomi (1999)

Sparks and Seeds: Medieval Literature and its Afterlife; Essays in Honor of John Freccero, ed. by Dana E. Stewart and Alison Cornish (2000)

Nirit Ben-Aryeh Debby, *Renaissance Florence in the Rhetoric of Two Popular Preachers: Giovanni Dominici (1356–1419) and Bernardino da Siena (1380–1444)* (2001)

Ian Robertson, *Tyranny under the Mantle of St Peter: Pope Paul II and Bologna* (2002)

Stephen Kolsky, *The Ghost of Boccaccio: Writings on Famous Women in Renaissance Italy* (2005)

Rituals, Images, and Words: Varieties of Cultural Expression in Late Medieval and Early Modern Europe, ed. by F. W. Kent and Charles Zika (2006)

Camilla Russell, *Giulia Gonzaga and the Religious Controversies of Sixteenth-Century Italy* (2006)

Stefan Bauer, *The Censorship and Fortuna of Platina's 'Lives of the Popes' in the Sixteenth Century* (2006)

Nirit Ben-Aryeh Debby, *The Renaissance Pulpit: Art and Preaching in Tuscany, 1400–1550* (2007)

Fabrizio Ricciardelli, *The Politics of Exclusion in Early Renaissance Florence* (2007)

Practices of Gender in Late Medieval and Early Modern Europe, ed. by Megan Cassidy-Welch and Peter Sherlock (2008)

Kate Cregan, *The Theatre of the Body: Staging Death and Embodying Life in Early-Modern London* (2009)

Andrew James Johnston, *Performing the Middle Ages from 'Beowulf' to 'Othello'* (2009)

Old Worlds, New Worlds: European Cultural Encounters, c. 1000 – c. 1750, ed. by Lisa Bailey, Lindsay Diggelmann, and Kim M. Phillips (2009)

Francesco Benigno, *Mirrors of Revolution: Conflict and Political Identity in Early Modern Europe* (2010)

Gunnar W. Knutsen, *Servants of Satan and Masters of Demons: The Spanish Inquisition's Trials for Superstition, Valencia and Barcelona, 1478–1700* (2010)

Mark Amsler, *Affective Literacies: Writing and Multilingualism in the Late Middle Ages* (2012)

Richard Rowlands Verstegan: A Versatile Man in an Age of Turmoil, ed. by Romana Zacchi and Massimiliano Morini (2012)

Middle English Religious Writing in Practice: Texts, Readers, and Transformations, ed. by Nicole R. Rice (2013)

In Preparation

Adelina Modesti, *Elisabetta Sirani 'Virtuosa': Women's Cultural Production in Early Modern Bologna*

E. J. Kent, *Cases of Male Witchcraft in Old and New England, 1592–1692*

Francis W. Kent (†), *Princely Citizen: Lorenzo de' Medici and Renaissance Florence*, ed. by Carolyn James

Medieval and Early Modern Performance in the Eastern Mediterranean, ed. by Arzu Öztürkmen and Evelyn Birge Vitz